D1013770

BEST
HIKES
WITH
KIDS
WESTERN
WASHINGTON

BEST HIKES WITH KIDS

SUSAN ELDERKIN

WESTERN WASHINGTON

MOUNTAINEERS
BOOKS

MOUNTAINEERS BOOKS is the publishing division of The Mountaineers, an organization founded in 1906 and dedicated to the exploration, preservation, and enjoyment of outdoor and wilderness areas.

1001 SW Klickitat Way, Suite 201 • Seattle, WA 98134
800.553.4453 • www.mountaineersbooks.org

Printed in China
Distributed in the United Kingdom by Cordee, www.cordee.co.uk

First edition: 2018

Copyeditor: Kristi Hein
Cover Design: Jen Grable
Design and layout: Jennifer Shontz, www.redshoedesign.com
Cartographer: Martha Bostwick
Cover photograph: *Crossing the Icicle Gorge bridge*
Frontispiece: *Overlooking Dewey Lakes on the Naches Peak Loop*
All photos by author unless credited otherwise

The background maps for this book were produced using the online map viewer CalTopo. For more information, visit caltopo.com.

Library of Congress Cataloging-in-Publication data is on file

Mountaineers Books titles may be purchased for corporate, educational, or other promotional sales, and our authors are available for a wide range of events. For information on special discounts or booking an author, contact our customer service at 800-553-4453 or mbooks@mountaineersbooks.org.

ISBN (paperback): 978-1-68051-014-0
ISBN (ebook): 978-1-68051-015-7

CONTENTS

⑤	Interstate highway	⊤	Bench
②	US highway	■	Building of interest
⑤③⓪	State route	⬭	Cave
1230	Forest road	⛺	Campground (backpacking)
------	Main trail	▲	Campground (established)
········	Continuation of main trail	→	Direction of travel
········	Other trail	↦	Gate
═══	Paved road	↻	Good turnaround point
┅┅┅	Gravel road	⍟	Lookout
-‡-	Bridge	℗	Parking
≋	Pass	)(	Pass
-⊣⊢-	Underpass or tunnel	▲	Peak or mountain
┝┿┥	Railroad	𝅭	Picnic table
⬭	Body of water	✪	Playground
────	River or stream	•	Point of interest
-----	Underground river	⬥	Restroom or privy
▬	Park, forest, or wilderness area	·	Tarn
//////	Bluffs	❶ ⓣ	Trailhead; alternate trailhead
⣿	Sand dunes	─	Underground lava tube
⣿	Tidal area	❶	Viewpoint
⣿	Wetlands	⬋	Waterfall
65	Hike number	▬▪▬	Land management boundary

A QUICK GUIDE TO THE HIKES

There's a little something for every kind of hiker within these pages, and a "best of" list is a good way to get you started. Each list is ordered by the hike's number in this book, so the "best of the best" is not necessarily listed first. By no means are these exhaustive lists of each category—I could double or triple some of them. These are simply really good choices. In the main descriptions, check the symbols at the beginning of each hike to identify more hikes that feature big trees and wildlife or opportunities for water play and backpacking.

BEST HIKES TO PITCH A TENT

- **Ptarmigan Ridge–Mazama Lake** (hike 33): This family-friendly alpine delight is the most easily reached of Mount Baker's Chain Lakes. You may explore beyond for additional sparkling lakes.
- **Barclay Lake** (hike 48): You don't have to work too hard to get to these big lakeside campsites, and the swimming is great.
- **Sourdough Ridge–Shadow Lake Loop** (hike 64): Many years ago, Sunrise Camp was a drive-in campground. Now it's a short jaunt from the Sunrise Visitor Center at Mount Rainier National Park and a perfect place to try backpacking for the first time.
- **Ozette Triangle: Cape Alava–Sand Point** (hike 109): Backpack to one of the most heralded beaches on the Olympic Coast. You won't be alone, but a variety of camping locations do spread out the visitors.
- **Third Beach** (hike 112): A short hike to a mile-long beach provides endless sandy ocean fun. Second Beach is no slouch either, but Third Beach allows for exploring the headlands at Taylor Point.

BEST HIKES TO HUG REALLY BIG TREES

- **Boulder River** (hike 39): This slice of wilderness preserves one of the few low-elevation old-growth forests left in the Cascades. Plus you get to see a very lovely waterfall.
- **Asahel Curtis Nature Trail** (hike 57): One of the few groves of old-growth forest left in the Snoqualmie Pass corridor makes you contemplate what might have been.
- **Federation Forest** (hike 62): These are some BIG trees! And what's more, the state park has helpfully labeled many of them so you can actually learn to identify each species.
- **Hoh Rain Forest Nature Trails** (hike 113): The copious amount of rain this forest receives each year feeds the growth of these old-growth giants.
- **Quinault Rain Forest Trails** (hike 114): The Quinault Rain Forest boasts some of the largest old-growth specimens in the country, and you can see their enormous cousins on hikes just upslope from the lake.

With its wide, paved, and level trail, toddlers can successfully circumambulate Gold Creek Pond all by themselves.

BEST HIKES FOR STROLLERS AND LITTLE LEGS

- **Point Whitehorn Marine Reserve** (hike 1): It's smooth sailing on boardwalk and level trail all the way to a bluff, where toddlers will need a hand on the stairs to the beach.
- **West Hylebos Wetlands** (hike 24): This gem tucked away in the heart of Federal Way showcases wildlife, boardwalks, and two historic cabins.
- **Gold Creek Pond** (hike 60): This level stroll atop Snoqualmie Pass is one of my favorite toddler hikes. There's water, flowers, mountain views, and a level, barrier-free stroll around the pond.
- **Nisqually Vista** (hike 70): Recently repaved, this is the easiest hike at Mount Rainier's Paradise, and suitable for wheelchairs, strollers, and just walkers.
- **Rainy Lake** (hike 81): A jewel-hued lake is a short jaunt down a barrier-free path in the North Cascades. This is a great leg-stretcher when heading over the North Cascades Highway.

(See also "Best Longer Hikes That Can Easily Be Shortened.")

BEST HIKES FOR PEAK-BAGGING

- **Sugarloaf Mountain** (hike 6): The views of Puget Sound and the Olympics from Fidalgo Island are sublime, and you can even climb this mountain in the winter!
- **Sauk Mountain** (hike 36): The views start in the parking lot and are constant all the way to the summit.
- **Steamboat Mountain** (hike 73): Four volcanoes are visible from the top, but Mount Adams reigns supreme.
- **Red Top Lookout** (hike 90): Short, steep, and sweet. Volunteers maintain the lookout and welcome visitors in the summer.
- **Beacon Rock** (hike 121): A mind-boggling series of overlapping catwalks has been hammered into the side of the mountain—with handrails!

BEST HIKES TO TAKE A CURIOUSLY REFRESHING DIP

- **Kelcema Lake** (hike 42): This is the former site of a Boy Scout camp, and you know those kids spent much of their time swimming in the lake.
- **Barclay Lake** (hike 48): Giant trees have fallen into the lake perpendicular to the shore, providing excellent access to the deeper parts.
- **Denny Creek Waterslide** (hike 59): It's no secret that hours of splashy fun can be had at this natural waterslide. Bring a picnic and be prepared for company.
- **Eightmile Lake** (hike 85): This big lake in the Enchantments Zone is cold but refreshing after the long, hot hike.
- **Hyas Lake** (hike 91): Because the lake is fairly shallow, it's warmer than the typical alpine lake, and the trail is easy enough that you could haul in an inflatable raft.

BEST WATERFALL HIKES

- **Boulder River** (hike 39): Two lacy waterfalls in a shady old-growth forest are a special attraction in spring when they are full of snowmelt.
- **Wallace Falls** (hike 45): A series of spectacular cascades drops more than 1000 feet in a vertical mile and can be seen more than 5 miles away. It's even more impressive up close.
- **Franklin Falls** (hike 58): A waterfall hike that even the smallest hikers can do, and it's less than an hour from Seattle.
- **Lewis River Falls** (hike 72): A series of waterfalls, with a bit of the Hawaiian tropics thrown in. These are not the tallest in the state, but they are my favorites.
- **Sol Duc Falls** (hike 108): A thundering waterfall roars among giant old-growth fir, hemlock, and spruce on an easy Olympic National Park trail.

BEST HIKES TO WEIRD PLACES

- **Chambers Bay** (hike 26): This trail circumnavigates a sand and gravel pit–turned–golf course that has only one tree. It's strangely wonderful.
- **Mima Mounds** (hike 30): No one knows exactly why the grassland here looks like bubble wrap.

■ **Ape Cave** (hike 79): No apes, but you can explore the longest continuous lava tube in the country on this one-of-a-kind hike.

■ **Ginkgo Petrified Forest** (hike 92): The remains of a lush tropical rain forest are petrified in the now-arid climate of Central Washington.

■ **Beacon Rock** (hike 121): This engineering marvel features fifty-three switchbacks—some right on top of each other—up the side of a stone monolith above the Columbia River.

BEST HIKES TO SEE BIRDS AND ANIMALS

■ **Nisqually National Wildlife Refuge** (hike 27): You can return over and over and always see something new. From turtles and seals to great blue herons and bald eagles, this place is a slam dunk for wildlife.

■ **Skyline–Golden Gate Loop** (hike 69): I have seen a marmot or three every time I've hiked this trail from Mount Rainier National Park's Paradise.

■ **Umtanum Creek Canyon** (hike 93): This place is alive! During one spring visit I saw kingfishers, ospreys, turkey vultures, a marmot, and bighorn sheep. Plus a dozen other birds and visible beaver activity.

■ **Steigerwald Lake National Wildlife Refuge** (hike 120): More than two hundred species of birds and waterfowl have been spotted at this wildlife refuge on the Columbia River, and you are guaranteed to see at least a dozen of them.

■ **Horsethief Butte** (hike 125): Sunny, warm days bring out curious and seriously adorable lizards.

BEST HIKES TO STUFF YOURSELF WITH BERRIES

■ **Blue Lake (West)** (hike 34): Berries taste so much better when they are wild, and hikers can sample both blues and huckles on this short trail.

■ **Mirror Lake** (hike 61): An entire open hillside of tasty berries awaits hikers who time their hike just right.

■ **Placid and Chenamus Lakes** (hike 74): Winner for tastiest fruit! I could spend days eating these sweet blueberries.

■ **Eightmile Lake** (hike 85): I credit the thimbleberries with getting my six-year-old to the lake. It was slow going, but worth it!

■ **Hyas Lake** (hike 91): This is not a pathway, but a fruitway, with huckle-berries, blueberries, thimbleberries, and salmonberries lining the trail all the way to the lake.

BEST HIKES FOR HISTORY BUFFS

■ **Ebey's Landing** (hike 10): One of Washington's earliest pioneer settle-ments has a complicated and bloody history (a beheading!) and is now preserved as a rural historic district by the National Park Service.

■ **Old Robe Canyon** (hike 44): A railway once ran through this canyon, transporting gold and silver ore mined in Monte Cristo to Everett. The trains are long gone, but there is still old junk littering the trail for hikers to discover.

In August, berries are plentiful and tasty near Placid Lake in the Indian Heaven Wilderness.

- ■ **Iron Goat Loop** (hike 51): Wander past the concrete walls of snowsheds and poke your head into tunnels on the path of the old railway over Stevens Pass.
- ■ **Fort Flagler State Park** (hike 101): Play a great game of hide-and-seek in one of Fort Flagler's military batteries. This is history you can touch.
- ■ **Fort Cascades Historic Site** (hike 123): Long before dams altered the course and character of the Columbia River, this place was a flurry of human activity. Walk an interpretive loop around the site of Cascades Townsite, which was abandoned after the Great Flood of 1894.

BEST HIKES TO FIND THE WILD NEARBY

- ▪ **Hertz Trail: Lake Whatcom Park** (hike 4): Just beyond the housing developments of Bellingham is the uninterrupted eastern shoreline of Lake Whatcom. It's stroller-friendly, with picturesque covered bridges.
- ▪ **North Creek Park** (hike 14): This little wetland between Mill Creek and Bothell is a welcome surprise, as is the fun, bouncy boardwalk.
- ▪ **Mercer Slough Nature Park** (hike 18): Wedged between I-90, I-405, and Bellevue Way is an urban oasis where you can escape traffic and watch the ducks.
- ▪ **Point Defiance Park** (hike 25): Tacoma's largest city park has something for everyone: a zoo, a historic fort, a big beach, and miles of hiking beneath big trees and out to several Puget Sound vistas.
- ▪ **Lacamas Creek** (hike 119): Vancouver's suburb of Camas features one of my favorite urban parks, with a lake, waterfalls, and rocky balds with its namesake flower.

Although many hikes around Mount Rainier are vertical, there are plenty of trails that can be shortened for little ones. (photo by Jon Stier)

BEST HIKES FOR A WINTER'S DAY

- **Nisqually National Wildlife Refuge** (hike 27): The wildlife changes with the seasons, and one of the highlights of winter is the opportunity to see dozens of bald eagles who flock here to feast on chum salmon.
- **Old Sauk** (hike 40): Enjoy the peaceful sounds of the Old Sauk River while staying fairly dry under the thick forest canopy.
- **Twin Falls** (hike 53): This all-season, low-elevation waterfall hike is even more impressive after a big rain, as you stand on a sturdy bridge that straddles two big waterfall plunges.
- **Cape Disappointment State Park** (hike 117): From the high perch of two lighthouses you can see the impressive winter surf pummel the shore. Plus razor clamming in Long Beach!
- **Catherine Creek** (hike 124): Flowers begin blooming as early as February on the sunny, south-facing slopes of the Columbia River Gorge.

BEST LONGER HIKES THAT CAN EASILY BE SHORTENED

- **Nisqually National Wildlife Refuge** (hike 27): Youngsters who have just mastered walking can confidently stride around the 1-mile Twin Barns Loop, and if they are quiet they might just see a motionless great blue heron or a bald eagle high in a tree.
- **Iron Goat Loop** (hike 51): Skip the full loop and hike the gentle lower grade to two historic railroad tunnels on an interpretive trail for a 2.4-mile round-trip.
- **Sourdough Ridge–Shadow Lake Loop** (hike 64): Options abound to scale this hike to suit the family while still retaining gobsmacking views of Mount Rainier.
- **Skyline–Golden Gate Loop** (hike 69): On the vertical trails at Paradise, young kids may tire quickly, but the first half mile of this trail climbs gently on a paved trail to picturesque Myrtle Falls.
- **Spruce Railroad** (hike 107): Two of the highlights of this trail along Lake Crescent—a crescent-shaped pool and a newly opened railroad tunnel—are just 1.2 miles down the wide path.

Making memories: my family rings in the New Year on Sugarloaf Mountain.

INTRODUCTION: HIKING WITH KIDS

I researched these hikes during a twenty-month period when my children were between the ages of six and eleven, but my experience and writing are informed by hiking with them on many of these same trails as babies, toddlers, and preschoolers. In the course of eleven years of hiking, I have seen my kids express wonder and glee at discovering insects and snow, melt down in defiance in the middle of the trail, and triumphantly reach a summit. They are just regular kids whose mom wanted to write a hiking book, and I am pleased to say that they rose to the occasion time and again as they accompanied me across the state in search of trails their peers would enjoy. As they gained two years of maturity, the whining and bickering subsided—usually—and they became more observant, stronger hikers. The book is better for their input, as they helped me gauge which types of trails are interesting for kids, tuned me into what proves difficult along the way, and helped me see hiking from a kid's point of view.

As a family, it was rewarding to spend time together without the distractions of our normal life. It was during these hikes and car rides that my children would open up and share their inner thoughts or demonstrate new creativity. We took several long weekends and a few weeklong trips to complete the research, camping out under the stars or visiting towns and places we'd never been to before. The time when the kids are young is so fleeting, and I feel fortunate to have had an opportunity to share the outdoors with them.

With this book, I hope that you will be able to share the abundance and beauty of Washington with your children, connecting with them in ways that transcend today's wired world and that have lasting impacts. Many of the hikes in this book are in or near urban areas and are ideal for a half-day or day trip. Others are farther afield—in the mountains, along the beach, or in our national parks—and may require an overnight stay or two. As a result, I've included thirteen "Great Getaways" that provide ideas about how you can spin two to four days into a nice mini-vacation with the family.

Please use this guide to weave together a series of short trips close to home and longer excursions to explore the great state of Washington. It's not always easy, but it is ultimately one of the most rewarding ways to spend time with your family.

TIPS FOR HIKING WITH CHILDREN

Hiking with young children is an altogether different experience than hiking with adults. As a parent new to hiking with kids, I found the hardest thing was to adjust my own expectations. We walked at a snail's pace and on numerous occasions turned around short of our destination. It was tough, but I was determined that my kids have good experiences on their hikes so that they'd willingly return to hike another day.

Bringing a friend along helps make the miles fly by. (photo by Jon Stier)

I've included some strategies you can use to encourage and motivate kids along the way. At some time or another I've used all of these ideas to move my two along, often to great success, yet sometimes not. Every kid is motivated differently, and some strategies work better for older kids than younger ones. Pick and choose those that appeal most to your child.

Choose the Right Trail

You know your children the best—what motivates them, how much stamina they have, their impulse control and anxieties. Choosing a trail that fits their abilities is one of the most effective ways you can make sure they are still smiling at the end of the hike. But while every hike in this book has something for kids to like, it doesn't mean that every hike here will please your child. What is easy for one kid may be more difficult for another whose gross motor skills are still developing. Some routes and destinations have steep drop-offs that may be inappropriate for kids who lack balance or impulse control. Read through the descriptions thoroughly and choose a trail that will build their self-confidence and their love for the outdoors.

Set Expectations

Our most successful hikes come when the kids have some idea of what they are getting into. I always cue them in on how long we will be in the car, whether there is elevation gain, how long the hike should take, and what they might see. When they were younger, I used words like "explore" and "walk" instead of "hike," while I enthusiastically sold the hike by mentioning some of the things that motivated them (beaches, wildlife, berries, and so on).

Bring a Friend

Having a friend along is a powerful motivator and can be just the ticket to win over a reluctant hiker. When my children's friends accompany us, I'm amazed by the newfound spring in their steps. They move along the trail more quickly, there is far less squabbling and whining, and they express greater interest in little things along the trail. One of my favorite moments during my research was observing two moms with six kids under five years old who had successfully wrangled their spirited and happy gang all the way to the top of Heybrook Lookout. I also ran into new parents hiking with other parents they had met in hiking meet-up groups, supporting each other while getting outside with their little ones.

Dress for Success

Conditions can change quickly in Washington, and it is wise to be prepared with long-sleeved layers, extra socks, and rain jackets, even on nice days. Fog can roll in over the Puget Sound, clouds and rain can sneak in over the mountains, and it's almost always colder at the trailhead than it is at home. Equally as likely, someone will submerge their foot in a creek or get chilled at the destination when they take a break. Make sure you are prepared for all weather.

Go at Their Pace and Be Flexible

Kids can be slow hikers. Glacially slow. As toddlers and preschoolers, kids care only about their journey, not the destination. My advice: go with the flow. Slow down and explore the wonder of every fern, slug, mossy stump, and creek. At this age, it's about sparking their curiosity and love for the outdoors, not about your desire to reach a lake or a waterfall. You may not attain your destination, or it may take you a very long time to get there, but I guarantee you will gain a new appreciation for the natural world around you if you look at it through the eyes of a kid.

For older kids who move slowly, be patient and be sure to praise good effort. Remember that their legs are still shorter than yours, so it takes more effort to move up hills and down the path. It won't be long until they gallop ahead of you, but in the meantime you may decide to employ some of the other strategies here to keep them going.

HIKING WITH KIDS WITH SPECIAL NEEDS

Hiking with kids who have special needs is an enriching and rewarding experience, but getting everyone outside poses specific challenges and risks, depending upon the disability. Children with mobility issues may be confined to a wheelchair or lack muscle tone, coordination, and stamina. Kids with hearing or sight impairment need trails that may be barrier-free or provide other sensory experiences. Children with autism, ADHD, or other sensory issues may have a compromised attention span, have particular sensitivities to temperature or moisture, or lack common sense.

The good news is that there are plenty of hikes to fit families who have kids all across the special needs spectrum. Many of the trails in this book are barrier-free and paved—perfect for kids who have mobility issues. More than two dozen trails are quite short, which allows for families to take their time over easy terrain. And there is something here to fit every passion or obsession—birds, big trees, bugs, water, and much more.

You know your kid best. Start small, plan in advance, and manage expectations. Wherever possible I have drawn attention to trails that are barrier-free or, alternatively, have characteristics like steep drop-offs that pose a danger to kids who are unpredictable or lack balance. Indulge in what interests your kids and go at their pace. The physical activity and outdoor environment are so healthy for them.

National parks are overseen by the most well-equipped land management agency for people with disabilities. The National Park Service's website details which trails and campgrounds have accessible facilities. Families with children with disabilities may also qualify for a free lifetime Access Pass, which allows admission to all federal sites. Getting your kids outside may be a little more work, but it is definitely worth it.

Take frequent rest breaks to refuel along the way. (photo by Ryan Ojerio)

Pack Snacks and Take Brief Breaks

Kids metabolize food more quickly than adults. Instead of eating a meal at your destination, snack your way along the trail with frequent (but short) stops to refuel. Pack high-energy snacks, like nuts and jerky, but also something they love. I usually have a pocket full of Skittles that I dole out when they need motivation to get to the top of the hill or around the next bend. One family I know takes this to another level, with one parent going ahead and placing Skittles along the trail for the children to find.

Be sure to also pack an adequate supply of water. Whenever I notice my kids flagging, I know they need water. On hot days it's amazing how a few gulps can rejuvenate the body. To encourage water consumption, consider purchasing hydration packs for your kids. My kids love the novelty of sucking on the hose, and they drink two to three times more water when they have their hydration packs in their backpack.

Play Games along the Way

Playing games or storytelling along the way helps kids to forget how tired they are. With younger kids, entertain them with your own tale or tell a classic fairy tale. With older kids, make up a story together, with each person making up a part of the tale, then passing it off to someone else. The time and miles just fly by. Other easy games to try are I Spy, Twenty Questions, ABC games, and scavenger hunts.

BACKPACKING WITH KIDS

While backpacking with children takes extra planning and a strong back, it's also a great way to truly get away from it all. When my husband and I first took our kids backpacking, they were three and six years old, and we carried everything. It almost broke us, but watching our kids frolicking on an ocean beach away from crowds and traffic for three days made up for a few aches and pains. And it got easier over time: The kids started carrying their own backpacks when they were seven. My pack is still heavy when I take the kids into the backcountry on my own, but it helps that the kids carry their own sleeping bags, sleeping pads, water, and a few communal items.

Backpacking allows a lot of time for rest and relaxation.

In this book, I have noted several hikes that are excellent beginning backpacking trips; they're marked with the backpacking icon, like the one above. These trails are short and usually don't have too much elevation gain. The destinations are kid-pleasers too: lakes and ocean. I usually spend two nights, so we can relax and explore on the off-day. If you are new to backpacking, borrow some gear and go with friends, so you can spread the work and the weight. Most of all, enjoy the quiet and solitude away from roads and lights.

Walkie-talkies are guaranteed to make the hike more fun. (photo by Jon Stier)

Bring Tools for Kids

Encourage your kids to explore and record their hike by bringing along cameras, binoculars, magnifying glasses, walkie-talkies, bird and plant identification guides, journals, or art supplies. For beach hikes, a bucket and shovel are fun to bring along. Each of these tools allows kids to deepen their experience and practice their observational skills.

HELPING YOUR KIDS BECOME HIKERS

Getting your child out in nature from an early age is an ideal way to combine exercise with an exploration of our wild and beautiful world. When the kids are young, you don't have to travel far from home. Visit your city or county park systems and discover the bounty of nature nearby. I've included a smattering of hikes within urban areas of Western Washington, but there is so much more to discover just beyond your back door.

Babies and Toddlers

I carried my son in a baby backpack, but my daughter preferred to snuggle up in a front carrier. Many parents like to push a jogging stroller. It depends what is comfortable to you and to your baby. Some kids love riding in the carriers into their toddlerhood, tucking in for a nap when they are sleepy. Not my kids. As soon as they could walk, they squirmed to get out—and I let them, carrying them only when they were tired. By the time the kids were three, however, we left the backpack at home and transitioned away from carrying them. Instead, we chose easy hikes that they could do without being carried, usually 2 miles or less. This way the kids developed self-confidence, strength, and independence.

A big sun hat offers the best protection for little ones. (photo by Kevin Hall)

Preschoolers

During preschool years, kids develop more strength and stamina, and that means you can begin to choose more difficult hikes, perhaps a short hike with a little elevation gain or a longer hike that is relatively flat. How far a four- or five-year-old can hike is really variable. Some can sprint up a mountain happily, while others struggle on a paved, flat trail. As you encourage kids to move beyond their comfort zone, make sure you employ the previously mentioned tips and tricks. Snacks, games, walkie-talkies, and other fun tools are all very useful distractions at this age.

Grade-Schoolers

Once kids hit grade school, they can start to keep up with you. My daughter hiked one of the toughest trails in this book, Eightmile Lake, when she was six. It took us seven hours to hike 6 miles, but she made it. I will never forget her look of pride as she arrived at this big, beautiful lake, and the confidence it gave her to try other difficult trails. Gradually try more difficult trails as your kids get older, and if you find them lagging, consider bringing along a friend for extra motivation.

WHAT TO WEAR AND PACK

In addition to the Ten Essentials (explained shortly), you will want to be prepared for your hike. It doesn't have to be complicated, but you should be properly equipped for both safety and enjoyment. Let's start from the feet up.

Footwear

Tennis shoes or hiking boots? Everyone has a pair of tennies, but hiking shoes or boots for fast-growing feet can be an added expense that keeps families off the hiking trail. Here's the good news: most of the hikes in this book can be hiked by kids in tennis shoes. Kids generally will be happiest hiking in shoes that are light and comfortable, and if it is a nice day on a trail that is rated from easiest to moderate, sneakers are the way to go. However, a sturdier sole and ankle support are important on more difficult hikes, especially those where you will be hiking over roots and rocks. If the hike is rated more difficult or difficult, kids may be happier in hiking shoes or boots that are worn in, although this is not a hard-and-fast rule. If price is an obstacle, visit a local consignment store for lightly used shoes and boots.

For hiking socks, I like a tightly knit polyester blend. Make sure to pack an extra pair or two; kids are notorious for dunking their feet into the water. And when feet become wet and cold, that may spell an end to your hike or create a dangerous situation.

This happens most trips. Always bring dry socks and leave extra shoes in the car. (photo by Jon Stier)

Adjustable baby backpacks are often available as hand-me-downs from friends or at consignment stores.

Clothing and Raingear

In the Pacific Northwest it is always important to bring extra layers of clothing. At a minimum, I pack a long-sleeved shirt and a raincoat for everyone in the family. I've seen too many sunny days turn gloomy to leave these essentials at home. What I do leave at home are cotton T-shirts and jeans. Hikers have a saying: "Cotton kills." That's because when cotton gets wet, it becomes cold and is very slow to dry. In fact, it can suck away body heat and put you at risk of hypothermia. Instead, dress your kids and yourself in synthetics that wick away moisture and dry quickly. Most athletic wear is available in this comfortable, durable material; anyway, that is what my kids—and many of their friends—wear most of the time.

Packs

You've got extra clothes, food, water, and your other essentials to carry. You need a backpack to carry your stuff. For short hikes, it may be fine for just the adults to carry the load, but for longer trails, kids should carry their own backpacks. I always have them carry something communal—like the snacks or the first-aid kit—along with their water or raincoat. You can certainly have them wear their school backpack, but make sure that these are not too ill-fitting or big. I invested in small backpacks with hydration bladders and chest straps that have served both of the kids for the past five years.

If you're carrying your baby or toddler, consider what is most comfortable for you. I found that wearing my baby in a front baby carrier worked best for the first year. Then I switched to an external frame baby backpack for the toddler years. When searching for a baby backpack, make sure that (1) it can be adjusted to fit both parents, (2) it has comfortable shoulder and waist straps, and (3) there is some kind of protection from rain and sun.

Food and Water

On the trail, as everywhere else in life, food and water are a necessity. When kids' energy sags, they generally are either hungry or thirsty, and probably the latter. Always pack more water than you think everyone will drink. Dehydration is the single biggest reason kids lose their energy, and they almost never realize it. Time and again I've seen a few sips of water completely revive a kid who appeared unable go one step farther. However, do not trust that lakes or streams will provide you with safe water to refill your canteen. Invisible and nasty parasites can infect even the clearest water, and only a good filter (these days they are light and filter very quickly), iodine purification tablets, or boiling will remove them.

For food, pack several energy-boosting snacks—nuts, jerky, string cheese, whole-grain crackers, energy bars, cold pizza, and the like. If it is cool outside, search the refrigerator for favorite perishable snacks, like hummus, softer cheeses, or yogurt.

Kids need to drink plenty of fluids to keep their energy up. (photo by Jon Stier)

TEN ESSENTIALS

Over the years, The Mountaineers has developed a systems approach to items that should be carried on every hike. These Ten Essentials will allow you to hike safely and comfortably and to respond positively to an accident or emergency situation.

1. **Navigation (map, compass, GPS):** A good map is one of the most important tools for hiking safely. It is not always intuitive which direction is the right one, and smartphones usually lose reception in the mountains. Take the opportunity to teach your kids how to read a map and use a compass too.

2. **Headlamp (or flashlight):** Hedge your bets and bring some source of illumination in your pack and pack extra batteries. If your return is delayed, you will be relieved to have a way to light the trail.

3. **Sun protection (sunglasses, hat, sunscreen):** Most parents are well-acquainted with slathering sunscreen on their kids. It is doubly important when hiking in the mountains, where the rays are stronger, or near water or snow, which reflects the sun.

4. **First aid:** Always bring a well-stocked first-aid kit and hope you never have to use it. For kids, I make sure to include adhesive bandages in several sizes and antiseptic for cleaning cuts. I also suggest bringing children's Tylenol and Benadryl, a small vial of baking soda for nettle encounters and insect stings, and additional medicine that your kids may need, such as an inhaler or EpiPen.

5. **Knife (repair kit and tools):** A multitool pocketknife is indispensable, for both everyday versatility and use in an emergency. Consider also bringing a small amount of duct tape, which can help repair tears to your clothing or pack.

6. **Fire (firestarter and matches):** If you must unexpectedly stay the night outside and make a fire, these items are lifesavers.

7. **Shelter (space blanket, tarp):** Your local sporting goods store is likely to carry emergency space blankets and tarps. The shiny space blankets roll up into a tiny ball and can save your life if you have to spend the night outside. A tarp can also be useful on a rainy-day lunch stop.

8. **Extra food:** Too much food is better than not enough.

9. **Extra water:** Always pack more water than you will need and ideally carry a filter or tablets to purify stream or lake water in an emergency.

10. **Extra clothes:** Our Northwest weather is fickle: without warning, it can rain or turn cold and windy. Always bring extra layers and a rain jacket. Mittens and a stocking cap are good choices too.

There are a few other essentials I like to mention for families.

▪ **Whistle:** Consider outfitting each kid with a whistle. In case they ever get separated from the group, teach them to blow on the whistle three times to summon you.

▪ **Insect repellent:** I try to use insect repellent as little as possible, but when the bugs are bad, it is important to have it handy. For children,

Build important skills as you hike; teach kids how to read a map.

choose a repellent with no more than 30 percent DEET for their safety. I also bring an anti-itch stick or baking soda for bites.

- **Wet wipes:** Not just for babies! Wipes are useful in many situations.
- **Toilet paper and trowel:** You never know when nature will call. I bring a trowel to dig a cathole, if it is allowed, and toilet paper and a sealable baggy to pack it out.

WILDERNESS PERMITS, PASSES, AND FEES

As our public lands have become more popular, and state and federal recreation budgets have shrunk, wilderness permits and passes, with associated fees, have become a necessity. These nominal fees help fund trail maintenance, trailhead amenities, upkeep of structures, and basic services. Unfortunately, the fee system is confusing, because different passes are required depending upon who owns the land you will be hiking on. Here's a short primer:

- **National parks:** To enter Mount Rainier or Olympic national parks you will need to purchase a pass good for one week, or an Interagency Pass (also called America the Beautiful) that allows admittance to all federal lands for one year. No pass is required at North Cascades National Park.
- **National forests:** In Washington and Oregon, a Northwest Forest Pass or Interagency Pass is required at developed trailheads. A daily Northwest Forest Pass can be purchased at some (but not all) trailheads and online. Annual passes can be purchased online, at sporting goods stores, and at some nearby businesses.

▪ **National wildlife refuges:** A nominal group fee is often required. The Interagency Pass works for a car group.

▪ **Mount St. Helens:** This national monument has a confusing fee program depending on where you are. A Northwest Forest Pass or Interagency Pass works in most places, but an additional fee may be required for adults at Johnston Ridge.

▪ **Washington State Parks, Washington Department of Natural Resources properties, and State Fish and Wildlife lands:** Washington State has a different fee program from the federal government's. A daily or annual Discover Pass is required when parking at state-owned trailheads. These are available online, at some parks, and at many sporting goods stores.

In addition, permits are required for backcountry camping in national parks and some popular wilderness areas. Be sure to research and acquire your permits before you leave on your trip. Note also your party size. If you are entering a federally designated wilderness area, your party size must be less than twelve, which includes pets and stock. Finally, if you plan to visit a refuge or other area that may have seasonal closures or reduced hours, contact them by phone or email to confirm before you go.

SAFETY

Like any activity, hiking entails some risk. Safety isn't always related to how challenging a hike is. It's possible to get lost, whether you wander off-trail on an easy hike or a difficult one; you can twist an ankle on a paved trail or a rocky one. Whole books are devoted to backcountry safety, but there are some commonsense measures you can take to be knowledgeable, prepared, and alert. While I have made every effort to describe each hike's trail and its hazards, conditions change. Always be willing to turn around if your kids aren't up for the challenge, it is starting to get dark, weather conditions deteriorate, or the trail is too dangerous to be passable. Safety is paramount.

Hypothermia

Hypothermia is sneaky, especially as it manifests in children. Because of their small size and body weight, it is possible for them to begin showing the signs well before it would develop in adults. A dip in a cold lake, a chilly rain, or a windy rest stop after a sweaty climb can lower the body temperature and bring on hypothermia. It doesn't have to be freezing out; hypothermia can happen at temperatures up to 50°F. Before more advanced signs like shivering, slurring, or stumbling begin, children are apt to appear irritable, listless, and uncooperative. It's hard to assess, because that's also the way kids are when they are bored or upset.

The best way you can prevent hypothermia is to ensure your kids are dressed in dry clothing and stay hydrated. Make sure you pack a change of clothing if your children will be swimming, and that you have an insulating wool or synthetic layer stashed in your backpack.

Stay Found

Kids naturally like to explore their surroundings or race ahead on a trail. Freedom is one of the fantastic benefits about getting kids outside, but it comes with the risk of getting lost or separated from the rest of the party. To keep everyone found, first set ground rules. If they want to hike ahead, they need to stay on the trail and wait at all trail junctions. Assign a hike leader and give them the responsibility to stop at regular intervals and let the slower members of the hiking party catch up.

Establish exploration boundaries at your destination or camp. Again, outfit each child with a whistle that they use only in emergencies. Three whistles is an international distress call. If they get lost, they should stay together in one place, preferably in an open area, and wait to be found.

Trailhead Crime

Unfortunately, this is an issue at trailheads in Washington. Never leave valuables in your car. Bring your wallet, phone, and electronic devices with you—or leave them at home.

WILDLIFE ENCOUNTERS

Wildlife encounters on trails are usually a cause to celebrate. In Washington, you are most likely to see deer, chipmunks, and squirrels. Especially in popular areas like national parks, these animals may have no fear of humans because humans have fed them. Please do not perpetuate the problem and feed wildlife. It upsets the natural balance and puts hikers in jeopardy of encountering aggressive animals.

Marmots can be found in alpine rocky areas.

You are less likely to come upon large mammals like elk, mountain goats, bear, or cougar, especially the latter two. In more than twenty years of hiking in Washington I have never seen a bear or a cougar in the wild. Usually, these animals want nothing to do with humans. Should you encounter a bear or cougar, never turn your back, and, if it's a cougar, look it in the eyes. (If it's a bear, avoid eye contact.). Pick up children and small dogs. Retreat slowly until safely out of sight of the animal.

PLANT SAFETY

One common characteristic of many Washington trails is lush plant life. Young hikers love to examine plants along the trail, and it is worth bringing along field guides to help them learn all of the varieties of ferns, mosses, shrubs, and trees. There are a couple of types of plants that I'd like to call out in particular: the ones you can eat and the ones that can hurt you.

Edible Plants

My kids love to forage along the trail, and there is no better hike than one where they can stuff their mouths with berries. Ripe blueberries, huckleberries, salmonberries, and thimbleberries thrive in our environment and are

Mountain blueberries—yum!

a tasty treat and motivational reward for hiking. Make sure you can distinguish edible berries from those that are inedible by looking up photos before you go, and don't eat berries you can't identify. This is doubly true for mushrooms. While our forests have many edible varieties, there are look-alikes that can fool you. Unless you have taken a class or have an expert with you, leave mushrooms alone.

Poison Oak and Stinging Nettles

"Leaves of three, let it be." That's the motto in poison oak country. Poison oak can take on many guises—ground cover, vine, bush, woody plant—and can sport leaves in several shades of green or red. In this book, I have mentioned the trails where poison oak is prevalent. On these trails, stick to the middle of the path and avoid touching plants.

Stinging nettles are more prevalent. They produce an instant and intense inflammatory reaction, which usually dissipates after an hour or so. A paste made from the baking soda in your first-aid kit can soothe the itching. Learn how to identify and avoid this plant, which grows in forests and meadows.

TRAIL ETIQUETTE

Teach your children to be good trail and wilderness stewards by following a few key rules to ensure that you've left the environment just as you found it and that you have respected other hikers along the way.

Stay on the Trail

Ask your kids to walk down the middle of the trail. Walking along the sides widens it and tramples the vegetation. Cutting switchbacks causes erosion and saves little time or energy. It takes resources land managers don't have—and many seasons—to repair damage caused by hikers who don't stay on the trail.

Pee and Poop in the Proper Place

Use toilets at the trailhead or on the trail whenever possible, and teach your kids where and how to relieve themselves in the backcountry. As a rule, hikers should pee 200 feet from a water source and poop 200 feet from water, camp, or trails. It's no longer acceptable to bury toilet paper (animals dig it up), so bring along a ziplocking bag to pack it out. There are places where you may be asked to pack out human waste as well, or where it is impossible to dig a cathole for poop. Where digging is possible, dig your cathole six to eight inches deep; after use, cover it completely with soil and vegetation. I bring along a trowel to help dig the hole, but a strong stick can work too.

For dogs, pack out all dog poop, just as you would if walking in your neighborhood. Do not stash the baggy of waste along the trail to pick up later. Instead, tie the bag of waste to the dog's leash and dispose of it properly when you get home.

Many hiking destinations, especially lakes, have backcountry toilets.

Pack It In, Pack It Out

We all know that we shouldn't litter, especially in a natural environment, but it is worth underscoring that you should pack out whatever you pack in. That includes orange peels and apple cores. Even though these are biodegradable, they do not belong in the environment and can take months or years to decompose. I suggest you go a step further and leave the trail better than you found it by bringing along a sack and picking up wrappers, peels, and other litter you find on your hike.

Take Only Photographs

Please leave plants and natural objects where you find them. Picking flowers is tempting for children, but the interest in them will only be fleeting. Let others enjoy their blooms too, and give the plants a chance to spread their seeds in their short growing season. In addition, many of the hikes in this book feature historical relics and structures. Spend time examining these objects, but leave them where they are for the next hikers to discover.

Leash Your Dog

Dogs are allowed on most, but not all, trails outside of national parks and wildlife refuges. I have noted wilderness areas and wildlife preserves outside of parks and refuges where they are prohibited. Where they are allowed, your pooch should be leashed. Even if your dog is lovable, many people—especially young children—are very afraid when a dog bounds up to them without its owner. It is also important to leash your dog to prevent encounters with wildlife and other off-leash dogs, and to keep him safe from hazards along the trail.

Be Respectful of Other Hikers

Be courteous to other trail users. By keeping your voices down, you will be respecting others and have a greater chance of spotting wildlife. Try to give other groups of hikers space, and yield to groups hiking uphill. When encountering horses or pack animals, step to the downhill side of the trail to let them pass.

Also limit the stick-wielding and rock-throwing. Kids love to pick up sticks as they hike, but often these become a hazard for other hikers and the vegetation along the trail. Kids like to throw rocks too. At a big body of water when there is no one else around, this is a pretty harmless activity. But please don't let kids throw rocks off of summits or cliffs.

A NOTE ABOUT SAFETY

Safety is an important concern in all outdoor activities. No guidebook can alert you to every hazard or anticipate the limitations of every reader. Therefore, the descriptions of roads, trails, routes, and natural features in this book are not representations that a particular place or excursion will be safe for your party. When you follow any of the routes described in this book, you assume responsibility for your own safety. Under normal conditions, such excursions require the usual attention to traffic, road and trail conditions, weather, terrain, the capabilities of your party, and other factors. Keeping informed on current conditions and exercising common sense are the keys to a safe, enjoyable outing.

—Mountaineers Books

HOW TO USE THIS GUIDE

This book contains 125 hikes handpicked for children that are located west and north of the Columbia River. It is by no means a complete list of kid-friendly Western Washington trails. Because of the vast geographic area and the limited number that could fit into this guide, I was forced to make hard choices. Many wonderful trails did not make this guidebook, and another volume would be needed to begin to do justice to what is out there. Included in this volume are thirteen "**Great Getaways**," which serve as a resource for extending your hike into a weekend vacation or longer.

The book is written for parents with young children, with the sweet spot being between ages three and nine. These are ages when kids are up for some adventure, but not quite ready for long mileage, elevation gain, or hazards along the trail. With a few exceptions, the hikes in this book are less than 6 miles long and require an elevation gain of less than 1000 feet. Once kids can handle longer and tougher hikes, I suggest you purchase the excellent series of day hiking guides by Mountaineers Books, in which you will find hikes of all difficulty levels.

Taking a well-deserved rest atop Sauk Mountain

BEFORE YOU GO

Map: The name and number of the topographic Green Trails map is included, if one exists for the hike. Green Trails maps are the most accurate and updated hiking maps in Washington. If there isn't one for a hike, I've included the best possible alternative, usually available online.

Contact: Lists the land management agency for the hiking trail, with contact information provided in the Resources. To avoid disappointment at the trailhead, be sure to check the agency website—or call or email them—for open hours and possible seasonal trail or road closures.

Notes: Look here for important information specific to this hike, including required permits, whether dogs are allowed, the availability of restroom or privy facilities, hazard warnings, and seasonal closures.

GPS: The GPS coordinates listed correspond to the trailhead location.

ABOUT THE HIKE

Season: Look here for the best months to hike each trail. Many trails can be hiked year-round.

Difficulty: This subjective measure is calibrated to the average five- or six-year-old.

> *Easy:* Generally less than 2 miles long, with little or no elevation gain. The trail may be paved or barrier-free.
>
> *Easy to moderate:* Up to 4 miles long, with less than 300 feet of elevation gain.
>
> *Moderate:* These trails are longer with less elevation gain, or shorter with a steeper gain.
>
> *Moderate to difficult:* These trails require some stamina, with more elevation gain and rougher trail conditions. Stiff-soled hiking shoes or boots may be necessary.
>
> *Difficult:* The toughest hikes in the book, these may exceed 6 miles or 1000 feet elevation gain. They are classics that just had to be included, but are best for older kids. Hiking shoes or boots may be necessary.

Distance: Trail length is measured in miles, specifying whether it is one-way, a roundtrip, or a loop. For some trails, a mileage range is given.

High point: The highest point of elevation the trail will reach is included.

Elevation gain: This is the total elevation gain from the trailhead.

GETTING THERE

The driving directions listed for each hike begin at the nearest reference point, whether a major highway exit or intersection or a town. The road is paved unless otherwise specified. A few roads are called out for their potholes and other poor conditions, but please note that mountain roads in Washington wash out with regularity, so check with land management agencies for their status before setting out. The driving directions will also note whether the hike is accessible by public transportation.

ON THE TRAIL

Each trail description begins with an overview of the hike and then provides information about how to hike it from start to finish.

EXPLORING FURTHER

For families wishing to backpack or add length or challenge to the hike, I've included information about how to extend your trip. On occasion, I mention other short trails, sights, or family-friendly attractions nearby.

KEY TO ICONS

Stroller accessible. These trails are easily passable for strollers, usually paved or with barrier-free soft surfaces.

Dog-friendly. These trails allow leashed dogs and are well-suited to bringing your dog along.

Backpacking. These hikes can be extended into short overnight trips, ideal for beginning backpackers and families.

Interpretive trail. Interpretive signs enhance the learning experience on these trails.

Splash zone. These trails provide opportunities to wade or swim in water.

Wildflowers. Seasonal wildflowers can be enjoyed along the trail.

Waterfalls. One or more waterfalls can be found on these hikes.

Wildlife. There is a good, but not guaranteed, chance of spotting wildlife on these hikes.

Old growth. Walk beneath giant old trees on these trails.

Opposite: *Kids explore Teddy Bear Cove's eroded bank at low tide.*

PUGET SOUND REGION AND FOOTHILLS

BELLINGHAM AREA

1 POINT WHITEHORN MARINE RESERVE

BEFORE YOU GO
MAP Available online from website
CONTACT Whatcom County Parks and Recreation
NOTES Dogs prohibited; privy available
GPS N 48 53.236, W 122 46.815

ABOUT THE HIKE
SEASON Year-round
DIFFICULTY Easy
DISTANCE 1.6 miles roundtrip
HIGH POINT 115 feet
ELEVATION GAIN 75 feet

Water laps gently on the rounded cobblestones at Point Whitehorn. (photo by Jon Stier)

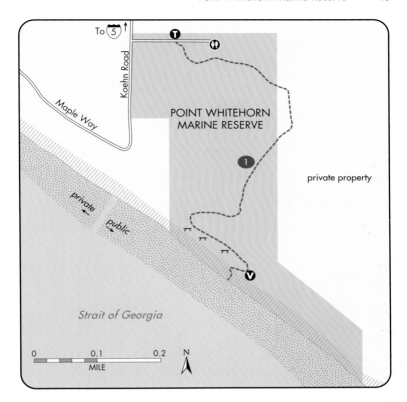

GETTING THERE

From Bellingham, take Interstate 5 northbound 13 miles to exit 266, Grand-view Road (State Route 548). Head west on Grandview for 8.5 miles, following signs for Birch Bay State Park. At Holeman Avenue, Grandview will become Koehn Road. Continue straight on Koehn Road, which takes a 90-degree turn to the left/south. In less than half a mile past the turn, look for the large Point Whitehorn parking area on the left.

ON THE TRAIL

A wheelchair-accessible trail winds through wetlands and upland forest to a bluff with views out across the Strait of Georgia to a dozen San Juan Islands, including Orcas, Lummi, Cyprus, and Sucia. Stairs to the cobblestone beach below offer opportunities to bask in its south-facing sun and dip bare feet into the chilly waters. The preservation of this sweet 54-acre tract is owed to a series of deft and creative land transactions by the Whatcom Land Trust in the early 2000s, which protects this habitat near the heavy industrial footprint of the Cherry Point Refinery.

Start your hike at the sign located in the middle of the parking area. Because it is a designated marine reserve, dogs are not allowed. The trail is wide enough to walk side by side and suitable for strollers. Interpretive signs add context for kids.

The forest includes a variety of native conifers like Douglas fir, Sitka spruce, western hemlock, and western red cedar. It's also boggy, but your way is dry thanks to a series of small bridges and boardwalks. Soon the conifers give way to deciduous forest of black cottonwood, big-leaf maple, and more. Emerging from the forest, the trail travels along the bluff for a short distance, with three overlooks graced by lovely, polished stone benches at 0.75 mile.

This is where strollers must stop, but hikers can proceed 75 feet down the steep bluff and stairs to the beach. When the tide is low, you can explore and investigate tide pools (please step lightly and leave all marine life where you see it). The public tidelands can be explored to the east (toward the refinery), but the stretch to the west is private. Several large boulders grace the beach, the remains of the last ice age. Your kids may enjoy sunning themselves on their flat tops. Note there may be no beach at the highest tides; make sure to watch the tide, so you can safely make your way back to the stairway at the base of the bluff before the water rises too high.

2 TEDDY BEAR COVE

BEFORE YOU GO
MAP Available online on county website
CONTACT Whatcom County Parks and Recreation
NOTES Dogs prohibited on beach; privy available; watch for cars and trains; drop-offs on headland
GPS N 48 42.036, W 122 29.318

ABOUT THE HIKE
SEASON Year-round
DIFFICULTY Easy to moderate
DISTANCE 1.9 miles roundtrip
HIGH POINT 250 feet
ELEVATION GAIN 250 feet

GETTING THERE
From Interstate 5 exit 250 in Bellingham, follow State Route 11 South/Old Fairhaven Parkway west toward Chuckanut Drive. After 1.3 miles, turn left on 12th Street, staying on SR 11. In just 0.1 mile, SR 11 turns slightly left, becoming Chuckanut Drive. Drive another 1.6 miles and turn left into the North Chuckanut Mountain parking area.

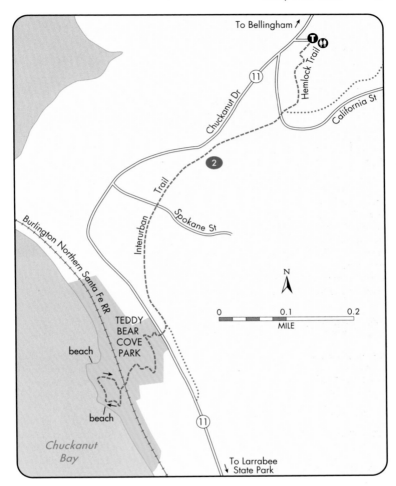

ON THE TRAIL

Mountains meet the sea just minutes from downtown Bellingham in the Chuckanut Mountains. This unique area offers day hiking opportunities that attract hordes of hikers year-round. Unfortunately, many of these trails are too vertical for little legs and so popular that parking areas fill early, requiring long road walks on a busy highway just to reach the trailhead. Enter Teddy Bear Cove! This easy hike is sized just right for kids, leading to two adorable little beaches and a headland at the edge of Chuckanut Bay.

Shells decorate little niches in the rock at Teddy Bear Cove.

Start at the amply sized North Chuckanut Mountain parking area and follow the gentle switchbacks of the Hemlock Trail 0.2 mile to an intersection with the Interurban Trail. The Interurban runs from Bellingham on a right-of-way all the way to Larrabee State Park. Turn right onto this trail, watching for bikes and horses, as it parallels Chuckanut Drive southward.

You might find that this part of the hike stretches your definition of a trail. Crossing first California and then Spokane streets, it becomes a road walk through a woodsy neighborhood. (Your kids, like mine, may enjoy imagining living in one of these trailside homes, riding bikes on the trail, and playing in the large yards.) After a level 0.5 mile, reach a mailbox marked "1464." Just beyond, stairs descend to Chuckanut Drive. Cross the busy road very carefully.

A large Whatcom County sign welcomes you to Teddy Bear Cove. This section of trail is short but steep with switchbacks. Kids will want to fly down the trail. Make sure they don't cut the switchbacks, and that they stop and wait before crossing the railroad tracks at the bottom. Trains whiz along this corridor several times a day, and the sight lines are adequate but not long.

Crossing the tracks, choose right or left—both lead to beaches. The path to the right (north) is more secluded, but the beach to the left (south) is more fun. At first, the south beach looks to be covered in white sand. As you approach, you'll see it consists of crushed clamshells. Archaeologists have posited that this could be a midden left over from hundreds of years of shellfish gathering. Equally interesting is the geology of the headland, which is pockmarked with little holes perfect for decorating with shell fragments and rocks. At low tide, this is a stellar place to tidepool. Don't forget to look to the water and sky for seals, eagles, and other wildlife.

TIDEPOOL ETIQUETTE

Kids love all kinds of creatures, and there is no better way to get them interested in the marine environment than to take them tidepooling. Puget Sound and Washington's abundant coastline offer many opportunities to look for anemones, sea stars, crabs, and more. I like to bring waterproof boots to keep toes dry and a marine field guide. Every visit is different, and you never know what you will find.

Whether you're in your local city park or a national park, the tidepool environment is fragile. Set expectations before you go out, and be a good role model. Watch where you step to avoid smashing creatures under your feet. If you turn over a rock to examine what's underneath, make sure to carefully tip it back to where it was. You may touch gently or simply have a look. Finally, refrain from collecting shells or animals from the beach. While you may have fond memories of collecting shells as a kid, biologists have found that the loss of these items has negatively impacted the intertidal environment.

Make sure to climb up the steps to the top of the headland for even better views of the Olympics, Orcas Island, and other smaller islands in the sound. Note: this is best to explore with adults, as there are steep drop-offs all around. Admire the majestic madronas and Garry oaks, then make your way down the stairs to check out the north beach before returning the way you came—up the switchbacks, through the neighborhood, and back to the trailhead.

3 SEHOME HILL ARBORETUM

BEFORE YOU GO
MAP Available online on Sehome Hill Arboretum website
CONTACT Western Washington University
NOTES Dogs must be leashed; tunnel and tower accessible to strollers from upper parking area; no restroom facilities
GPS N 48 43.630, W 122 29.130

ABOUT THE HIKE
SEASON Year-round
DIFFICULTY Moderate
DISTANCE 2.4 miles loop
HIGH POINT 625 feet
ELEVATION GAIN 450 feet

GETTING THERE
From Interstate 5 in Bellingham, take exit 252 for Samish Way and head west. At the first major intersection, turn left on Bill McDonald Parkway. Take this 0.9 mile to 25th Street. Turn right on 25th Street and find two lower parking areas almost immediately to your left. The hike starts at the trailhead here. To

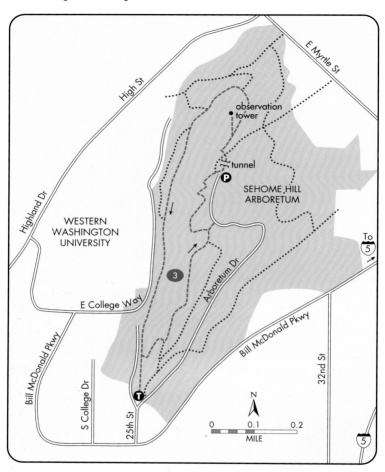

reach the upper parking area near the tunnel and observation tower, veer right onto Arboretum Drive and follow it to its end, about 0.8 mile. This trail can be reached by public transportation.

ON THE TRAIL

At Sehome Hill Arboretum there are no manicured lawns with labeled plant specimens. Instead, you'll find a 180-acre wooded hill adjacent to the Western Washington University campus with more than 5 miles of hiking trails. At the top of Sehome Hill, an 80-foot-tall observation tower rises above the canopy and gives hikers a bird's-eye view of North Puget Sound.

GREAT GETAWAY: BELLINGHAM

Don't overlook sweet Bellingham as a destination. This small city, particularly the Fairhaven neighborhood, has a quirky and comfortable college town feel, with old storefronts, good food, and a thriving art scene. It's the perfect place to do a town mouse/country mouse weekend. Take a short hike in the morning, check out the excellent Whatcom Museum or the Marine Life Center in the afternoon, and then top it off with a tasty dinner and ice cream.

Lodging options abound in the city and are usually available on short notice unless it is a big parents' weekend at the university. For camping, check out Larrabee or Birch Bay state parks—both can keep a family happily occupied with hiking, clamming, sandcastles, and sunsets for a long weekend.

A 2.4-mile loop provides a brisk workout, highlighted by a historic auto tunnel as well as the observatory. Before going, print out an online map; some of the trails are well marked, but others, especially around the observation tower, are not.

Start at the trailhead between the two lower parking areas, taking a dirt path to the first intersection. Go right to reach the Douglas Fir Trail, climbing twenty steps to just below the ridgeline. Take a left on the Douglas Fir Trail and gain 325 feet in 0.4 mile. The arboretum property was logged until 1904, so while the trees are not old growth, some are quite old and tall. Look for Douglas fir, cedar, and hemlocks, as well as maples and alders. This canopy keeps hikers cool on warm days and dry on rainy ones.

Hand-chiseled tunnel in Sehome Arboretum

The trail will intersect with Arboretum Drive. Hikers can either take the road, watching carefully for vehicles, or walk a slightly longer, more sinuous route through the trees. Both reconnect at the upper parking lot, an alternative and quicker access point for the observation tower and tunnel. While this parking area is a good starting point for toddlers or hikers with disabilities, older kids may feel a greater sense of accomplishment if they have to work to reach their destination.

From the upper parking area, follow the trail to the right of the communications tower. Here you will find a hand-chiseled tunnel, carved out of sandstone in 1923 for drivers on a weekend auto tour. The tunnel is irresistible to kids, and you will want to supervise closely any climbing they may want to try.

Emerge from the tunnel and at the junction choose the paved Tunnel Trail to reach the nearby observation tower. Even if the kids are tired, they will scamper up the six flights of tower steps with renewed energy. You'll want a clear day—especially in the fall or winter when the trees are leafless—to fully appreciate this perch in the treetops. There's Bellingham in panorama: downtown, the port, the pier, and many neighborhoods. The Coast Range of British Columbia looms on the northern horizon, and Mount Baker is visible between two tall conifers.

After getting your fill of the view, return to the junction and follow the Huntoon Trail down the paved path to the left. A few old interpretive signs remain, but trail signage is lacking and choosing the correct route can be confusing. The trail you want is at the end of a big paved turnaround on the left. The online trail map says this path is also paved, but it is actually gravel. Pass sandstone cliffs and an amphitheater, and descend so that you are parallel with the Western Washington University campus and East College Way. It's about 0.8 mile to return to your car or the bus stop.

4 HERTZ TRAIL: LAKE WHATCOM PARK

BEFORE YOU GO
    MAP Available online from county website
    CONTACT Whatcom County Parks and Recreation
    NOTES Bikes allowed; privy available
    GPS N 48 43.815, W 122 18.508

ABOUT THE HIKE
    SEASON Year-round
    DIFFICULTY Easy
    DISTANCE 0.4 to 6.2 miles roundtrip
    HIGH POINT 415 feet
    ELEVATION GAIN 100 feet

GETTING THERE

From Interstate 5 northbound, take exit 254 in Bellingham and turn right on Iowa Street. In 0.7 mile, veer left onto Yew Street. In 0.5 mile, turn right on Alabama Street and drive until you reach Lake Whatcom, about 1 mile. Here

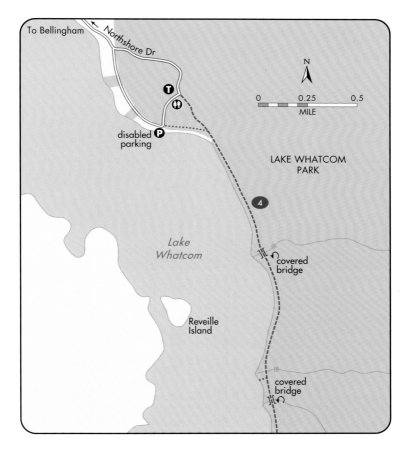

turn left onto Northshore Drive and proceed all the way around the lake, a full 7.2 miles through lakeside neighborhoods. Look for the sign for Lake Whatcom Park and turn left; the parking lot is 0.5 mile on the left. A wheelchair-accessible lot is slightly farther on. Trails from both lots meet at the lake.

ON THE TRAIL
Trails don't come more family-friendly than this one. It travels along the east side of Lake Whatcom on an old railroad corridor ideal for strollers, wheelchairs, bicycles, and walking. The lake sparkles in the sunlight, with several small rocky beaches for swimming or throwing rocks. Two waterfalls tumble down the side of Stewart Mountain, and a pair of charming covered bridges beg to be photographed. This hike rewards no matter where you turn around.

Lake Whatcom offers a quiet place to reflect. (photo by Jon Stier)

From the main parking area, descend 0.2 mile through ferny, mossy second-growth forest to the shore of Lake Whatcom, Washington's fourth-largest freshwater lake and the source of Bellingham's drinking water. Hop onto an abandoned railway, carved improbably into the side of Stewart Mountain. This short spur operated between 1902 and 1919 to and from the Blue Canyon coal mine. The rich history of the railroad and surrounding area is described on interpretive signs.

Beach access is best here, enticing kids to swim or chuck rocks (hopefully not at the same time!). It may be difficult to get them to continue hiking. But those who march onward will enjoy dappled sunshine as the trail hugs the shoreline. Take a left at the lake and let the kids loose. Long sight lines make it possible to let the kids run ahead, and the wide trail allows families to walk three abreast.

At 1 mile, reach an idyllic spot. A 50-foot waterfall cascades down a steep creek, flows under a covered bridge, and trickles through a beach to the lake. Many people opt to turn around here, which makes for a pleasing 2-mile roundtrip. Soon thereafter, the trail narrows a bit and becomes rockier. Look for remnants of the former railroad in this section. Old support pylons poke up out of the lake even after one hundred years. A weeping, rocky cliff face shows signs of blasting. Listen carefully for the sound of cascading water and a second waterfall.

Just before the 1.5-mile marker, a side trail leads to a good place to lay out a picnic, with broad views up and down the lake and Reveille Island directly across the water. If everyone is up for a little more, press on to a second covered bridge, another 0.25 mile down the trail. It's after this point that the other walkers really thin out. The scenery changes gradually, but as you round a corner after the bridge, new views open up at the far end of the lake. Those hiking the full length will find a private property sign marking the end of the trail at 3.1 miles. When you are ready, turn around and return to the trailhead.

SKAGIT COUNTY AND ISLANDS

5 PADILLA BAY SHORE TRAIL

BEFORE YOU GO
 MAP Available online on county website
 CONTACT Skagit County Parks and Recreation
 NOTES Dogs must be leashed; privy available at both trailheads
 GPS N 48 27.420, W 122 27.971

ABOUT THE HIKE
 SEASON Year-round
 DIFFICULTY Easy
 DISTANCE 2 to 4.6 miles roundtrip
 HIGH POINT 20 feet
 ELEVATION GAIN none

GETTING THERE
From Interstate 5, take exit 230 in Burlington and head west on State Route 20 toward Anacortes. In 7 miles, turn right on Bayview-Edison Road. In 0.9 mile, look for the dike and a small parking area on the left. This is the south lot. If it is full, continue another 2.1 miles for the northern trailhead. Parking is located at the Skagit County Historical Society. Turn right on Second Street and left in 200 feet into the large parking lot.

ON THE TRAIL
An amble atop an earthen dike gives visitors an intimate glimpse of an intertidal estuary so special that it has been designated as a National Estuarine Research Reserve. It teems with waterfowl and birds, attracted by plentiful clams, shrimp, and other invertebrates in Padilla Bay. The trail is ideal for families, whether pushing a stroller, skipping along the level path, or taking bicycles for an easy ride.

There are two entrances to the Padilla Bay Shore Trail. The north entrance has the larger parking area, but requires a short road walk and a longer trek along the bay, where wildlife is not as plentiful. The trail from the south entrance is more interesting, but parking is limited. If you are able, park in the south lot and walk north.

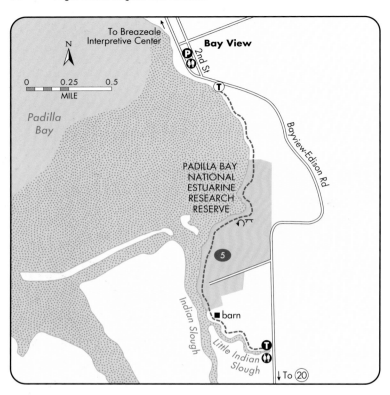

Follow Little Indian Slough along the dike, heading to the barn in the distance. The setting is inspiring, especially on a sunny day. Green farm fields and the glistening bay are ringed with peaks—the Chuckanut Mountains and Canadian Cascades to the north, Mount Baker and Glacier Peak to the east, and Mount Erie nearby to the west. The barn, shaded by a lone tree, is particularly photogenic. The only thing marring the vista is the Anacortes refineries' billowing exhaust stacks across the bay.

After the barn, the dike curves along a portion of the bay heavily influenced by tides. Look for great blue herons, kingfishers, sandpipers, gulls, and a variety of ducks near the water, and don't be surprised if you see bald eagles, northern harriers, or owls swooping in the fields for a meal. A part of the Pacific Flyway, in winter the bay attracts migratory birds; this is considered the best time to visit, but summertime walks are rewarded with more songbirds. It's best to time your visit to when the tide is coming in or going out. Too low, and there is mud as far as you can see; too high, and the best wildlife viewing areas are submerged.

Birds are plentiful in Padilla Bay's mudflats. (photo by Jon Stier)

The dike runs a full 2.3 miles from end to end—ideal if you have two cars or lots of energy. A satisfying turnaround, however, can be found at the 1-mile marker, where two benches provide a pleasant spot to rest before returning the way you came.

EXPLORING FURTHER

Don't miss the nearby Breazeale Interpretive Center. This top-notch educational facility was one of the highlights of our trip to Padilla Bay. There are several hands-on exhibits inside that kids (and adults) of all ages can enjoy, and a small aquarium with some superb specimens. Outside the center, the short Upland Trail winds through meadow and forest. The center is not open every day, so before you go, check the website for days and times.

SUGARLOAF MOUNTAIN

BEFORE YOU GO

MAP Green Trails, Deception Pass/Anacortes Community Forest Lands No. 41S; Whistle Lake Area Map available from the Friends of the ACFL online at www.friendsoftheacfl.org

CONTACT City of Anacortes–Parks and Recreation

NOTES Dogs must be leashed; unsigned trail junctions; no restrooms or privies; trail can be scaled for younger hikers

GPS N 48 27.945, W 122 37.779

Sweeping views from the summit of Sugarloaf Mountain (photo by Jon Stier)

ABOUT THE HIKE (LONGER ROUTE)

SEASON Year-round
DIFFICULTY Moderate to difficult
DISTANCE 2.2 miles roundtrip
HIGH POINT 1044 feet
ELEVATION GAIN 825 feet

ABOUT THE HIKE (SHORTER ROUTE)

SEASON Year-round
DIFFICULTY Easy to moderate
DISTANCE 0.5 mile roundtrip
HIGH POINT 1044 feet
ELEVATION GAIN 300 feet

GETTING THERE

From Interstate 5, take exit 230 in Burlington and head west on State Route 20 toward Anacortes. After driving SR 20 11.8 miles to Sharpes Corner, turn left. You will remain on SR 20 and follow the signs for Deception Pass State Park. Go 1.8 miles and turn right on Campbell Lake Road. Drive 1.4 miles to the Lake Erie Grocery and veer right on Heart Lake Road. Go another 1.4 miles and turn right at the sign labeled "Mt Erie Viewpoint." Trailhead parking for the longer route is about 200 feet up the road, just past the road to Mount Erie. To find the trailhead for the alternative shorter route, turn onto Mount Erie Road and drive 0.7 mile to a small pullout.

ON THE TRAIL

Sugarloaf's glorious summit is attainable by young and old via two separate routes. Both are short, but one has considerably more elevation gain and the other is more appropriate for toddlers and preschoolers. The trails top out on a broad, open, and safe summit with views over Puget Sound of the Olympics and San Juan Islands to the west and of Mount Baker and the Cascades to the east.

Sugarloaf Mountain is part of the impressive and vast Anacortes Community Forest Lands, managed by the City of Anacortes. Fifty miles of trails encircle lakes, traverse meadows, and scale mountains. There are a baffling number of trails and junctions, all marked with numbers (not names), and you will definitely want a map to help guide you. The Lake Erie Grocery carries a full set; download maps from the Friends of the Anacortes Community Forest Lands website, or snap a photo of the map at the trailhead kiosk.

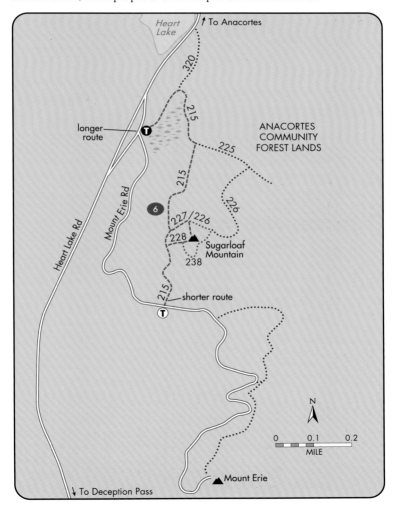

Longer Route

The more challenging course wends its way 1.1 miles and 825 feet up through a shady forest with a salal and fern understory. It begins on Trail No. 215 in a marshy level area, but soon gets down to business. After a heart-pumping 0.5 mile, reach an intersection and go right, remaining on Trail No. 215. Power up a steep hill to another intersection, where you will go straight. At 0.8 mile is yet another intersection. Here, turn left onto Trail No. 227 (it may also be signed Trail No. 226) for your final push. At this point, all upward-trending trails lead to the summit. Take a seat on the grassy knoll and catch your breath beneath a swooping limb of one of the pines that grace the summit. The views invite quiet reflection, but also further exploration. Take some of the paths to find seasonal wildflowers, chartreuse mossy rocks, and new views.

Shorter Route

If you drive to the small pullout on Mount Erie Road, the route to Sugarloaf Mountain is only 300 feet of elevation gain over 0.25 mile. That's steep, but so short that just about anyone can make it. This trail is also more direct. Take Trail No. 215 until you reach Trail No. 228, and go right to the summit.

Whatever route you take, make sure to retrace your steps from the summit upon your return. It is easy to head downhill on a different trail than you arrived on, and then you must navigate among the tangle of trails to get back to your car.

7 SHARPE PARK–SARES HEAD

BEFORE YOU GO

MAP Green Trails, Deception Pass/Anacortes Community Forest Lands No. 41S
CONTACT Skagit County Parks and Recreation
NOTES Dogs must be leashed; privy available; steep drop-offs
GPS N 48 25.849, W 122 39.880

ABOUT THE HIKE

SEASON Year-round
DIFFICULTY Easy to moderate
DISTANCE 1.5 miles roundtrip
HIGH POINT 150 feet
ELEVATION GAIN 400 feet

GETTING THERE

From Interstate 5, take exit 230 in Burlington and head west on State Route 20 toward Anacortes. After driving SR 20 11.8 miles to Sharpes Corner, turn left. You will remain on SR 20 and follow the signs for Deception Pass State Park. Go 5.1 miles, passing Lake Campbell and Pass Lake, to Rosario Road. Turn right on Rosario Road and proceed 1.7 miles to Sharpe Park Montgomery-Duban Headlands and pull into the parking area on the left.

Happy kids celebrate their arrival at Sares Head. (photo by David Elderkin)

ON THE TRAIL

Not far from the madding crowds at Deception Pass State Park is this little-known, easy trail to a breathtaking headland overlooking Puget Sound. Just a mile up the road from Rosario Head, Skagit County's Sharpe Park is an excellent destination when you need a short hike that the kids will like. It has a wetland full of birds and a big broad rocky bald dotted with wildflowers, gnarled old trees, and great views. This is an ideal place to watch the sunset.

From the parking area, pass alongside the boggy picnic area and Rachel Carson Memorial sundial to a wetland. Watch for red-winged blackbirds

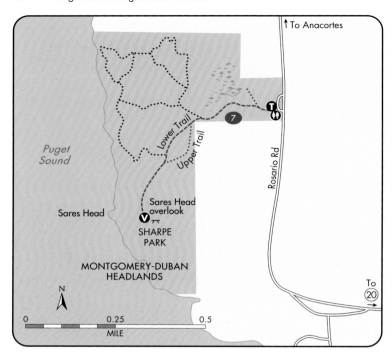

bobbing on cattails and hooded mergansers, Canada geese, widgeons, and mallards among the lily pads on the pond. At 0.3 mile, reach a junction. Stay on the well-maintained trail and veer left to Sares Head. Almost immediately you will reach another junction—both the Upper and Lower trails go to the same place, but the Lower Trail is a much smoother choice.

As you approach Sares Head at 0.75 mile, take hold of little ones' hands. The first viewpoint has some steep drop-offs, but if you round the headland a bit, you will reach a bench atop a broad rock in a safer environment. If it is windy, follow a side path for a view of Deception Pass Bridge and Whidbey Island. My kids were rather mesmerized by this place. We looked up and saw bald eagles soaring on the wind currents. We counted the islands on the horizon. We listened to the wind and inspected the variety and colors of lichen and moss covering the rocks. I hoisted them up into a gnarly old tree blackened with soot from a long-ago fire. They actually thanked me for taking them there!

On your return, take a closer look at the huge Douglas firs on the lee side of the headland, and the ferns, red-flowering currants, and Oregon grape alongside the trail. You may opt for the Upper Trail on the return, but be aware that the trail is rooty and rocky and a tad bit steep. Return past the pond and to your car.

GREAT GETAWAY: WHIDBEY ISLAND

Whidbey Island offers an ideal retreat for families, with less hassle than traveling to the San Juan Islands. If the ferry line is long in Mukilteo, you can drive up to Burlington and take State Route 20. Follow the signs to the Deception Pass Bridge onto the island. That's where the best recreation is anyway. Deception Pass State Park is one of our state's crown jewels, with ample camping, hiking, and dramatic bluffs overlooking the Puget Sound and the Strait of Juan de Fuca.

Whidbey Island has a fascinating history as part of our nation's maritime defense. Don't miss poking around the old military buildings at Fort Casey and Fort Ebey state parks, which also offer excellent campgrounds. Bring shovels, buckets, and a shellfish license to dig for clams, or ride bicycles along the back roads. Hotels can be found on the island in Oak Harbor, Coupeville, and farther south in Langley. Make sure to plan your visit in advance, however, as motels and campgrounds fill early in the summer and may require a two-night stay.

EXPLORING FURTHER

Several loop options are possible, but note that the other trails cover much rougher terrain than the trail to Sares Head, with lots of roots, rocks, and mud that make it difficult for short legs, as well as steep drop-offs that might give you pause. A trail descends to a cove near the water, and there are fine views along the bluff. But the ones at Sares Head are just as good. Venturing out on these trails would be suitable for older kids, but not for younger children. If you do explore further, make sure you have a copy of the park map.

8 GOOSE ROCK

BEFORE YOU GO

MAP Green Trails, Deception Pass/Anacortes Community Forest Lands No. 41S
CONTACT Washington State Parks
NOTES Discover Pass required; dogs must be leashed; restrooms and water available
GPS N 48 24.197, W 122 38.835

ABOUT THE HIKE

SEASON Year-round
DIFFICULTY Moderate
DISTANCE 2.4 miles loop
HIGH POINT 484 feet
ELEVATION GAIN 460 feet

GETTING THERE

From Interstate 5, take exit 230 in Burlington and head west on State Route 20 toward Anacortes. After driving SR 20 11.8 miles to Sharpes Corner, turn left. You will remain on SR 20 and follow the signs for Deception Pass State

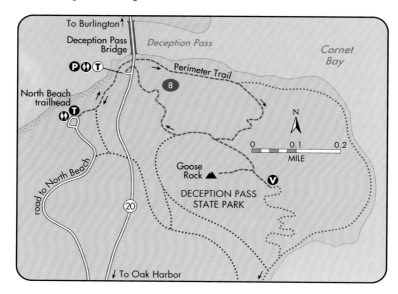

Park. Travel 6 miles and cross the Deception Pass Bridge onto Whidbey Island. If there is room in the small lot on the Whidbey Island side, you can park there and save 100 feet of elevation gain. In the summer this lot is packed with bridge-gawking tourists, and you'll need to travel another mile to the turnoff for Deception Pass State Park. Turn right into the park, and right again at the sign for North Beach. In 0.7 mile you will arrive at a large parking area and the trailhead. This trail can be reached by public transportation.

ON THE TRAIL

Here's a mountain even the youngest can climb! With an elevation of 484 feet, it's not a very tall mountain, but the open rocky balds at the top provide such sweeping views that most kids will feel the achievement of reaching a summit. The Perimeter Trail encircles Goose Rock, with entry trails approaching from several directions. This northern approach via a 1.8-mile lollipop loop is the easiest and shortest way to the top.

If you're beginning at the North Beach trailhead, find the trail between the parking lot and the beach and huff it uphill in the direction of the Deception Pass Bridge. In just 0.25 mile and 100 feet of elevation gain, you'll reach the alternative trailhead next to the bridge. Duck under the impressive arched steel tresses and reach a junction. Take the Perimeter Trail to the left; your return will be on the trail to the right.

The trail is cooled by shaded forest and breezes flowing through Deception Pass, with peek-a-boo views of the water and Cornet Bay. At 0.6 mile, reach another junction. The trail to the left contours around Goose Rock and at one

BALDS

Balds are areas that were scraped to bedrock by retreating ice sheets. Today, they are ecologically important, with fragile plants that are unique to that environment.

point drops to the shores of Cornet Bay before ascending steeply to the summit from the south. As a simpler option, veer right and ascend 200 feet in 0.3 mile. It may seem steep, but it is well graded and short. Take your time and admire the stately Douglas firs as you climb. At the next junction, go left and in no time at all emerge from under powerlines onto a rocky bald. (Please follow the existing trails here so that you don't trample these sensitive plants.)

Powerlines aside, this first bald offers good views of the Cascades. However, the real treat—and the actual summit—is just a short uphill climb to the right, topping out at 1.4 miles and 484 feet. And what a panorama it is! Between the snowy heights of Mount Rainier and the distinctive humps of the San Juan Islands, you can take in the full Olympic range, Deception Pass State Park's

Having a snack atop Goose Rock (photo by David Elderkin)

Cranberry Lake, and even planes taking off and landing at Whidbey Naval Air Station in Oak Harbor.

Having scored your fill of summit views, head back to your last junction. At the fork below the summit, choose the trail to the left. It's a bit steeper and shorter than the way you ascended and joins up again with the main trail at the bridge.

EXPLORING FURTHER

On your way back, detour onto the Deception Pass Bridge with the many sightseers. You can walk along the east side of the bridge, admiring the swirling currents and picturesque Strawberry Island below, then cross under the bridge and pop out on the west side for the return to the trailhead.

9 LIGHTHOUSE POINT

BEFORE YOU GO
MAP Green Trails, Deception Pass/Anacortes Community Forest Lands No. 41S
CONTACT Washington State Parks
NOTES Discover Pass required; dogs must be leashed; privy available; steep drop-offs
GPS N 48 24.197, W 122 38.835

ABOUT THE HIKE
SEASON Year-round
DIFFICULTY Easy to moderate
DISTANCE 2 miles roundtrip
HIGH POINT 135 feet
ELEVATION GAIN 50 feet

GETTING THERE
From Interstate 5, take exit 230 in Burlington and head west on State Route 20 toward Anacortes. After driving SR 20 11.8 miles to Sharpes Corner, turn left. You will remain on SR 20 and follow the signs for Deception Pass State Park. Go 5.1 miles, passing two lakes, to Rosario Road. Turn right on Rosario Road and immediately left on Bowman Bay Road. Descend 0.3 mile, turning left into the large parking area with the boat launch and small playground. This trail can be reached by public transportation.

ON THE TRAIL
Deception Pass State Park sports more than 14 miles of saltwater shoreline, and on this hike you can explore some of the most rewarding of them. Lighthouse Point juts out into Puget Sound from Fidalgo Island, and as you round it you can clamber up headlands with ever-changing views, including the Deception Pass Bridge, North Beach on Whidbey Island, little Deception Island, and farther west to the San Juan Islands.

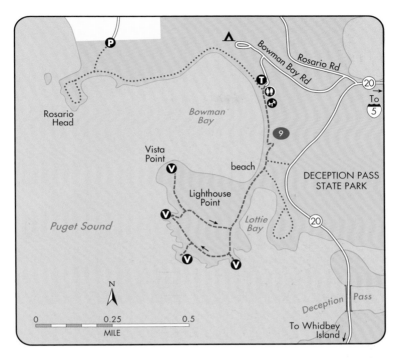

Bowman Bay, where the hike begins, was the site of a bustling Samish village until the late 1880s when white settlers moved into the area. With its protected cove and abundant shellfish, you can see why this would be an attractive place to settle, and in fact, archaeologists have found shell middens throughout this area. From the parking area, take the trail going south (left) along the water, passing a long pier. Climb up and over a headland on a good trail to the first of two junctions. Take the trails to the right at each of them, following the signs for Lighthouse Point.

After the second junction, cross a grassy spit between Lottie Bay (left) and Bowman Bay (right). A sandy beach beckons, but is best saved as a reward for after the hike. Ascend through pleasant forest above Lottie Bay with places to view the Deception Pass Bridge. At 0.6 mile, reach a junction with the loop trail at a hollowed and burned stump. Choose the left fork; the right will be your return. Soon arrive at a knockout view of the bridge where you may notice that it is actually two bridges with a small island in the middle. There's a pocket beach and a small headland to scramble up and survey the scene. Search for a slice of rock that resembles the prow of a ship. Enjoy this spot, but please tread lightly on the little plants that grow here.

Kayaking around Lighthouse Point

Continue looping your way around the point, going up and down over more rocky headlands. Short side trails lead off from the main one to other vistas. Explore some of these and notice how the scenery changes as you round the point. However, keep kids close by, as there are steep drop-offs and no railings; this is not the trail for recklessness. But as long as everyone is sitting down, it's fun to try to identify landmarks in a panorama that stretches from Whidbey Island to Rosario Head and to look for harbor seals plying the water below. At a final stunning promontory 135 feet above the water, aptly named Vista Point, the side trail peters out in thick underbrush. If you reach that point, you'll know it is time to turn around and return to the main trail.

The trail returns to the original junction at Lottie Bay. Go left, retracing your steps and possibly stopping to play at the beach or the playground before returning to your car.

EXPLORING FURTHER

Two other fine trails radiate from Bowman Bay. The short, lollipop-loop trail around Lottie Point offers even better views of Deception Pass Bridge. And the 1.7-mile roundtrip to Rosario Head passes by the CCC Interpretive Center (open during summer months, with displays about the Depression-era Civilian Conservation Corps) and the campground to another stunning rocky headland.

GREAT GETAWAY: THE SAN JUAN ISLANDS

The San Juan Islands offer a unique escape from the hustle and bustle of mainland urban and suburban life. Long, pebbly beaches, abundant wildlife, island bluffs and hilltops, and the chance for quiet reflection attract thousands of visitors each year. It's a great place to camp and bicycle, eat good food, and get away from it all. The four main islands accessible by the state ferry system—San Juan, Lopez, Orcas, and Shaw—also boast excellent hiking.

With a limited amount of space in this volume, I felt I couldn't do justice to what each island has to offer for hiking. Nearly every hike on the islands is kid-friendly. Venture out and discover resting seals, spouting whales, and soaring eagles. Feast your eyes on mountains, open water, ships, and sailboats.

If you are headed to any of the San Juan or Gulf islands, get a copy of Craig Romano's *Day Hiking: The San Juans and Gulf Islands*. It's the most comprehensive source for hiking trails in the islands and will provide you with tips and insights for visiting this fascinating archipelago.

10 EBEY'S LANDING

BEFORE YOU GO
    MAP Available online from the preserve
    CONTACT Ebey's Landing National Historical Reserve
    NOTES Discover Pass required; dogs must be leashed; privy available
    GPS N 48 11.552, W 122 42.519

ABOUT THE HIKE
    SEASON Year-round
    DIFFICULTY Moderate
    DISTANCE 3.5 miles loop
    HIGH POINT 250 feet
    ELEVATION GAIN 250 feet

GETTING THERE

There are two approaches to long, narrow Whidbey Island: via ferry to the south end, or by bridge to the north end; Ebey's Landing is at roughly the midpoint. The state ferry runs from Mukilteo to Clinton on Whidbey. From there, drive State Route 525 north 22 miles to the junction with State Route 20. Bear right onto SR 20 and proceed 5.5 miles to a traffic light in the town of Coupeville. At the next left, turn left onto S Ebey Road. This road will veer right and become Ebey's Landing Road. Take it to its end and park in the small lot (Discover Pass) or on the road (no pass). By bridge, from Interstate 5, take exit 230 in Burlington and head west on SR 20 toward Anacortes. After driving SR 20 11.8 miles to Sharpes Corner, turn left. You will remain on SR 20 and follow the signs for Deception Pass State Park. Drive 6 miles and cross the Deception Pass Bridge onto Whidbey Island and continue through Oak

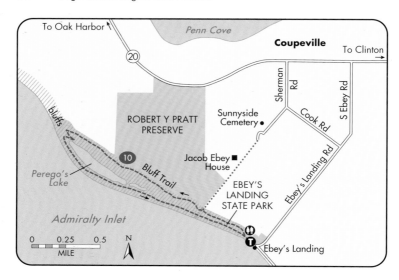

Harbor on SR 20 west. The turnoff to S Ebey Road is approximately 9 miles south of Oak Harbor.

ON THE TRAIL

With something for everyone, this hike is the star of Whidbey Island: the Olympic Mountains rising regally across the water, cargo ships passing through the Strait of Juan de Fuca, raptors gliding on the wind currents, a saltwater lagoon teeming with wildlife, a long stretch of beach full of driftwood and colorful tide-tumbled stones, and a rich (and bloody!) history. When the fog rolls in, ships sound their horns in a musical dance to avoid collision. In the sunshine, bluffside grasses glow, set off by the water below.

Most trail guides have hikers do a 5.6-mile loop, starting at a historic cemetery that includes a small visitor center and blockhouse that belonged to the area's namesake, Colonel Isaac Ebey, one of the first white settlers in the area. While these are good to visit, the mile-long walk to the bluff is apt to tire out young people before they reach the good stuff. Instead, consider parking in the small beachside lot at the end of Ebey's Landing Road on Washington State Parks land and explore a bluff-beach loop from there.

Take time to read the informational panels at the trailhead. These tell of the wildlife, the types of ships plying the water, and the long history of this land. Drawn by an abundance of food and materials, Skagit Indians established permanent villages in Penn Cove in the 1300s. By the time Captain George Vancouver landed on Whidbey's shores in 1792, the Native American community exceeded 1500 people. With the promise of free land to homestead, white settlers began arriving in the 1850s. During that time this area served

A trail along Perego's Lake provides an alternative to the beach walk.

as a ferry landing, allowing the trade of goods from Port Angeles. The Ebey family homesteaded on adjacent farmland and ran the dock. In 1857, Colonel Ebey met an untimely end, beheaded by natives from the north seeking revenge for killings of their tribal members by whites. To preserve this tangled yet rich history, the area was named the country's first National Historical Reserve in 1978.

Climb the stairs and ascend the Bluff Trail, promising the kids beach time upon the return. It's steep, so take your time and savor the views. This place is glorious. Not only is the full breadth of the snowcapped Olympics visible, but you can see Mount Baker to the east. In season, an astonishing variety of wildflowers graces the sand bluffs and rare prairie environment: paintbrush, camas, even prickly pear cactus! Bald eagles soar through the air or gaze watchfully from snags, spying their next meal.

At about a mile, Perego's Lake comes into view and you start your descent. Many people opt to turn around before descending all the way to the beach. Beach walking is always more difficult than trail walking, and if the tide is in, you will be forced to walk on rounded cobblestones for much of the way. If you choose the beach, descend on two long switchbacks to the water and let the kids enjoy themselves before proceeding. There is also a path alongside Perego's Lake. Consider taking it for at least part of your return journey. The lake—actually a lagoon—is one of the least-disturbed coastal wetlands in the state and supports a diverse array of wildlife. The walk along here is quiet and peaceful compared to the loud beach just yards away. Whichever route you choose, in a little over a mile you will be back to the trailhead.

EXPLORING FURTHER

If the history of Ebey's Landing left you wanting to know more, make sure to visit the historic buildings and cemetery at the other end of Ebey's Prairie Trail. From Ebey's Landing Road, turn left on Cook Road. It ends near the Sunnyside Cemetery, where you can walk down the trail to the Jacob Ebey House and Visitor Contact Station. The town of Coupeville, where you can get excellent ice cream and pizza, is a worthwhile stop too.

11 CAMANO ISLAND STATE PARK

BEFORE YOU GO
MAP Available online on state park website
CONTACT Washington State Parks
NOTES Discover Pass required; dogs must be leashed; beach access may be limited at very high tides; privy available
GPS N 48 07.315, W 122 29.445

ABOUT THE HIKE
SEASON Year-round
DIFFICULTY Easy
DISTANCE 1.5 miles loop
HIGH POINT 130 feet
ELEVATION GAIN 125 feet

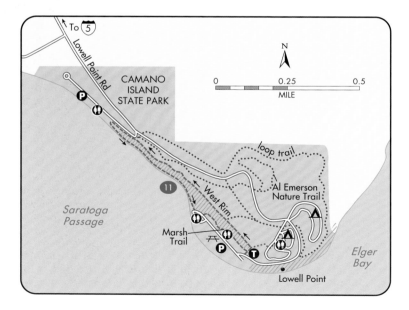

It's exhausting to ride in a backpack!

GETTING THERE

From Interstate 5, take exit 212 and travel west on State Route 532 through Stanwood 10 miles to the junction of NE Camano Drive and E North Camano Drive. Bear left onto NE Camano Drive and follow it 5.8 miles. At E Monticello Drive, turn right and drive 1.9 miles. Turn left onto W Camano Drive and drive 1.3 miles. Turn right onto Lowell Point Road and drive 0.8 mile to the Camano Island State Park entrance. Follow the park drive through the campground 1.1 miles to its end at a large parking area.

ON THE TRAIL

While everyone else is piling onto ferries and visiting the San Juan Islands and Whidbey Island, consider a more accessible island getaway: Camano Island. It's far easier to get there, and at the southern end of the island are two unique state parks with hiking, camping, and cabins. Camano Island State Park is the wilder of the two, with about 5 miles of trails looping along the beach, the bluff, and the campground. For families visiting for the day or staying in the campground, an easy 1.5-mile beach-bluff loop takes in the highlights of this park.

Start at the south end of the long beachside day-use lot. The trailhead is at the bottom of the drive from the campground. Head up the ravine a short distance to the second of two successive and well-signed trail junctions. Go left on the Loop Trail, climbing about 100 feet up onto the West Rim. The trail traverses a bluff overlooking Saratoga Passage. Dappled light radiates through the trees, and every so often there is a bench with peek-a-boo views of the water and the sweep of the Olympic Mountains in the distance.

At 0.6 mile, you'll emerge from the trees onto a road. Carefully walk on the left-hand side of the road down toward the beach. It's only a tenth of a mile. When you reach the kiosk in the parking area, head left on a path to the beach and pick your way over drift logs until you reach the pebbles. Now walk back the way you came, this time at the foot of the bluff. It is an excellent place to linger and play on a sunny day, with no shortage of rocks to heave into the water and fine views of Puget Sound.

At 1.2 miles, reach the park's boat dock. Hikers can take one of two routes back to the trailhead at the other end of the long parking area: they can continue walking along the beach, or they can take the Marsh Trail. I prefer the Marsh Trail, because it offers something you haven't seen on the hike and because it is more direct.

To reach the Marsh Trail, cross the access road opposite the privy. The trail cozies up next to the bluff and meanders for 0.3 mile through a wetland full of birdsong and butterflies. Before you know it, you'll reach the trail where you began your adventure and you can retrace your steps to your car.

EXPLORING FURTHER
Alternatively, take the longer 2.5-mile loop around Camano Island State Park by proceeding through the campground to the bluffs over Elger Bay and into a forest on the northern edge of the park, before dropping to the West Rim Trail.

SNOHOMISH COUNTY

12 SPENCER ISLAND

BEFORE YOU GO
MAP Available online on county website
CONTACT Snohomish County Parks and Recreation
NOTES No dogs or bikes on Spencer Island; northern part of island open seasonally for hunting; porta-potty on Smith Island and flush restrooms back at the Langus Riverfront Park boat launch
GPS N 47 59.648, W 122 10.767

ABOUT THE HIKE
SEASON Year-round
DIFFICULTY Easy to moderate
DISTANCE 3.4 miles roundtrip
HIGH POINT 20 feet
ELEVATION GAIN 10 feet

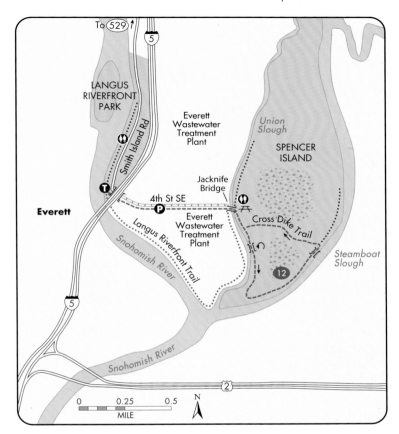

GETTING THERE

Getting to the trailhead is complicated, so follow these directions closely. In Everett, take exit 195 (Marine View Drive) off of Interstate 5. Turn left on E Marine View Drive. In 1.4 miles, reach a light at the intersection with State Route 529. Turn left, curving over Marine View Drive and across a steel drawbridge. After crossing the bridge, take your first right onto 28th Place NE (signed Langus Park/Animal Shelter). Then take an immediate right on 35th Avenue. At the next intersection, go left on Ross Avenue, passing a marina. The road is now called Smith Island Road. You will veer right at the Y-intersection and drive alongside the Snohomish River to a small parking lot under I-5. On your return, instead of turning right onto 35th Avenue, duck left under SR 529 to access the frontage road to southbound SR 529.

ON THE TRAIL

Who would think that a wildlife-rich oasis could be wedged between three major highways and just beyond the industrial footprint of Everett and Marysville? Thanks to the Snohomish River and a system of braided sloughs, a wildlife-rich saltwater river estuary thrives on Spencer Island. For generations, farmers built earthen dikes to tame the Snohomish as it neared its mouth. Now Snohomish County and the Washington Department of Fish and Wildlife have breached some of the dikes, allowing the tides to return to this unique ecosystem.

There are two ways to approach Spencer Island. The first is a Snohomish River route that begins on the paved Langus Riverfront Trail as it goes under I-5 and upstream along the Snohomish River. This way is smooth, with the deceptively lazy river floating past and an active rail yard on the other side. Via this trail, it is 1.75 miles to Spencer Island. The alternate route is to walk from the parking area on the gravel 4th Street SE for 0.75 mile, bisecting the Everett

Jackknife Bridge delivers hikers to Spencer Island.

SHHH!

You will see much more wildlife if you walk quietly. Listen for the distinctive call of the red-winged blackbird bobbing on cattails or the honking of geese in the wetland. See if you can locate any of the songbirds whose tunes carry on the wind.

Wastewater Treatment Plant operations. The Snohomish River route is ideal for pushing a stroller or wheelchair, but young walkers may tire before they get to the island. For this reason, it's best to take the road.

Kids will no doubt find hiking past a wastewater treatment plant fascinating. There are holding ponds with aeration sprinklers and a slightly off smell hanging in the wind. Carefully watch for traffic on 4th Street SE as you make a beeline for Spencer Island. Jackknife Bridge, a historic counterbalanced steel bridge, welcomes hikers to the island, its story told on diagonal beams. Picnic tables provide a good place to rest before taking the 1.9-mile loop around the south side of the island. Scamper down to a floating observation platform for a water-level view of the wetland, home to mallards, pintails, widgeons, herons, and much more. It's helpful to bring an identification guide so that you can differentiate among the many species of waterfowl. Don't forget to look to the sky and treetops as well for bald eagles, harriers, red-tailed hawks, and osprey searching for their next meal.

Beyond the Jackknife Bridge, proceed right on property managed by Snohomish County and stay right just beyond at the junction after the interpretive displays. The dike along this stretch has been breached to allow for tidal influences. You can see cattails thriving, competing for space with invasive reed canary grass. Take a bearing on a log in the water and check back on it later to determine whether the tide is ebbing or flowing.

The smooth pathway ends after the second bridge. This is the turnaround for strollers; past this bridge the trail becomes too hummocky. Continue with caution on the uneven surface, following Union Slough downstream and then heading left by Steamboat Slough and walking upstream. Listen for birds and look for movement in the trees. Kids may also enjoy peeking through to the slough and boats (some quite derelict) that are tied up along here. Emerge from this thicket to a junction at 2 miles. The trail straight ahead peters out at a breach in the dike. Parents should also be aware that the northern end of the island is open to hunting during winter.

Instead, close the loop by turning left on the Cross-Dike Trail, a levee between two wetlands. Linger here to see what emerges from the cattails. It's also a great place to take in the view—Mount Pilchuck, Whitehorse, Three Fingers, and even Mount Baker on a clear day. Take note of whether the water has risen or fallen while you were hiking. When you reach the junction on the other side, go right and then back over Jackknife Bridge, choosing your return route to the trailhead.

13 LUNDS GULCH

BEFORE YOU GO

MAP USGS Edmonds East

CONTACT Snohomish County Parks and Recreation

NOTES Dogs must be leashed; under some conditions, water may be too high to reach beach; playground, picnic area available; porta-potty at trailhead, restrooms at beach

GPS N 47 51.427, W 122 18.990

ABOUT THE HIKE

SEASON Year-round

DIFFICULTY Moderate

DISTANCE 2.3 miles roundtrip

HIGH POINT 415 feet

ELEVATION GAIN 415 feet

GETTING THERE

In Lynnwood, take exit 183 from Interstate 5. Follow 164th Street SW west for 1.7 miles, curving with the arterial onto 44th Avenue SW. At a traffic light, turn right onto 168th Street SW. Cross over State Route 99, and turn right on 52nd Avenue W. At 156th Street SW, turn left and follow it into Meadowdale Beach

Gulls gather on Meadowdale Beach.

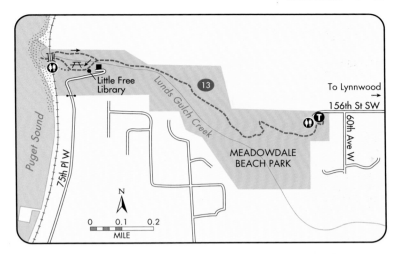

Park. The parking lot has room for about thirty cars and fills quickly on week-ends. If parking in the neighborhood, be sure to comply with posted signs.

ON THE TRAIL

Lunds Gulch is a quiet oasis in a busy metropolitan area, a chance to dial into your senses not too far from home. The forest is earthy, the beach salty, and the views to Whidbey Island and the Olympics are an ample reward for hiking more than a mile through the forest to reach the beach.

Begin on a wide gravel trail that swings down into a wooded ravine. De-ciduous alders sprinkled generously among conifers provide welcome shade in the summertime, light in the winter, and habitat for birds. Down, down, down you will go—sometimes at a significantly steep angle. Recent volunteer efforts by Washington Trails Association have improved the stairs and drainage, but it is an ongoing effort to fight erosion. After 0.5 mile, reach Lunds Gulch Creek and a more level section of trail. This is the most pleasant part of the hike, with the soothing sounds of the creek and a mossy, mature tree canopy.

At 1 mile, reach a trail junction. Go left toward the ranger's residence, out-side of which is a Little Free Library. Bring a book for the library and see if there is one to suit you. It's an unexpected treat. You'll then walk past a picnic shelter, volleyball court, and a set of restrooms near the train tracks. A small tunnel, through which the creek flows, leads under the tracks to Meadowdale Beach. The access has been officially closed because there is no reliable dry path under the tracks that also will accommodate safe fish passage, but during the dry season it is easy to walk through without getting your feet wet. Other times of year, consider bringing sandals for a quick, cold wade. Meadowdale Beach is expansive, and it would be a shame to miss it. At low tide, the beach extends out for a significant distance as the creek braids through the rocks and gravel to reach salt water. Look for ferries plying the water—the route to Kingston on the left and Whidbey Island on the right—and gathering seabirds at the water's edge. On clear days, enjoy looking to the snowcapped Olympics and the big bluffs of Whidbey Island.

When you are done, tiptoe back through the tunnel, then turn left to complete a little loop around the park. At the intersection, veer left and return up, up, up to the trailhead.

14 NORTH CREEK PARK

BEFORE YOU GO
MAP Available online on county website
CONTACT Snohomish County Parks and Recreation
NOTES Boardwalk has no handrails; playground, picnic tables, and porta-potties available
GPS N 47 49.967, W 122 13.149

ABOUT THE HIKE
SEASON Year-round
DIFFICULTY Easy
DISTANCE 1.8 miles roundtrip
HIGH POINT 235 feet
ELEVATION GAIN 25 feet

Great blue herons can be found at North Creek Park. (photo by Jon Stier)

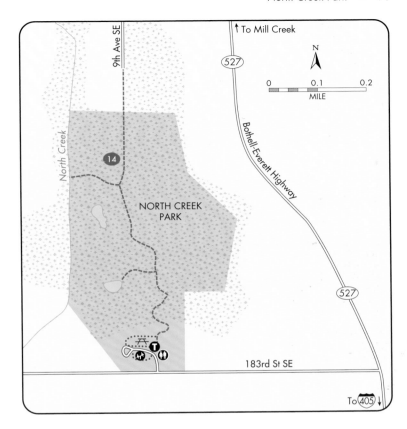

GETTING THERE

From Interstate 5 in Lynnwood, take exit 183 and follow 164th Avenue SW east for 1.8 miles. At the intersection with State Route 527, turn right (south), and follow it for 1.3 miles. Turn right on 183rd Street SE. Go 0.5 mile and turn right into North Creek Park. This trail can be reached by public transportation.

ON THE TRAIL

A little slice of tranquility has been protected amid the suburban hustle and bustle between Mill Creek and Bothell. At North Creek Park you can combine a nature walk in the wetland with free play on an excellent jungle gym and a picnic in the park. Babies can spot birds from the comfort of strollers, and older kids can sway lightly on the floating boardwalks. This is a walk to try in all seasons, but it's arguably at its most satisfying in the spring when plants are returning to life and the birds are most plentiful.

Once a dairy farm, this 85-acre parcel is now a fully functional wetland that serves an important purpose for urban storm water control. The wetland acts as a sponge, soaking up and filtering runoff from rains, roads, and roofs. The wetland cleans the water, making it safe for fish and other wildlife. Be sure to read the interpretive signs to fully appreciate the importance of wetlands.

The trail drops slightly from the picnic area to the wetland, passing through grasses onto the boardwalk. Has it rained recently? When the wetlands are full of water, the boardwalk floats. Swallows and hawks swoop in and out of the reeds, and red-winged blackbirds sing their distinctive song while bobbing on cattails. In the spring, you may catch sight of a great blue heron from a nearby rookery. If you're lucky, you may even spot a frog or muskrat.

The boardwalk extends northward through the wetland to a neighborhood on the other side, with two side trips on boardwalks that dead-end at a seasonal pond and a copse of trees at the edge of the wetland. The destinations are not particularly noteworthy, but at each turn, you may spot some new wildlife. Wander about, listening to birds singing and the grass rustling, until it's time to turn around and head home.

SEATTLE METRO

15 DISCOVERY PARK—SOUTH BEACH

BEFORE YOU GO
MAP Pick up at the visitor center or online from the park website
CONTACT City of Seattle–Parks and Recreation
NOTES Dogs must be leashed; privy available at trailhead; restroom and water on the trail
GPS N 47 39.280, W 122 24.606

ABOUT THE HIKE
SEASON Year-round
DIFFICULTY Easy to moderate
DISTANCE 2.5 miles roundtrip
HIGH POINT 300 feet
ELEVATION GAIN 275 feet

GETTING THERE
There are several ways to get to Discovery Park; none of them are straight-forward. One of the most direct routes is from Interstate 5, north of the Ship Canal. Take exit 169 and go west on N 50th Street, following the arterial past the Woodland Park Zoo. It will jog onto Phinney Avenue N and N 49th Street until it merges onto NW Market Street. In a mile, turn left on 15th Avenue W, cross over the Ballard Bridge, and take the first exit for W Emerson Place (not to be confused with W Emerson Street, later in the route). Cross railroad tracks

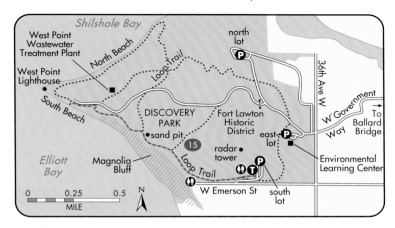

and turn right on Gilman Avenue W. This street turns into W Government Way as it curves near Discovery Park. To reach the south lot where this trail begins, pass by the main entrance (where the visitor center is located), turning left on 36th Avenue W. Go three blocks and turn right on W Emerson Street. Look for the park entrance at the chain-link gate on the right. Alternatively, many bus routes reach Discovery Park.

ON THE TRAIL

Seattle's largest city park boasts more than 550 acres of forests, meadows, beaches, and ravines with 12 miles of trails. These trails weave through and skirt a historic fort, a sewage treatment plant, and an Indian cultural center. But despite this eclectic mix of uses, the park is so big that it has plenty of wild spaces to explore. Our family's favorite hike, described here, includes a long beach, a lighthouse, a sand pit, and impressive views of Elliott Bay through peely-barked madronas atop a windswept bluff.

The Discovery Park Loop Trail, which hikers follow until reaching the junction to South Beach, encircles the park. It can be accessed from all of the main parking areas, but the most convenient is the south lot. The Loop Trail leaves from the south end of the lot at the bulletin board. It parallels West Emerson Street for a short distance, traveling beneath some enormous big-leaf maples, before popping out into a vast meadow of golden grasses. On the other side of the meadow is the Fort Lawton Historic District, with stately old officers' homes and a distinctive radar tower. Fort Lawton, first opened in 1899, was a small army post that saw its most active duty during World War II. But by the 1960s it was deemed surplus and was turned over to the City of Seattle in the 1970s as a park.

Pass restrooms and walk along Magnolia Bluff. The views open with West Seattle's Alki Beach to the left and Bainbridge Island straight ahead and surprisingly close. Please heed all signs to stay back from the edge of the bluffs.

As crabs grow, they shed their shells in a process called molting.

This is a fragile environment, and the impact of many feet near the edge makes the bluffs more susceptible to landslides. Instead, focus the kids on the big sand pit at 0.6 mile, which is absolutely irresistible. They will thank you for remembering sand toys, but it's possible you won't make it to the beach once they start digging.

If you can pry them away from their sandy fun, the trail down to the beach is not far away. Look for the trail to South Beach veering off of the Loop Trail to the left. Descend through a tree tunnel of maples, past several observation platforms, smelling the salty air. As you reach the access road at 1.1 miles, note the West Point Wastewater Treatment Plant camouflaged across the way. They've done a remarkable job of hiding it, and we've found it doesn't intrude on our fun. Follow the road to the left until you reach the opening to the beach.

You've arrived! Now spend time scanning the skies and shores for bald eagles, great blue herons, and swallows; building forts out of driftwood; or tidepooling to spot crabs, sea stars, and anemones.

EXPLORING FURTHER

Just around the corner from the West Point Lighthouse is North Beach. A trail runs alongside it for 0.5 mile before curving back up into the woods and eventually hooking up with the Loop Trail. The Loop Trail winds through forests, crossing several frontage roads and passing by the visitor center until reaching the south lot again. This full loop is more than 4 miles.

16 WASHINGTON PARK ARBORETUM WATERFRONT TRAIL

BEFORE YOU GO
MAP Pick up at Graham Visitor Center or online
CONTACT University of Washington
NOTES Dogs must be leashed; restrooms at the visitor center
GPS N 47 38.452, W 122 17.654

ABOUT THE HIKE
SEASON Year-round
DIFFICULTY Easy
DISTANCE 1.25 miles roundtrip
HIGH POINT 35 feet
ELEVATION GAIN 15 feet

GETTING THERE

From Seattle, take State Route 520 east to the first exit at Montlake Boulevard/ University of Washington (before the toll bridge). Proceed straight on Lake Washington Boulevard across Montlake Boulevard, following the brown signs for "Washington Park." (From Bellevue, take SR 520 west to Montlake Boulevard. Turn right on Montlake and then make a legal U-turn, doubling back and over SR 520. Turn left after the bridge on Lake Washington Boulevard.) At the first stop sign, go straight. At the second stop sign, take a left onto Foster Island Road and follow the signs to Graham Visitor Center. Park in Lot 13 on the left (trailhead) or at the visitor center just beyond. This trail can be reached by public transportation.

ON THE TRAIL

Word has it that you need hip waders to visit Washington Park Arboretum, and it's true that some parts of the University of Washington's 230-acre living laboratory are notoriously sloppy and muddy. But not all! The shoreline trail to Foster and Marsh islands is wide and well-maintained and can easily be navigated by hikers in tennis shoes. The trail is a true mashup of urban and wild: transportation, wildlife, and the built environment are on full display.

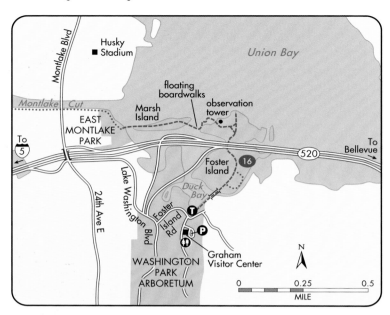

After picking up a map at the Graham Visitor Center, start your hike on the gravel path adjacent to the Foster Island parking lot (#13), walking toward Duck Bay. You will likely see ducks in their namesake bay, but other water-fowl may be present too: grebes, bitterns, great blue herons, and Canada geese, among others. Cross a bridge and enter Foster Island, staying on the path to avoid wet shoes. Spend some time spotting what's in bloom. There are more than 5000 plants in the arboretum, and something is usually flowering or sprouting year-round. If you can't identify a flower, snap a photo. On week-ends, Master Gardeners who volunteer at the visitor center can help put a name to what you find.

The roar of State Route 520 grows as you approach and walk under the spans. Emerge on the other side and reach a junction. Detour to a small beach by going straight or veer left toward Marsh Island, where you will soon reach an observation tower with similar views.

On a sunny day, a flotilla of watercraft ply Union Bay. Look for rowing sculls, canoes, kayaks, motorboats, and yachts cruising to and from the Montlake Cut. This spot provides an intriguing perspective from which to view Seattle. Across the water is the sprawling campus of the University of Washington and imposing Husky Stadium, rising like two fighting cobras. And there's the Montlake Cut, a channel carved in 1916 between Lakes Union and Washington to provide an easier passage to get logs and coal from the Cascade foothills to Elliott Bay. This narrow channel had far-ranging impacts on the environment,

Floating boardwalks extend into Union Bay.

dropping the water level of Lake Washington by several feet, altering the courses of rivers, and ultimately reshaping the greater Seattle region.

Keep this in mind as you walk along the floating boardwalks, the highlight of the hike for most kids. You are walking on water! Do keep ahold of toddlers' hands, as there are some areas without handrails and with gaps between sections. Watch the cars whiz by on the newly expanded highway as you approach Marsh Island. Meanwhile, look for waterfowl placidly swimming, birds singing in the grasses, and dragonflies flitting near water lilies. It's a strange oasis that may produce conflicting feelings about the human impact on the environment.

The Arboretum Waterfront Trail ends in East Montlake Park, the former site of the Museum of History and Industry, but you can continue walking along the waterfront through the Montlake Cut. When you are done exploring, return the way you came or meander back through the neighborhood.

EXPLORING FURTHER

If the kids still have energy, take the time to visit other parts of the Washington Park Arboretum. Fall and winter favorites are the winter garden and the Pinetum, a conifer collection. Spring and summer destinations include the soggy, yet gorgeous, Azalea Way and Rhododendron Glen. Wear boots!

17 EVANS CREEK PRESERVE

BEFORE YOU GO
MAP Availalble online and on trail signs
CONTACT City of Sammamish–Parks and Recreation
NOTES Dogs must be leashed; privy located in the meadow
GPS N 47 38.733, W 122 02.463

ABOUT THE HIKE
SEASON Year-round
DIFFICULTY Easy
DISTANCE 0.5 to 3 miles loop
HIGH POINT 245 feet
ELEVATION GAIN Up to 100 feet

GETTING THERE

From Bellevue, take State Route 520 east 7 miles to Redmond Way/SR 202. At the light, turn right onto SR 202 (Redmond-Fall City Road). Drive 4 miles, and go right on 224th Avenue NE. The trailhead is in about 500 feet on the right with room for about ten cars. This trail can be reached by public transportation.

ON THE TRAIL

Evans Creek Preserve is one of the newer trail systems in the Seattle area, with more than 3 miles of trail through woodland and meadows between Sammamish and Redmond. The land was deeded to the City of Sammamish in 2000,

Excellent signage at Evans Creek Preserve makes getting lost nearly impossible.

and Washington Trails Association helped design the trails, building them with volunteer efforts over a few years. Today families can venture out on a system of boardwalks, bridges, and dirt pathways to enjoy natural wonders such as birds, butterflies, and other wildlife. There are many potential loops and helpful maps at each intersection that keep hikers from getting lost.

From the small parking area, head down the trail to the meadow, where a wheelchair-accessible trail takes a short 0.25-mile loop. Parents with toddlers and strollers can easily proceed to the woodland trails for a longer walk. Several loop options of varying lengths are available, with the outermost circuit clocking in at about 3 miles. Choose a direction and start exploring. There are trail maps at each of fifteen intersections to guide your way.

All intersections are numbered. My favorite segments are between #10 and #13, where a long boardwalk stretches over a swampy area dotted with big-leafed skunk cabbage and under a canopy of red alder, and between #5 and #6, where the trail goes uphill in a quiet forest next to the tinkling sounds of a creek. The most difficult section is between #10 and #11, which can be slippery when wet.

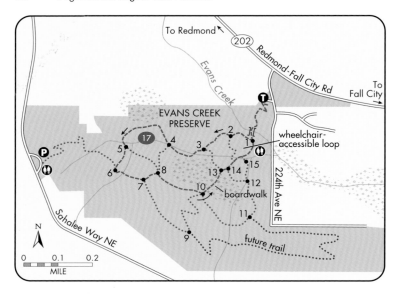

Evans Creek Preserve attracts a variety of wildlife, from frogs and swallows to deer and even black bear. You're unlikely to spot a bear, but do be aware of your surroundings as you hike. You might miss an owl swooping through the trees or a salamander trundling across the trail. The best time to spot wildlife is in the morning or near dusk, when you may encounter bird-watchers with binoculars staring into the trees. But really, this sweet place is a good destination any time you need a dose of the outdoors without driving too far. When you are finished exploring, return to the meadow and make the short climb to your car.

18 MERCER SLOUGH NATURE PARK

BEFORE YOU GO
MAP Available on the City of Bellevue website
CONTACT City of Bellevue–Parks and Community Services
NOTES Dogs must be leashed; restrooms available
GPS N 47 35.596, W 122 10.983

ABOUT THE HIKE
SEASON Year-round
DIFFICULTY Easy
DISTANCE 1.1 to 2.2 miles loops
HIGH POINT 90 feet
ELEVATION GAIN 50 feet

GETTING THERE

There are many access points to Mercer Slough Nature Park, but Sound Transit construction has closed most of the parking and the trail along Bellevue Way until 2020. Instead, start on the eastern side of the park by driving Interstate 405 to Exit 12/SE 8th Street. Travel west on SE 8th Street and take an immediate left onto 118th Avenue SE. Drive south for 0.7 mile to the small Bellefields Trailhead parking area. If it is full, double back to the Mercer Slough Environmental Education Center and park in its large lot (which will add 0.4 mile roundtrip to your total distance).

ON THE TRAIL

Once a water-filled bay of Lake Washington, Mercer Slough is now the lake's largest wetland and one of Bellevue's largest city parks. It beckons in all four seasons—winter brings migrating birds, spring heralds the bloom of rhododendrons, summer treats with a U-pick blueberry farm, and fall dazzles with crimson colors.

Two short loops allow you to experience the full flavor of the park, from its diverse wildlife and plant life to its unique history. If you had stood here just over a hundred years ago, Lake Washington's waters would lap at your feet. That all changed when regional leaders decided to link Lake Washington to

Blueberry bushes at the Overlake Farm turn crimson in the fall.

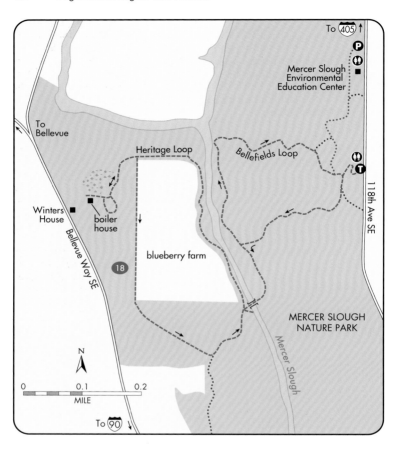

Lake Union and Puget Sound. When the project was complete in 1917, Lake Washington dropped more than 10 feet, leaving behind this wetland. Attracted by rich soils, owners of the property planted flower bulbs, then rhododendrons, and finally blueberries.

New construction is underway even now with Sound Transit building light rail along Bellevue Way through 2019, displacing parking and part of the trail, so begin your visit at the Bellefields Trailhead. Follow the sidewalk south over the ravine, then drop down to the right beyond the fence. At an intersection at the bottom of the hill, go first left and then right just past a small seating area. As you walk, notice how springy the trail is. The organic peat soil here is up to 70 feet deep and is excellent for filtering out pollutants and recharging the wetland environment.

At 0.4 mile turn left onto a boardwalk and cross Mercer Slough on a picturesque iron bridge. Take some time to linger here, watching for buffleheads, mergansers, great blue herons, and canoeists plying its waters (canoes can be rented in summer at Enatai Beach Park). If it is autumn, you may even spot salmon migrating to Kelsey Creek. Some families may opt to turn around and complete the Bellefields Loop to finish their hike at this point, but it is well worth continuing onto the Heritage Loop.

At the intersection beyond the bridge, turn right and walk beside rows and rows of blueberry bushes. Beyond the blueberry farm, the trail briefly enters a watery world of cattails and rushes on a boardwalk. In the springtime, take the tiny loop around the remnants of the abandoned rhododendron farm. Otherwise, go right at the intersection to view a derelict historic boiler house that is sinking into the bog (1.1 miles). When Sound Transit construction is complete, you will be able to continue up to the Winters House on a wider circuit. Until that time, return to the northwest corner of the blueberry farm. Depending on planting and construction conditions, you may be able to hike 0.4 mile along its western edge to close the loop. If it is closed you will have to retrace your steps to reach the Mercer Slough bridge.

Cross over the slough and reach the intersection with the Bellefields Loop. Take the trail clockwise and hike a pleasant half-mile under arching trees. Take time to read the information panels along the trail. If you parked at the education center, take the first left; if you parked in the Bellefields lot, take the second left up to your vehicle.

19 COAL CREEK FALLS

BEFORE YOU GO
   MAP Green Trails, Cougar Mountain No. 203S; county trail map from kiosk or website
   CONTACT King County Parks
   NOTES Stay on path to avoid coal mining cave-in holes and stinging nettles; porta-potty located past the trail gate
   GPS N 47 32.094, W 122 07.722

ABOUT THE HIKE
   SEASON Year-round
   DIFFICULTY Moderate
   DISTANCE 2.2 miles roundtrip
   HIGH POINT 1050 feet
   ELEVATION GAIN 400 feet

GETTING THERE
From Seattle, take Interstate 90 eastbound 13 miles to exit 13. Go right on Lakemont Boulevard SE and follow it for 3 miles. Cougar Mountain Regional Wildland Park's Red Town trailhead is on your left just as the road makes a hairpin turn. The parking lot can fit fifty or more cars but fills on weekends.

ON THE TRAIL

Of King County's two hundred parks, Cougar Mountain Regional Wildland Park stands out as one of the best. At 3100 acres, it is also the largest—part of a contiguous and protected urban wilderness corridor known as the Mountains to Sound Greenway. It wasn't always this wild. For one hundred years, Cougar Mountain miners dug tunnels and strip-mined more than 13 million tons of coal, and although nature has reclaimed much of this area, there are telltale signs throughout the park of its working days, some of which you will hike past on your way to Coal Creek Falls.

First, pick up a trail map at the kiosk near the parking lot. More than 35 miles of trails crisscross the park, and the many trail junctions can be confusing to the uninitiated. The way to Coal Creek Falls is relatively straightforward but requires some navigation. It's an excellent choice for families, because much of the trail is wide, and the waterfall is a nice reward after putting in the hard work of getting there.

Pass the gates and go left on the Red Town Trail (W2) at the porta-potties. Ascend this old road a short distance to a junction with the Cave Hole Trail (C3). Peel off to the left on the Cave Hole Trail, walking among moss-covered maples and bursts of sword fern. Shortly beyond, reach another junction, this time going right and remaining on the Cave Hole Trail.

The trail steadily gains elevation—about 200 feet in less than a half mile. This is the hardest part! Remind tired kids about the fun they will have going down on the return. Stop at the "cave-in hole" and talk a little about the coal mining history. Kids will find its warning sign hilarious, but it is a good reminder that it is important to stay on the trail. Depressions in the ground indicate the instability of old mine seams and are much deeper than they appear. What's more, a coal seam fire has been burning underground for sixty years. On cold winter days you may even spot vapor rising from the holes. Fortunately, if you stick to the trail, you'll be safe.

Kids think this sign is hilarious, but it is a good warning not to wander off-trail.

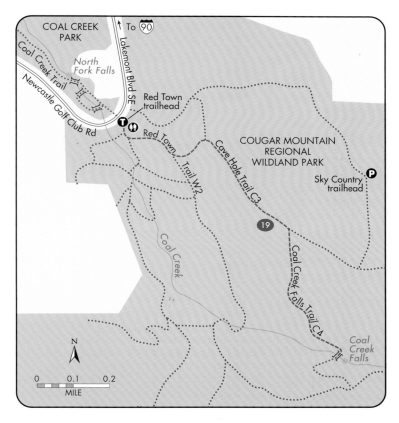

After climbing 0.6 mile, reach the Coal Creek Falls Trail (C4). From here, go right and enjoy how the trail levels off, becomes dirt-packed, and narrows. Listen for the gentle sound of water. That's Coal Creek, and when you hear it, the waterfall is near. Coal Creek Falls (1.1 miles, 990 feet) is impressive after a big winter rain, but in the summer it slows to a trickle.

Children will want to play around the waterfall, and it will be important to set ground rules. The biggest attractive nuisance is scaling the falls. My advice: don't let them do it. It is muddy and slippery, with drop-offs, and nearly impossible to climb down without slipping. Downstream on a hot day, kids may want to play around the creek. There are round rocks, sticks, social paths, and many ways to get dirty. Consider bringing an extra pair of socks or shoes.

A sturdy wooden bridge with a handrail offers a good perspective of the falls and provides an opportunity for a loop trip upon the return. Otherwise, pack up and head back the way you came.

GEOCACHING AND LETTERBOXING

Insert a treasure hunt into your next hike by trying out geocaching or letterboxing. For reluctant hikers, a little mystery may be what they need to motivate them down the trail. Both activities involve navigating to a hidden cache in the outdoors. Geocaching requires a smartphone or GPS unit to guide the way and trinkets that you can trade for those in the cache. Letterboxing provides a written set of clues to the cache, which includes a logbook with rubber stamps. You leave the book inked with your stamp, and use the stamp inside to stamp your own book.

Both activities can be a lot of fun with kids. Many caches are near campgrounds, while others are located off the trail you may be following. Do your research before you leave home and, if possible, practice in a city park beforehand. Note also that cell phone coverage can be spotty or nonexistent in the mountains.

EXPLORING FURTHER

Consider crossing Lakemont Boulevard (carefully) and hiking the first 0.25 mile of the City of Bellevue's Coal Creek Trail. The grassy field is the site of the old Coal Creek Hotel, and the concrete foundation is still visible. Descend the trail and almost immediately come to what looks to be a cool cave. It's actually an airshaft to an old mine that descends more than 1000 feet. Read the signs to learn about the history of this now-tranquil creek, then look for mining evidence along the trail: lumps of coal, metal debris, wooden support beams along the creek for transporting coal, concrete footings from coal bunkers, even a hard-to-spot locomotive turntable. Another waterfall, North Fork Falls, also bears signs of the past. What appears to be red stone is in fact leached iron salts from the coal seam. Turn around here and plan to come back and visit this trail another time.

20 TRADITION PLATEAU

BEFORE YOU GO
MAP Green Trails, Tiger Mountain No. 204S
CONTACT Washington Department of Natural Resources
NOTES Discover Pass required; dogs must be leashed; bus has sharp, rusty edges; privy available
GPS N 47 31.779, W 121 59.727

ABOUT THE HIKE
SEASON Year-round
DIFFICULTY Easy
DISTANCE 1.1 miles loop
HIGH POINT 540 feet
ELEVATION GAIN 20 feet

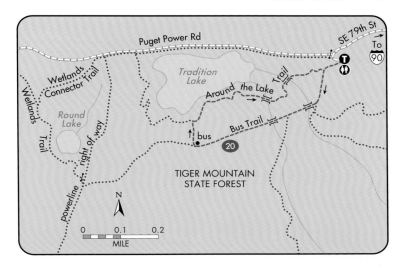

GETTING THERE

From Issaquah, take Interstate 90 east 2 miles to exit 20 (High Point Way). Turn right on 270th Avenue, then take an immediate right on SE 79th Street. Parallel the interstate a short distance until you reach a gate. This gate closes at 7:00 PM daily, so plan accordingly. Beyond the gate, travel a bumpy 0.4 mile on a gravel road to the trailhead at road's end.

ON THE TRAIL

Just outside of Issaquah, alongside a mossy, barrier-free trail in Tiger Mountain State Forest, lies the rusting hulk of a 1930s-era split-level bus. Its insides were salvaged long ago, but the exterior remains on its side, abandoned in the 1950s after serving logging crews for several years. The bus is by no means the only reason to venture out on this easy trail, but it is a fun discovery. Beyond the bus, the Tradition Plateau offers a variety of looping trail options that include wetlands, ponds, big trees, and lots and lots of moss.

From the parking area, follow signs for the Bus Trail. Once you reach the main path, take the second right onto a wide, barrier-free trail ideal for strollers and toddlers. Ramble under a leafy canopy and over a creek, observing how the moss embraces the trees in a big green hug. Upon closer inspection, note how small ferns are growing out of the moss on the sides of the trees, all part of a symbiotic environment.

In just 0.5 mile, reach the derelict bus. Although there isn't much left of it, the relic does pique the imagination. How did it get here in the middle of the forest? Kids will undoubtedly want to inspect it more closely, but they should keep their hands off of it for safety. It is rusty, with many sharp edges—a tetanus shot just waiting to happen if they are careless.

This bus has seen better days.

Just beyond the bus is a connector trail that rounds out a 1.1-mile barrier-free loop past Tradition Lake. This is a good option for families with small children. In just 0.1 mile, reach another intersection at Tradition Lake. Go right, walking along the lake on the Around the Lake Trail. There are a few viewpoints, but no shoreline access. Interpretive signs add context to your short 0.5-mile journey back to the trailhead.

EXPLORING FURTHER

If you are seeking a longer adventure, press on straight after you reach the rusty bus. Cross under powerlines at 0.9 mile and through a gate onto the Wetlands Trail. In spring, the place is noisy with frogs and ducks. Meander past Round Lake, reaching the Wetlands Connector Trail at 1.3 miles. Take a right, rounding the lake, and arrive on Puget Power Road at 1.5 miles. Go right and walk along the gravel road, passing under the powerlines again. Immediately after, look for a trail back into the forest. This is the Around the Lake Trail, which leads back to the loop you began on. (Don't worry if you miss it; the road leads to the trailhead too.) Walk around Tradition Lake until you reach the barrier-free trail once again. Then follow the earlier directions. The entire loop is 2.5 miles.

KITSAP PENINSULA

21 GUILLEMOT COVE

BEFORE YOU GO
MAP Available online from county and at trailhead
CONTACT Kitsap County Parks
NOTES Dogs prohibited
GPS N 47 36.959, W 122 54.516

ABOUT THE HIKE
SEASON Year-round
DIFFICULTY Moderate
DISTANCE 2.5 miles roundtrip
HIGH POINT 360 feet
ELEVATION GAIN 350 feet

GETTING THERE
From Bremerton, follow State Route 3 north approximately 5 miles to the exit for Newberry Hill Road outside of Silverdale. Turn left (west) on Newberry Hill Road, following it for 3 miles to a T-intersection. Go right on Seabeck Highway for 5 miles to a junction. Take a right on Miami Beach Road, bearing left after a mile onto NW Stavis Bay Road. The Guillemot Cove Nature Reserve parking area is on the right in 4.5 miles.

ON THE TRAIL
All matter of hidden delights are scattered throughout the Kitsap Peninsula, and one of the best is at Guillemot Cove. Tucked into a marshy, wildlife-rich inlet along Hood Canal, Guillemot Cove provides a dazzling view of the Olympic Mountains, flocks of squawking seabirds, and a fairy-tale house for kids to play in.

Cross the road from the parking area, pick up a map of the reserve, and start your downhill journey to the cove. Several paths will join the main access trail; your job is to stay right at all of these intersections, first onto the Sawmill Trail and then onto the Margaret Trail. Listen to the insistent hammering of woodpeckers as you take the winding paths through elderberry, evergreen huckleberry, salal, and sword fern.

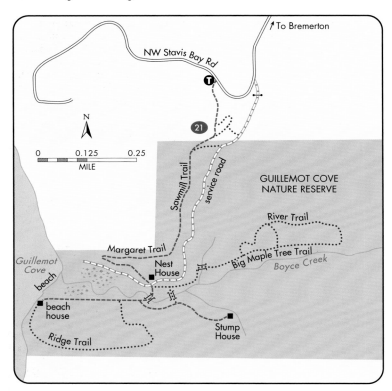

At 0.4 mile, the trail flattens out through an alder grove before descending again, steeply at times, until it reaches the bottom of the bluff at 0.75 mile, where the derelict Nest House sits next to the trail. The house is one of several structures in the reserve, a reminder of its previous use as a summer beach property. Kitsap County Parks acquired the property in 1993 when a 158-acre portion of a private estate was sold to the Trust for Public Land and county. Similar to a nearby barn that collapsed in 2014, the house has fallen into disrepair and is unsafe to enter, and it may be gone by the time you visit.

Cross a service road and Boyce Creek, traveling through a wetland of grasses and cattails. On the other side of the bridge, make a choice: Stump House or beach? All kids must go to the Stump House, which is just 0.25 mile to the left through a lush cedar forest. It's made from a hollow cedar stump, with a cute roof on top and a door—a perfect children's playhouse. But perhaps not always so. Urban legend has it that the stump was once used as a hideout for a criminal on the run named Dirty Thompson!

Returning the way you came, make a beeline for the beach and quiet Guillemot Cove. Another beach house, boarded up but in better shape, sits here at the edge of the beach. Kids can scamper over the retaining wall and find a nice place to relax and pick through shellfish shells. It was originally called Frenchman's Cove; the property owners renamed the area Guillemot Cove after the black-and-white seabird that can often be seen foraging here. If it is clear, this is also an ideal spot to stare at The Brothers peaks across the deep expanse of Hood Canal.

There are more trails to explore if you have the energy or time, including the Ridge Trail and the Big Maple Tree–River Trail loop. When you're done, pass the creepy house and return the way you came, remembering to stay left at each trail junction.

The Stump House is right out of a fairy tale.

22 THELER WETLANDS

BEFORE YOU GO
MAP Available online
CONTACT Washington Department of Fish and Wildlife–Union River Unit
NOTES Dogs prohibited; boardwalks slippery when wet; privy available at trailhead and picnic area
GPS N 47 26.274, W 122 50.185

ABOUT THE HIKE
SEASON Year-round
DIFFICULTY Easy
DISTANCE 0.4 to 3 miles roundtrip
HIGH POINT 50 feet
ELEVATION GAIN 15 feet

GETTING THERE
From Bremerton, head west on State Route 3 for 8 miles to Belfair. From the intersection with SR 300 (Old Belfair Highway), continue 1 mile on SR 3 to the Mary Theler Early Learning Center on the right. Pull in and proceed to the large parking area adjacent to the center. This trail can be reached by public transportation.

ON THE TRAIL
What began as a bequest to the North Mason County School District to provide local children and residents a place to gather and explore has blossomed into a 339-acre wildlife sanctuary and education center that includes artwork, trails, restoration, and teaching. The wide, flat, barrier-free trails at the Theler Wetlands are ideal for strollers, and they are open year-round for hiking and wildlife viewing.

There are several short trails to choose from, or a longer loop of up to 3 miles. To reach the trails, take the Rock Wall Trail through the decorative iron gate to the Wetlands Project Center. Be sure to linger here, checking out the native plantings (all labeled) in the demonstration gardens, the information on the kiosks, and the gray whale skeleton hanging in the breezeway between the two buildings. Kids will get a kick out of all of the whimsical animal sculptures dotting the gardens—search for bears, herons, salmon, and more.

If a short stroll is all your crew is up for, choose the 0.25-mile Sweetwater Creek Trail through the woods or the 0.5-mile South Tidal Marsh Trail out to an observation platform near Lynch Cove. The real prize, however, is the River Estuary Trail; this 2.3-mile loop can be extended to 3 miles and traverses a wildlife-rich estuary at the tip of Hood Canal. The tides fill and empty it twice a day, providing excellent habitat for a wide variety of waterfowl, other birds, and mammals.

To hike the River Estuary loop, begin on the trail to the right just beyond the second building and make your way out to the mouth of the Union River, first turning left at a T-intersection, then right, then left again. Spot colorful ducks, little striped killdeer, big-headed buffleheads, spread-winged cormorants, and regal great blue herons resting and feeding among bulrushes and salt grasses. Look to the sky for osprey and bald eagles, to the water for river otters, and to the ground for harmless garter snakes.

At 0.7 mile, reach a recently added 300-foot-long bridge. This, and a shorter bridge beyond, were constructed in 2013 when the Washington Department of Fish and Wildlife breached an earthen dike to restore estuary habitat on 30 acres of old farmland. Workers also built a new loop trail around the restored estuary, providing an up-close view of the saltwater marsh reclaiming its territory. The restoration efforts have added significantly to the enjoyment of this hike.

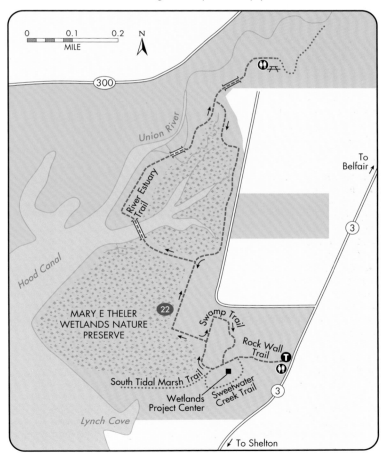

Wide trails with long sight lines provide a safe place for kids to run ahead.
(photo by Jon Stier)

The trail goes in and out of thickets of trees and seasonally flowering bushes, briefly running alongside the sinuous Union River. At 1.2 miles (the sign indicates 1 mile from the Wetlands Project Center), the trail loops back to the right. If you go less than 0.2 mile farther, you will reach a pleasant picnic area next to the river, with tables and a privy. The trail goes a bit beyond, before it ends at two observation platforms.

Return to the loop trail and head inland. In 2014, to speed up the recovery process, crews planted more than nine thousand native shrubs and grasses around the estuary and the new trail. Walk along the new dike for 0.5 mile until you connect up with the other end of the loop. Retrace your steps until reaching the original intersection. Return right, the way you came, or go left via the Swamp Trail, where gracefully drooping cedars and skunk cabbage thrive. Note that the boardwalk on the Swamp Trail can be extremely slippery after a rain. Once you've reached the Wetlands Project Center, return left, up the Rock Wall Trail, to the parking area.

23 PENROSE POINT STATE PARK

BEFORE YOU GO
    MAP Available online
    CONTACT Washington State Parks
    NOTES Discover Pass required; dogs must be leashed; restroom and
        water available
    GPS N 47 15.519, W 122 44.698

ABOUT THE HIKE
    SEASON Year-round
    DIFFICULTY Easy to moderate
    DISTANCE 1.6 miles loop
    HIGH POINT 90 feet
    ELEVATION GAIN 90 feet

Beaches beckon from both sides of Penrose Point.

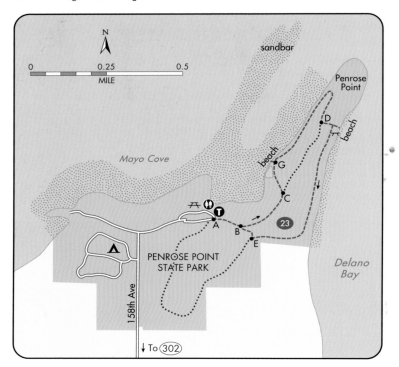

GETTING THERE

From Interstate 5 in Tacoma, drive north on State Route 16 over the tolled Tacoma Narrows Bridge for 13 miles. Exit in Purdy and take SR 302 west for 5.2 miles. At a light, bear left onto the Key Peninsula Highway (also called Gig Harbor–Longbranch Road) for 9 miles. South of the town of Home, take a left on Cornwall Road. Go 0.4 mile, then turn right on Delano Road. In 0.8 mile, take a left on 158th Avenue, which will lead into Penrose Point State Park.

ON THE TRAIL

Tucked away on Puget Sound's Carr Inlet is delightful Penrose Point State Park. It isn't easy to get to, but it's well worth the effort, especially if you stay in its shaded, friendly campground and spend a couple of days boating on Mayo Cove, digging for shellfish, and hiking its network of trails. The short circuit around Penrose Point is a fine outing, offering two beaches, a lagoon, and a mature forest graced with peely-barked madronas.

The trail system is well-signed, with maps at most intersections, to help alleviate the confusion of the many lettered trails and intersections. Start your saltwater adventure at the day-use picnic area. Gently ascend a bluff above the cove on Trail A. At just 0.2 mile, go left on Trail B, then, in rapid succession, another left on Trail C and again on Trail G, which runs out to a rocky beach on Mayo Cove. At low tide you may see people with shovels digging for clams, and the white crushed shells of clams and oysters surround a sweet little lagoon. This whole stretch of beach is ideal for tidepooling.

Returning to the junction with Trail G, turn left and enter a tunnel of lush, almost tropical flora. Evergreen leaves of Oregon boxwood line the trail, moss droops from tall Douglas firs, and seafoam-green lichen covers the bark of western red cedars. The red, peeling branches of madronas contrast with the greens of the forest. Traveling this corridor, round Penrose Point at 0.7 mile. There is no access to the point, but never fear, another beach awaits just a few hundred feet beyond the junction with Trail D, where you will turn left.

A short path leads out to a sand and rock beach on big Delano Bay. If it is a sunny day, you're in for a real treat: Mount Rainier, enormous, smack dab ahead in a gap between the Kitsap Peninsula and Fox Island. Enjoy the view from the beach or one of two well-placed benches just above. When you're ready to continue, go left at the benches, contouring the point. At 1.4 miles, reach the junction with Trail E. Go right here to begin closing the loop, then left at Trail B for the final downhill stretch to the trailhead.

TACOMA AND OLYMPIA

24 WEST HYLEBOS WETLANDS

BEFORE YOU GO
MAP Available online
CONTACT City of Federal Way–Parks and Recreation
NOTES Dogs and bikes prohibited; privy available
GPS N 47 17.373, W 122 19.754

ABOUT THE HIKE
SEASON Year-round
DIFFICULTY Easy
DISTANCE 1.4 miles loop
HIGH POINT 235 feet
ELEVATION GAIN 25 feet

GETTING THERE
From Interstate 5 in Federal Way, take exit 142B. Go west on State Route 18 toward South 348th Street and drive approximately a half mile to West Hylebos Wetlands Park on the left. Two historic cabins next to the parking area make it hard to miss. This trail can be reached by public transportation.

ON THE TRAIL

The West Hylebos Wetlands is one of those surprising places—a thriving oasis of green tucked away in a busy suburban area. Here, birds sing and frogs croak. Moss, lichen, and ferns attach to nearly every surface. Water oozes from the ground, flows, and pools. Very old trees, plus two historic cabins, give visitors a sense that they are entering a world of yesteryear. And a level boardwalk sweeps through it all, making it an ideal destination for feet and strollers (sorry, bikes and dogs are not allowed).

This is one of the last, and largest, remaining peat bogs in South King County. The spongy soil is 30 feet deep in places and supports a diverse array of plants and animals—from tiny fungi and shy garter snakes to a Sitka spruce more than four hundred years old. Begin your walk at the two historic cabins

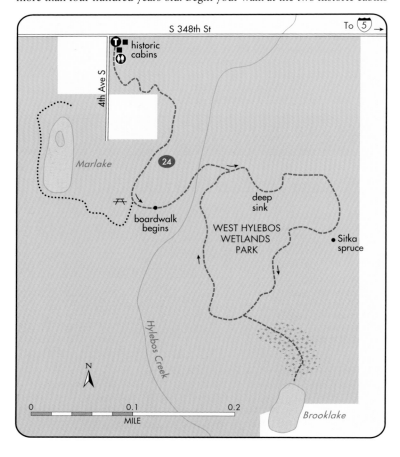

A welcome sign of spring: flowering currant

adjacent to the parking lot. These buildings date to the 1880s, but they didn't originate here. The distinctive Denny Cabin once housed a real estate office on Queen Anne Hill in Seattle, and the Barker Cabin sat a few miles away from this spot. Take time to peer inside and read the signs.

A wide crushed gravel pathway curves gently downhill, past a picnic area, about 0.2 mile to the beginning of the boardwalk. Shortly thereafter, reach a junction. The trail runs in a loop, and the interpretive signs tell a more logical story if you take it clockwise. Make sure to stop and read the first sign on the loop, which depicts the different kinds of wetlands you'll encounter—the younger scrub shrub and the older forested wetlands—then look for the transitions during your walk.

The trail visits a few interesting nooks and crannies. The first is called the "deep sink," a hole that used to be 20 feet deep, but is now filling in with mud and vegetation. Follow the boardwalk above the squishy wetlands, and at 0.5 mile reach an ancient Sitka spruce that's 175 tall, but leaning rather precariously. A curious, large, carved wooden mushroom sits to the side of the trail.

At 0.7 mile, take the short detour to Brooklake. It's just 500 feet, and worth the effort to walk over the swampiest part of the trail and to gaze at the lovely reflections on the lake. Take a seat on a bench and soak up the peacefulness of this place. Return to the junction, going straight, then meander 0.2 mile back to where you first began your circuit. Turn left, and return up the gravel pathway to the parking area. Make sure to return in a different season to see how the wetlands change.

25 POINT DEFIANCE PARK

BEFORE YOU GO
MAP Available online
CONTACT City of Tacoma–Metro Parks Tacoma
NOTES Dogs must be leashed; restrooms available
GPS N 47 18.532, W 122 31.874

ABOUT THE HIKE
SEASON Year-round
DIFFICULTY Easy to moderate
DISTANCE 4.3 miles loop
HIGH POINT 250 feet
ELEVATION GAIN 100 feet

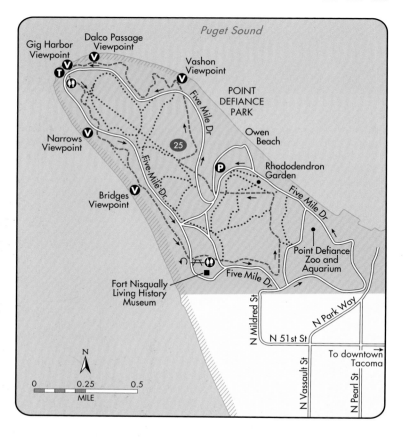

GETTING THERE

From southbound Interstate 5 in Tacoma, take exit 132B
on State Route 16 for 5 miles and take exit 4. Turn right o
and follow this arterial as it veers onto N Narrows Driv
mile, turn left to stay on N Narrows Drive, which beco
Continue to a four-way stop at N 51st Street. Go left on !
onto N Mildred Street. Turn left into Point Defiance P

There are many places to park that will allow you to hop onto
but the official trailhead is at the Gig Harbor Viewpoint about halfway around
the loop. Note that Five Mile Drive is closed until 10:00 AM Monday through
Friday and until 1:00 PM on Saturday and Sunday for runners and cyclists.
During those times, it is best to park at the upper end of the Owen Beach parking lot. This trail can be reached by public transportation.

ON THE TRAIL

Tacoma's Point Defiance Park is one of the wildest and largest urban parks in
the state. It truly has something for everyone: a zoo, a historical museum, a
beach, and a loop road that is closed daily for bikes and runners. It also has
miles of trails through quiet forest, punctuated by spectacular viewpoints that
provide the opportunity to spot bald eagles, seals, sea lions, and deer. The route
described here takes in the best on the 4.3-mile outside loop trail. With the
downloadable map, also available at intersections along the way, families can
adapt their outing to take in a shorter route that fits their needs.

Consult the big map at the main trailhead at the Gig Harbor Viewpoint.

Having fun with a big-leaf maple leaf at Point Defiance Park

be following the blue square trail counterclockwise. Most, but not the intersections are well marked, and you are never far from Five Mile e.

To begin, find the trailhead to the left of the picnic pavilion and proceed 0.25 mile, staying right at two intersections on your way to the Narrows Viewpoint. Cross the road and admire the views of the Narrows Bridge and across to Gig Harbor and the Olympic Mountains. The trail now continues on a high bluff among big cedars. If the bluff is too steep for your crew, the trail splits inland, offering a safer passage before reconnecting before the Bridges Viewpoint at 0.7 mile.

Walk along the parking area here, then duck into the madronas for a half-mile trek to Fort Nisqually at 1.2 miles. The Fort Nisqually Living History Museum makes a good destination for families; if you were to hike here and back it would be a 2.4-mile roundtrip.

To continue, pick up the trail on the far side of the picnic pavilion near the museum and cross the road. The trail loops around near the Point Defiance Zoo and Aquarium and ultimately connects, at 2.1 miles, with the park's main trails. The Rhododendron Garden is near here, and you'll spot a few growing along the trail. The trail now travels upward to a ridge, crossing the top of the Owen Beach parking area (an alternative trailhead when Five Mile Drive is closed) at 2.4 miles. This part of the trail has the best stretch of forest, with some big Douglas firs sheltering a mossy evergreen understory.

At a four-way intersection at 2.8 miles, turn right and head downhill to the Vashon Viewpoint. The trail beyond picks up at the far end of the tiny parking area and snakes its way between road and water to the Dalco Passage Viewpoint at 3.9 miles. My family loved the interesting vantages from these viewpoints and the opportunities to look for boats, marine mammals, and eagles. From here, it is just another 0.4 mile to the Gig Harbor Viewpoint and your drive home.

26 CHAMBERS BAY

BEFORE YOU GO
MAP Available online
CONTACT Pierce County Parks and Recreation
NOTES Dogs must be leashed; restrooms at trailhead and near north playground
GPS N 47 12.103, W 122 34.587

ABOUT THE HIKE
SEASON Year-round
DIFFICULTY Easy to moderate
DISTANCE 3.1 miles loop
HIGH POINT 235 feet
ELEVATION GAIN 215 feet

GETTING THERE

From Interstate 5 in Tacoma, take exit 130 and follow signs for Tacoma Mall and S 56th Street westbound. Turn left on Tacoma Mall Boulevard and immediately right onto S 56th Street. Drive west for five miles on S 56th; at a traffic circle it becomes Cirque Drive W. At the following traffic circle, take the third exit (left turn) onto Grandview Drive W. There are three parking areas for the park and street parking along Grandview, but start from the lower lot at the Central Meadow. To reach this parking area, enter Chambers Bay Golf Course and follow the road downhill to the large parking lot.

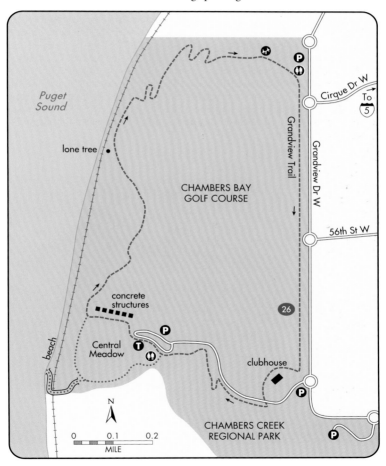

ON THE TRAIL

Cast aside any preconceived notions of what it's like to hike around a golf course. This place is different, almost surreal. Opened in 2007, the public links golf course at the center of this 3.1-mile paved loop is carved out of a former sand and gravel pit. The landscape has been sculpted into dozens of 30- to 40-foot-high sand dunes and planted with grasses. There is just one tree on the entire course. Enormous concrete slabs left over from the mine have been incorporated into freestanding art. Active train tracks run between the beach and the golfers.

You get to walk through all of this. That is, if you can convince the kids not to fly a kite in the Central Meadow or take an irresistible swooping bridge down to a 2-mile-long public beach along Puget Sound. You may have to promise them you'll come back.

To tackle the loop, walk toward the "ancient ruins," as my kids called these curious concrete structures. Shortly, the trail will bisect the golf course for a good half mile. Three holes of the course lie between the trail and the water, the rest on the other side of the trail. Due to the carefully placed dunes, walkers catch only glimpses of the golf course, which hosted the 2015 US Open tournament. Please keep the kids off the dunes, and do watch out for errantly hit golf balls in this section.

Pierce County left several "ancient ruins" as an architectural nod to the site's mining past. (photo by Jon Stier)

Because of the lack of tree cover, the views are constant. Four islands—Ketron, Anderson, McNeil, and Fox—dominate the waterscape. The Olympics glimmer in the west, especially when cloaked in a winter coat of snow. Ferries, barges, and other watercraft ply these waters. Trains race by several times each day.

As you approach the hike's only forested segment, look for the Tacoma Narrows Bridge jutting out from a far bluff. Now take a big breath for the short and steep climb of 200 feet in 0.3 mile. Fortunately, you will be in shade for the entire ascent, the only shade of the entire loop. As an enticement for the kids, a large and fenced playground with wooden play equipment waits for them at the top.

After stopping for some playtime and visiting nearby restrooms, join up with the Grandview Trail and walk south, paralleling the street. Lucky you if you're here at sunset on a clear day. The whole scene—golf course, golfers, water, islands, mountains—is laid out below like a map that is dramatically highlighted in low light. When you reach the clubhouse, go to the right, following the fence line, then cross the road and descend to the parking area where your car awaits.

27 NISQUALLY NATIONAL WILDLIFE REFUGE

BEFORE YOU GO
MAP At visitor center
CONTACT Billy Frank Jr. Nisqually National Wildlife Refuge
NOTES Refuge fee required; dogs prohibited; hunting permitted in season; restrooms at the visitor center and porta-potties at the Twin Barns
GPS N 47 04.350, W 122 42.779

ABOUT THE HIKE
SEASON Year-round
DIFFICULTY Easy to moderate
DISTANCE 1 to 4 miles roundtrip
HIGH POINT 20 feet
ELEVATION GAIN 10 feet

GETTING THERE
From Tacoma, drive 19 miles southbound on Interstate 5 to exit 114 (Nisqually). Turn right on the Nisqually Cutoff Road, then right again at the T-intersection with Brown Farm Road, following signs for the wildlife refuge. Park in one of the two large parking areas. From Olympia, drive 8 miles northbound on I-5 to exit 114. Turn left at the end of the exit ramp and follow the signs to the wildlife refuge.

ON THE TRAIL
Billy Frank Jr. Nisqually National Wildlife Refuge (to use its official name) is a slam dunk to see wildlife. In our visits over the years, I've seen bald eagles, owls, herons, snow geese, turtles, river otters, seals, and a huge variety of

shorebirds and waterfowl too numerous to mention. Every season has its charms, but my favorite is winter, when the tides are extreme and dozens of bald eagles rendezvous to dine on chum salmon in the river.

Make sure you stop in at the Nisqually Visitor Center, where you can learn about which birds and animals have recently been spotted, obtain a map, and borrow binoculars for your walk.

You can take two hikes at the refuge: the 1-mile, ADA-accessible Twin Barns Loop Trail or the 4-mile Nisqually Estuary Trail that also includes the Twin Barns Loop. The shorter trail is better for toddlers and the longer one for older kids. Either way, begin your hike on the Twin Barns Loop Trail to the right of the visitor center. After 0.2 mile, reach an intersection. The Riparian Forest Overlook is worth the extra 400 feet in springtime when bright yellow skunk cabbage blooms. As you continue on, encourage the kids to look around and be quiet. Can they spot any birds? Can they hear them?

At 0.5 mile, approach the Nisqually River. It is well worth going to the overlook at end of the trail here to see this river make its way to Puget Sound. In winter a large tree just beyond the path's end is a favorite perch for eagles.

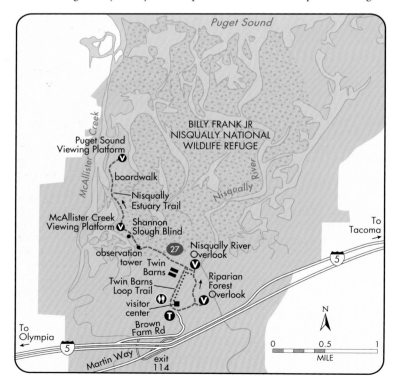

Observation towers, wildlife blinds, and telescopes provide ways to view the refuge's abundant wildlife.

This is also where I once saw a seal parked in the current, chowing down on a salmon.

Turn around and choose either one of the two trails you just crossed to make your way to the Twin Barns (last toilet stop). This whole area was once drained and farmed, and its recent restoration, explained on interpretive panels, is the largest such effort in the Pacific Northwest.

Now face your choice: are you going to loop back to the visitor center or venture out to the estuary? Wildlife awaits in the estuary. Look for ducks, great blue herons, geese, gulls, brants, sandpipers, and more in these tidal flats. After a 0.5-mile walk along the dike, reach one of the longest boardwalks on the Pacific Coast. This impressive structure, opened in 2011, extends a full mile into the Nisqually Delta, over mudflats when the tide is low and water when the tide is high. Wildlife is at its most abundant within two hours of high tide.

An observation tower at the beginning of the boardwalk provides a good bird's-eye view of the delta. If you want to venture only a short distance on the boardwalk, go to the Shannon Slough Blind and the McAllister Creek Viewing Platform. The blind is super fun for kids, with rectangular viewing slots at different levels from which to secretly peek out at the slough. The McAllister Creek Viewing Platform has excellent information about the estuary, birds, and Native American history.

The viewing platform at the end of the boardwalk is well worth the walk as well, especially on a clear day when hikers can enjoy views of Mount Rainier and the Olympics. Do note that the last 700 feet of boardwalk is closed seasonally for waterfowl hunting.

On your return, turn right at the Twin Barns to close your loop. Taking the gravel path is slightly faster, but you're more likely to see new wildlife along the Twin Barns Loop Trail. The trail ends on the opposite side of the visitor center from where you began.

28 WOODARD BAY CONSERVATION AREA

BEFORE YOU GO
MAP Available online on website
CONTACT Washington Department of Natural Resources
NOTES Discover Pass required; dogs and bikes prohibited; privy available
GPS N 47 07.622, W 122 51.219

ABOUT THE HIKE
SEASON Year-round
DIFFICULTY Easy
DISTANCE 1.4 to 2.1 miles roundtrip
HIGH POINT 60 feet
ELEVATION GAIN 50 feet

GETTING THERE
From southbound Interstate 5 in Lacey, take exit 109 (Martin Way) toward Sleater-Kinney Road. Turn right on Martin Way and right again on Sleater-Kinney Road NE. Travel 4.5 miles and continue straight onto 56th Avenue NE for 0.4 mile. At a T-intersection, turn right onto Shincke Road NE. After 0.6 mile the road curves left and becomes Woodard Bay Road NE. Drive 0.7 mile, cross the bridge over Woodard Bay, and the parking lot is on your right.

ON THE TRAIL
Snorting harbor seals. A colony of bats. Cormorants drying their wings. Woodard Bay Natural Resources Conservation Area is a hangout for wildlife. Some, like river otters, osprey, and great blue herons, live here year-round. Others, such as hooded mergansers and Barrow's goldeneyes, stop by for the temperate winter weather. There is a good chance you'll see or hear something that flies, swims, or slithers during your visit.

It wasn't always so idyllic. Until 1984, Weyerhaeuser used Weyer Point Peninsula as a loading point for logs bound for mills in Everett. A railway trestle crossed the bay, and a pier jutted far into Henderson Inlet. The South Bay Log Dump was a busy place, processing forty to sixty railcars of timber each day until logging activity slowed and the log dump closed. It has taken thirty years of active restoration to create today's tranquil wildlife sanctuary.

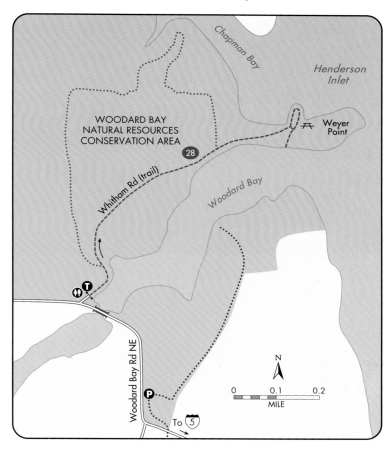

From the small parking area, pass through the gate onto Whitham Road. This wide, paved road is ideal for jogging strollers and little legs, but older kids (and adults) may want more challenge. A primitive loop trail takes off to the left just past the bike racks. It winds peacefully through the trees and out to Chapman Bay before it rejoins the road in half a mile, adding about 1.3 miles and a bit of elevation gain to your roundtrip.

For those sticking to the road, pass under mossy big-leaf maples and toddler-sized sword fern on the short trek to the point, every so often catching a glimpse of the emerald-green bay. It's just 0.6 mile to the peninsula and an additional 0.1 mile to Weyer Point. The first thing to notice is the large inter-pretive display and picnic shelter. Take time to read about the long human history of the area, the log dump, and the extensive restoration. Then wander

Although most recently a logging port, Woodard Bay has a rich history. This canoe is a reminder of its Native American past.

out toward Woodard Bay to your right. This is where the trestle, now removed, crossed the bay. There's a neat clay model of a canoe to climb in and a bench from which to watch shorebirds flitting in the water.

Now walk in the other direction. Notice how far the pier juts out into Henderson Inlet. A section of this pier remains as a bat roost; if you're here at dusk you may witness several thousand bats flying out for their evening meal. A bunch of old pilings serves as a haul-out point for harbor seals, their racket audible to all. Benches and another canoe to play in make this a good place to break out a snack before returning to the trailhead.

29 TUMWATER FALLS PARK

BEFORE YOU GO
MAP None
CONTACT Olympia Tumwater Foundation
NOTES Dogs must be leashed; restroom available
GPS N 47 00.875, W 122 54.299

ABOUT THE HIKE
SEASON Year-round
DIFFICULTY Easy
DISTANCE 0.7 mile loop
HIGH POINT 100 feet
ELEVATION GAIN 80 feet

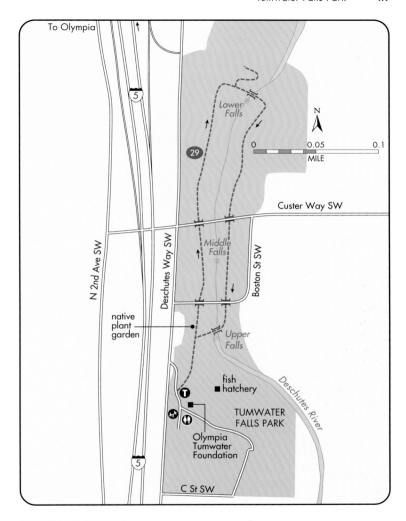

GETTING THERE

From Olympia, take Interstate 5 south 1 mile to exit 103 (N 2nd Avenue). Go left on Custer Way SW. After crossing I-5 and the river, take a right on Boston Street SW and then a quick left on Deschutes Way SW. Turn left on C Street SW into Tumwater Falls Park. Drive to the far parking area near the Olympia Tumwater Foundation.

ON THE TRAIL

History and natural wonder meet in historic Tumwater. Three waterfalls whose historic importance dates back hundreds of years roar improbably, just feet from Interstate 5. It's the final run of the Deschutes River before it pours into Capitol Lake and Puget Sound. Visitors today can take a 0.7-mile loop around the falls, stop to admire a native garden, read up on the extensive human history, and watch salmon flop their way up the fish ladders.

Not much of European settlement is truly old in Washington, but Tumwater qualifies as old. Used for fishing and shellfish harvesting by the Salish Indians for millennia, in 1845 this spot became the first American settlement north of

A pedestrian bridge spans the Deschutes River near the Upper Falls.

the Columbia River. Settlers used the power of the river to run their mills, and a community flourished. The area is probably best known as the original site of the Olympia Brewery.

All of that is gone now, but excellent interpretive signs tell both the native and settler stories, and there are foundations and old buildings to be seen from the trail. Start by the Olympia Tumwater Foundation building and make your way down to the roaring river. Here you will find manmade Upper Falls, where a sawmill used to operate. The metal grating beneath your feet is part of an extensive set of fish ladders installed in the 1950s to reestablish salmon runs on the Deschutes River.

After getting a good view, continue to the crushed gravel pathway. A short detour through the Salish native plant garden is worth your while to see what is in bloom. Then pass under the stone archway of Boston Street and parallel the river as it tumbles raucously down Middle Falls through a narrow gorge. What looks like a moss-covered puzzle is another fish ladder—water bouncing from one doorway to the next. In the fall, look for salmon jumping upstream toward the salmon hatchery above Upper Falls.

For a brief run, the river widens, slows, and quiets until it reaches the largest of the three waterfalls, Lower Falls, at 0.4 mile. There are two ways to view Lower Falls: above the waterfall on the bridge, or below the waterfall on the concrete patio. The lower viewpoint can get drenched in spray after a big rain. Don't be surprised if you get a face full of water, and it's okay to skip it if the conditions prove too dicey. Return to the bridge for the bird's-eye vantage and cross to the other side.

Now turn upriver for a walk of about 0.3 mile back to Upper Falls and the trailhead. A seasonal mini waterfall descends the hillside to your left and has been turned into a small splash pool for kids. And looking across the river, you can see the remnants of an old flour mill. A bridge takes walkers back over the river to where you started. In the fall when salmon are spawning, don't miss a visit to the salmon hatchery.

30 MIMA MOUNDS

BEFORE YOU GO
 MAP Capitol State Forest DNR map
 CONTACT Washington Department of Natural Resources
 NOTES Discover Pass required; dogs prohibited; do not pick flowers; privy available
 GPS N 46 54.321, W 123 02.860

ABOUT THE HIKE
 SEASON Year-round
 DIFFICULTY Easy
 DISTANCE 2.8 miles roundtrip
 HIGH POINT 225 feet
 ELEVATION GAIN 25 feet

Stroll among mysterious rounded mounds decorated with spring wildflowers.

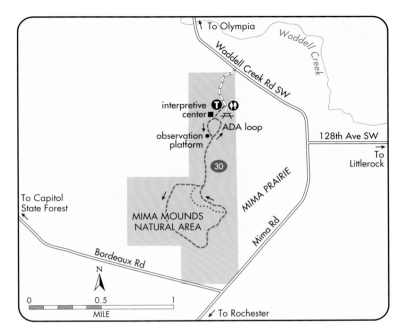

GETTING THERE

From Olympia, take Interstate 5 south 10 miles to exit 95. Turn right (west) on Maytown Road SW and follow it 3 miles to a stop sign in the tiny hamlet of Littlerock. Continue straight for 0.8 mile on what is now known as 128th Avenue SW. At the T-intersection, turn right on Waddell Creek Road SW and drive another 0.8 mile until you reach the signed drive for Mima Mounds Natural Area on the left. Park in the large lot.

ON THE TRAIL

Domelike mounds dot the prairie like bubble wrap as far as the eye can see. It's a grand mystery: what made these unusual little hills? Theories have abounded over the years, some rooted in science, others in the imagination. Were they made by glaciers or gophers? Aliens or humans? Volcanoes or earthquakes? No one really knows, and that's one of the reasons this place is compelling to visit.

Go in May or June to maximize your experience. A kaleidoscope of flowers, highlighted by purple camas, dot the hills, and with the flowers come an astonishing variety of butterflies. The Washington DNR website has a printable brochure that you can carry to help distinguish between painted ladies and western tiger swallowtails, or red admirals and great spangled fritillaries. Four species found on this prairie are candidates for the endangered species list.

Start your walk on the paved trail and follow it to the interpretive center. Here you can read up on all the geologic theories and the prairie environment. The best views of Mima Mounds are from above, but unless you're in a plane, you'll have to settle for climbing the stairs and thrusting a selfie stick high into the air. From here you can see how the landscape ripples across the prairie. Mornings and evenings, when the light is low, are the best time to capture the effect in photographs.

Continue on the paved trail toward the observation platform at 0.3 mile. This ADA-accessible loop makes for a pleasant half-mile outing, but if you want to get the feel of the mounds, continue south on the soft-surface trail past the platform. At 0.7 mile, reach a junction and follow it counterclockwise. Almost immediately, reach another junction where you can choose to make a 0.5-mile loop in the mounded prairie, or a longer 1.4-mile loop that takes in the full extent of the area. Either is a fine option.

As you wander among the mounds in a counterclockwise direction, help the kids identify flowers, butterflies, and animal scat. You'll likely encounter gobs of coyote scat. My kids gleefully accounted for each pile and imagined the tasty prey that live under these undulating mounds. A tantalizing two-tiered observation deck is visible on the loop but is unfortunately on private property. Your peaceful walk may also be disturbed by a nearby shooting range, but all of these present good opportunities to educate kids about the difference between private and public lands, and what people can do on them.

After you complete your loop, follow the paved trail back to the observation platform, then take the paved ADA loop to the right and into the trees. This section suggests what these mounds would look like if the forest was allowed to encroach onto the prairie. Walk past the interpretive center and back to the parking area. Picnic tables in the trees make this a good place to spread out a lunch.

Opposite: *Balance beam practice at Franklin Falls*

WEST SLOPE CASCADES

MOUNT BAKER

31 BAGLEY LAKES

BEFORE YOU GO
MAP Green Trails, Mt. Shuksan No. 14
CONTACT Mount Baker–Snoqualmie National Forest
NOTES Northwest Forest Pass required; dogs must be leashed; privy available
GPS N 48 51.701, W 121 40.937

ABOUT THE HIKE
SEASON July to mid-October
DIFFICULTY Easy
DISTANCE 1.6 miles to 2 miles loop
HIGH POINT 4250 feet
ELEVATION GAIN 75 feet

GETTING THERE
From Bellingham, follow State Route 542 east for 56 miles to the Mount Baker ski area. Where the road splits into a loop, drive less than a mile to Heather Meadows and a large parking lot on the right, signed Bagley Lakes.

ON THE TRAIL
While a steady stream of visitors amass at Artist Point, savvy family hikers will delight in two sparkling lakes and the potential to play in what is usually a year-round snowfield. The Bagley Lakes are just the right speed for young kids who dawdle and older kids who like to throw a snowball. It's a place the entire family can appreciate, and the hike can be adapted for additional challenge and length.

The views start from the parking lot and only get better. Descend 60 feet to Lower Bagley Lake and choose a direction when you reach the bottom. Start clockwise on the east side of the lake, which is so level that even toddlers can tackle it with ease. When the snow melts, the trailside blooms with electric pink and yellow monkey flowers, sunny cinquefoil, and lavender heather, then serves up tasty wild blueberries, and finally erupts into a fall display of orange and red foliage.

Lower Bagley Lake is like a string bean—long and skinny—shaped by the fact that it is a reservoir with a dam at its north end. It's not long before it reverts to a stream, braiding its way across the landscape. This is a nice place to break out a snack and observe your magnificent surroundings. The aptly named Table Mountain dominates the skyline, columns of basalt (actually ancient lava) emerge from the ground, and big boulders lounge like billiard balls in the valley.

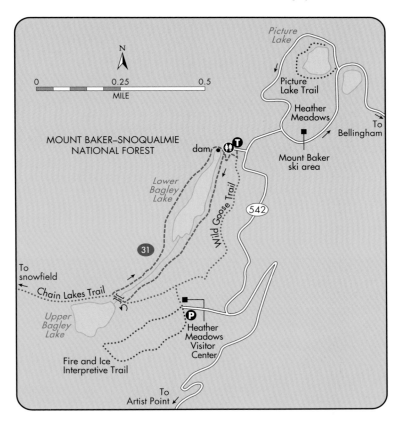

At 0.8 mile, reach Upper Bagley Lake, a natural deep cirque at the base of Table Mountain. An arched stone bridge—something you're more likely to find in New England than the Pacific Northwest—makes for an impromptu photo shoot with a dramatic backdrop.

Now you have several options that you may combine to suit your family. The easiest choice is to return the way you came. To return via a loop, double back on the Chain Lakes Trail on the west side of the stream to Lower Bagley Lake. It's a tad more difficult, with a few places that could require a hand for small children, but it offers a different perspective. To reach the visitor center, take the trail off to the left before the arched bridge. It climbs 175 feet for a bird's-eye view of Bagley Lakes, and then you can take the Wild Goose Trail from the visitor center back to your car. And finally, to reach what in most summers is a year-round snowfield, continue past Upper Bagley Lake on the

Chain Lakes Trail. Pass weeping walls, traverse (carefully—there is a drop-off here) a stone outcrop, then turn a corner and behold the immense snowfield below Herman Saddle.

Because alpine plant life is so fragile, please follow clear footpaths to the snowfield, and when you're there, stand only on the snow, not on the emerging grasses and flowers. This flora has a brief life every summer, and it takes years to recover from damage caused by people's feet. Pack a few snowballs, make a little snowman, and notice the snow cave where water runs out on its way to the lake. Then return via one of the three ways just noted.

EXPLORING FURTHER

The Chain Lakes Loop is one of the premier hikes of the North Cascades, and it is a great backpacking trip or strenuous day hike for older kids. The trail beyond the snowfield climbs to Herman Saddle (5400 feet) and then meanders down into a "chain" of alpine lakes. On its return, it climbs to Ptarmigan Ridge (5200 feet) and curves back to Artist Point. Although most guidebooks recommend starting at Bagley Lakes, it is easier to tackle it via Artist Point on the Ptarmigan Ridge–Mazama Lake Trail (Hike 33).

Meandering upstream to Upper Bagley Lake (photo by Jon Stier)

GREAT GETAWAY: MOUNT BAKER

Once you make your way to Heather Meadows and Artist Point, you'll want to figure out a way to stay there. On a sunny summer day this place shimmers with snowy peaks, icy tarns, and endless eye candy. It is packed midday on weekends, but is wonderfully empty in the early mornings and evenings. Why? Aside from a few small Forest Service campgrounds, there aren't many places where people can lodge in the area. Some folks stay in Bellingham to get a jump on crowds, while others rent cabins or houses in the few developments along State Route 542. Otherwise, Mount Baker is a far distance from almost everywhere.

If you plan to camp over the weekend, be sure to make reservations at one of the two nearby Forest Service campgrounds—Douglas Fir or Silver Fir—or at Whatcom County's Silver Lake Park. The latter has a swimming beach and boat rental, available to the public even if you aren't spending the night.

32 ARTIST RIDGE

BEFORE YOU GO
MAP Green Trails, Mt. Shuksan No. 14
CONTACT Mount Baker–Snoqualmie National Forest
NOTES Northwest Forest Pass required; dogs must be leashed; check snow conditions before you go; privy available
GPS N 48 50.800, W 121 41.606

ABOUT THE HIKE
SEASON Late July to September
DIFFICULTY Easy
DISTANCE 1 mile roundtrip
HIGH POINT 5225 feet
ELEVATION GAIN 100 feet

GETTING THERE
From Bellingham, follow State Route 542 east for 59 miles to the road's end at Artist Point. Due to heavy snowfall, this road is open only seasonally, and in some years not at all. Check road conditions before you go.

ON THE TRAIL
Artist Ridge is one of the most rewarding, super-short, and easy hikes in Washington. It's also one of the most overcrowded. But if you can arrive early on a sunny summer's day, you will be in for a treat. When my son first hiked here at age four, he was giddy—impressed by the massive snowiness of Mount Baker and Mount Shuksan and the magic iciness of the glacial tarns and summer snowfields.

If at all possible, arrive before 10:00 AM or after 5:00 PM on a summer weekend. Otherwise you will be competing for a parking place and following

Artist Ridge can remain partially snow-covered well into August. (photo by Jon Stier)

a long line of hikers on this much-loved trail. Along the way, you'll see many examples of where visitors' feet have damaged the fragile ecosystem. You will likely see people unwittingly cutting across the meadow, stomping on emerging plants. This is an excellent opportunity to set a good example by sticking to established trails and not picking the flowers.

The immense parking area may be walled in with snow until late summer. Usually, the trail melts out before the lot, so locate the trailhead to the right of the privies and venture forth. There is a paved trail to a viewpoint overlooking the Swift Creek drainage, with Mount Baker rising above.

It gets even better from here, so continue on a gravel path up a short ridge with Mount Shuksan before you, Mount Baker to your back, a little "V" of Baker Lake in the vast vista to your right, and the ribbon of highway to your left. White boulders—both big and small—pockmark the ridge, and snow-fields sometimes linger well into August. How fun it is to roll a snowball in the middle of summer!

You'll climb a series of sometimes steep stairs, but benches, boulders, and many photo opportunities ease the journey. Follow the trail to the left around a short lollipop loop that takes you to Huntoon Point and an unobstructed view of Mount Shuksan. You may find that the kids' favorite parts are the two turquoise glacial pools surrounded by ice and snow that you skirt. Linger here and notice how they reflect the light and mountains. The trail eventually peters out into many social trails near a second tarn. Be careful not to tread on tiny plants while determining your next steps. The loop will connect back to the main trail, and you'll be dazzled by Mount Baker, Table Mountain, and Ptarmigan Ridge on your return.

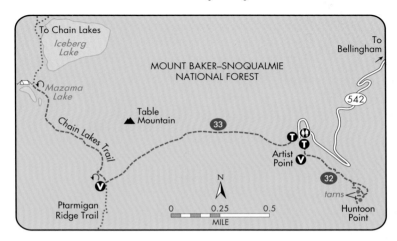

EXPLORING FURTHER

Because this trail is so short, consider combining it with a short jaunt along Ptarmigan Ridge (Hike 33), Bagley Lakes (Hike 31), the Fire and Ice Interpretive Trail, or Picture Lake. Stop at the visitor center at Austin Pass for advice.

33 PTARMIGAN RIDGE AND MAZAMA LAKE

BEFORE YOU GO

MAP Green Trails, Mt. Shuksan No. 14
CONTACT Mount Baker–Snoqualmie National Forest
NOTES Northwest Forest Pass required; dogs must be leashed; privy available; check snow conditions before you go
GPS N 48 50.800, W 121 41.606

ABOUT THE HIKE
(TO TRAIL JUNCTION)

SEASON Late July to September
DIFFICULTY Easy to moderate
DISTANCE 2.2 miles roundtrip
HIGH POINT 5200 feet
ELEVATION GAIN 50 feet

ABOUT THE HIKE
(TO MAZAMA LAKE)

SEASON Late July to September
DIFFICULTY Moderate to difficult
DISTANCE 3.8 miles roundtrip
HIGH POINT 5200 feet
ELEVATION GAIN 500 feet

GETTING THERE

From Bellingham, follow State Route 542 east for 59 miles to the road's end at Artist Point. Due to heavy snowfall, this road is open only seasonally, and in some years not at all. Check road conditions before you go.

Clouds part to reveal Mount Shuksan along Ptarmigan Ridge.

ON THE TRAIL

When you need a dose of alpine elixir, look no further. Dance along a lofty slope, bookended by two of Washington's most magnificent peaks: Mount Shuksan and Mount Baker. The earth here is raw and still forming, with lingering snowfields and glaciers hanging on steep slopes. Families can choose to hike the relatively easy and level Chain Lakes Trail 1.1 miles to the Ptarmigan

Ridge Trail junction, stopping at a destination-worthy panorama. Or they can continue into the Chain Lakes, dropping 450 feet in less than a mile to Mazama Lake, where excellent backcountry camping awaits.

Start your hike from the very popular Artist Point parking area. The Chain Lakes trailhead is opposite the restrooms at the northwest corner of the parking lot. The trail begins in shady trees but doesn't stay that way for long. Bring sunscreen, hats, and plenty of water, because it can feel very hot hiking in the bright summer sun. Be sure to also pack a jacket, because weather changes quickly here and it can get mighty chilly if the wind picks up and clouds appear.

Soon emerge on the long, sliding slope of Table Mountain, the trail carved into its side. If it is a clear day, mighty Mount Baker will beckon as you travel across boulder fields and through patches of fireweed and berries. This is an active volcano, and one of the most studied in the Cascades. It last erupted in the 1700s, and vents continue to emit gases near Sherman Crater. The volcanic history is written all over the landscape; layer upon layer of ash and pumice alternate with ancient columnar andesite lava, creating a rainbow effect on the surrounding slopes.

At 1.1 miles, find a rocky perch to spread out a snack at the Ptarmigan Ridge Trail junction. Say hello to Mount Shuksan, the other dominant peak that was at your back during your journey thus far. Observe the other valleys, ridges, and distant peaks of the North Cascades. I like getting out a map and helping the kids to identify the landmarks. While resting, you may be visited by a chipmunk (please don't feed them!) or spot a marmot, pika, or ptarmigan among the rocks. If you have binoculars, scan the slopes and ridges for mountain goats.

You may choose to turn around here, or continue on the Chain Lakes Trail. From this spot, the trail drops down to the right and visits a series of captivating alpine lakes. The closest is Mazama Lake (0.8 mile and a 450-foot descent), which has five lovely campsites that are well-suited for families. It is also a good destination for day hikers, though remember that the kids will have to climb back up to the ridge during the heat of the day.

Alternatively, the Ptarmigan Ridge Trail begins at the Chain Lakes intersection and proceeds straight, plodding ever closer to Mount Baker through an otherworldly moonscape of rocks and snow. While the elevation doesn't change dramatically, the trail gets extremely rocky and is often snow-covered well into August.

EXPLORING FURTHER

The Chain Lakes Loop is one of the premier hikes of the North Cascades, and it is a great intermediate backpacking trip. Families with older kids may want to push beyond Mazama Lake to Hayes and Arbuthnot lakes, where there are more campsites. This trail is a loop that climbs Herman Saddle (5400 feet) and emerges at Bagley Lakes (Hike 31) and Heather Meadows (7 miles, 4250 feet). A very steep 1.8-mile climb on the Wild Goose Trail (or a car shuttle) is required to return to Artist Point.

NORTH CASCADES HIGHWAY

34 BLUE LAKE (WEST)

BEFORE YOU GO
MAP Green Trails, Hamilton No. 45
CONTACT Mount Baker–Snoqualmie National Forest
NOTES Northwest Forest Pass required; dogs must be leashed; privy available
GPS N 48 39.252, W 121 47.061

ABOUT THE HIKE
SEASON Late June to October
DIFFICULTY Easy to moderate
DISTANCE 1.6 miles roundtrip
HIGH POINT 4000 feet
ELEVATION GAIN 200 feet

GETTING THERE
From Interstate 5 in Burlington, take exit 230 and follow State Route 20 east 26 miles through Sedro-Woolley to Baker Lake Road. Turn left on Baker Lake Road and follow it 12 miles. Turn left on Forest Road 12. Travel FR 12 for

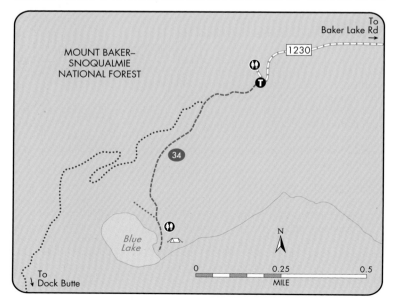

6.8 miles and veer left onto FR 1230. Drive FR 1230 to its end at the trailhead in 3.7 miles.

ON THE TRAIL

Travel through heather, blueberries, and tiny Christmas trees to a picturesque mountain lake high above Baker Lake. This Blue Lake is indeed blue, and is not to be confused with the other Blue Lake 80 miles east on State Route 20. The trail is relatively level and easy, although the final scramble down to its shore poses some obstacles. Consider bringing a pole to fish for brook trout or a tent to spend the night. You'll be glad you visited this little gem.

Lone tree at Blue Lake

Start high and stay high through a subalpine forest of firs and cedars. In just 0.3 mile, reach an intersection. The fork to the right leads to Dock Butte; the fork to the left leads to Blue Lake. Go left and walk through patches of heather, blueberries, and young conifers. After rains, there could be some mud. At 0.75 mile, reach Blue Lake and choose your route. It's a very short, but steep, descent to the lake. As you explore this alpine cirque, choose the most established paths. Social trails lead everywhere, and this place is in jeopardy of being loved to death.

There are attractive places to rest on either side of the lake, but my favorite is where a photogenic tree grows gracefully from a rocky peninsula. The lake is deep and filled with colorful, red-dotted brook trout. It's cold for swimming, though it could be curiously refreshing on a hot day! Blue Lake is an ideal place to hang out for the afternoon or a night, with a handful of choice campsites and a privy. When you can tear yourself away, return the way you came.

EXPLORING FURTHER

Older kids and adults may want to press on for Dock Butte and its incredible views of Mount Baker. It adds about 3.4 miles and 1200 feet of elevation gain to your hike, and certainly delivers a payoff. The trail is a steady, uphill climb to the ridge above Blue Lake and then meanders through meadows and around hills and tarns to the butte. Until late summer, when the snow melts, it can be a tough approach to the top. But even if you don't summit, the panoramic views below it are sublime.

35 BAKER RIVER

BEFORE YOU GO
MAP Green Trails, Mt. Shuksan No. 14
CONTACT Mount Baker–Snoqualmie National Forest
NOTES Northwest Forest Pass required; dogs not allowed into the national park; privy available
GPS N 48 45.025, W 121 33.305

ABOUT THE HIKE
SEASON Year-round
DIFFICULTY Moderate
DISTANCE 5.4 miles roundtrip
HIGH POINT 945 feet
ELEVATION GAIN 200 feet

GETTING THERE

From Interstate 5 in Burlington, take exit 230 and follow State Route 20 east 26 miles through Sedro-Woolley to Baker Lake Road. Turn left on Baker Lake Road and follow it 25.5 miles to its terminus at the trailhead. The final 5.5 miles of the road is a decent gravel surface, with some potholes.

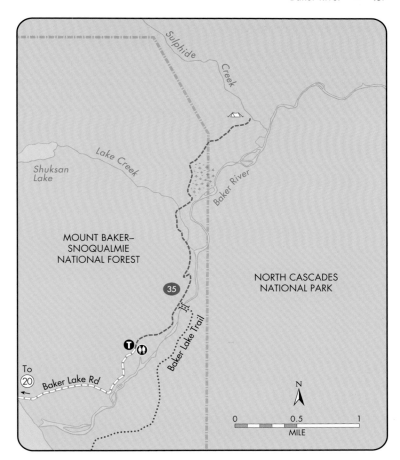

ON THE TRAIL

Don't let the size of the parking lot fool you. Most hikers will be traveling along the shores of big Baker Lake. And sure, you could join them on that family-friendly trail, but why not take the path less traveled? Beyond an impressive suspension bridge over the river, the Baker River Trail winds its way upstream, through cedar groves and mossy boulders, to Sulphide Camp in North Cascades National Park. From here, relax on the creek's wild shore and gaze up to the south side of Mount Shuksan and its flank of jumbo glaciers.

Share the first 0.5 mile to the suspension bridge where lake hikers turn off. The way is level and easy, with a couple of highlights: a gargantuan cedar tree and a hidey-hole in the boulders that you can explore like a cave. At the bridge,

Monster-size cedar along Baker River

continue straight upstream on the west side of Baker River, but make sure to detour onto its span to check out the river. In fall, you may be able to spot salmon swimming beneath your feet in the crystal clear water.

After the bridge, the trail winds and rolls up the wide river valley under cover of strapping cedars, hemlocks, and Douglas firs. Great mossy boulders squeeze the trail, and Baker River braids its way back and forth across the plain. At 1.5 miles, reach a fairy-tale grove, with outstretched branches of big-leaf maple and alders decorated with lush lichen and moss. Just beyond is Lake Creek, where a bridge carved out of a fallen giant reaches only halfway across the seasonal creek bed. This creek is dry for much of the year, but in spring and after big fall storms it is a torrent, as evidenced by the extensive debris in the creek bed and the erosion on the opposite bank. The scramble up the eroded bank is the hardest section for kids, and the water level may make it impassable after big storms.

Continuing along the river again, enter North Cascades National Park at 2.2 miles. If you are hiking with a dog, you must turn around here, as pets are not allowed in national parks. It is flat from here to trail's end at 2.7 miles, where there are two campsites tucked close together in the trees next to Sulphide Creek. Follow the sound of water and make your way out onto the rocks for a fine view of Mount Shuksan's pointy spires. Kids will enjoy playing on the cobblestone beach, and you can relax under the careful watch of the commanding peak. Enjoy your stay and return the way you came.

36 SAUK MOUNTAIN

BEFORE YOU GO
MAP Green Trails, Lake Shannon No. 46
CONTACT Mount Baker–Snoqualmie National Forest
NOTES Steep drop-offs; lingering snow patches warrant caution; privy available
GPS N 48 31.281, W 121 36.462

ABOUT THE HIKE
SEASON July to October
DIFFICULTY Difficult
DISTANCE 3.8 miles roundtrip
HIGH POINT 5537 feet
ELEVATION GAIN 1180 feet

GETTING THERE
From Interstate 5 in Burlington, take exit 230 and follow State Route 20 east 32 miles through Sedro-Woolley and Concrete to milepost 96 at the Rockport State Park boundary. Turn left on Forest Road 1030 (signed Sauk Mountain Road, also Drive) and drive 7.5 miles to its end. The road is gravel, with potholes and a washboard surface. Most sedans can make it, though low-clearance vehicles may have some trouble.

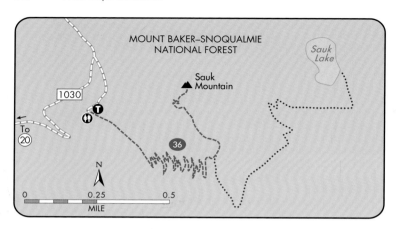

ON THE TRAIL

Sauk Mountain is a superlative hike in every way: the panoramic views; the twenty-six switchbacks; the plethora of blooms and vivid fall color; and, of course, the airy summit. It's a difficult hike, but one that provides enormous satisfaction to hikers young and old. It is not, however, ideal for all kids. If you don't trust your child's footwork, balance, or impulses, save it for when they are older. The mountainside is incredibly steep and the trail eroded in places; one wrong step could send a kid skidding downhill. It's also exposed to the sun and can get beastly hot on summer days. That said, confident school-age hikers can embrace the challenge to stand atop a prominent peak in the North Cascades.

The trailhead is pretty awesome in and of itself. From a well-placed picnic table you can trace your zigzag route up Sauk Mountain and gaze down at the sinuous Skagit River below. Immediately enter lush, humid meadows bloom-

DON'T CUT SWITCHBACKS

Many hikes in this book feature switchbacks, where the trail zigzags up the slope. Switchbacks serve two primary functions: they provide a more even grade for hikers, and they protect the slope from erosion. All too often, hikers cut across these switchbacks in an effort to save themselves a few steps. Unfortunately, when trails go straight up the hill, water channels down the path, hollowing out the trail and washing the soil down too. When hikers repeatedly cut switchbacks, they are affecting the trail for future users. It isn't easy to decommission established shortcuts or restore the slope. Please don't perpetuate the problem by cutting switchbacks—or using unofficial switchbacks. Teach your kids to stay on the established trail, and they will more likely grow up to be good trail stewards as adults.

The trail up Sauk Mountain provides sweeping views the entire way.

ing with paintbrush, columbine, tiger lilies, aster, and lupine, and buzzing with pollinators, grasshoppers, and flies. The trail gets to business quickly. I suggest counting switchbacks or different varieties of wildflowers to keep kids' minds off the incline. The switchbacks are intimidating—some right on top of each other—but notice how they keep the grade fairly mellow. Unfortunately, hikers have taken shortcuts on the switchbacks, which have eroded the trail, making it narrow and potentially dangerous in places. A small pebble kicked off the trail can be a significant hazard for hikers below; a misstep can turn into a slide. Be careful.

Continue crisscrossing the mountainside, gaining 900 feet over 1.4 miles, until you round a corner and proceed up the backside of the ridgeline. Here, the views open up to the south and east, revealing prominent Glacier Peak, Whitehorse Mountain, and the Picket Range. Peering downward, discern the confluence of the Skagit and Sauk rivers. As meadows give way to rockier terrain, listen for pikas and marmots and watch the skies for raptors. At an unmarked junction, stay to the right, and at the marked junction, remain to the left. Agate-hued Sauk Lake gleams 1000 feet below, and glacial Mount Shuksan makes a brief appearance before the last steep push up to the summit (5537 feet elevation). In the early season, lingering snow warrants caution.

GREAT GETAWAY: NORTH CASCADES NATIONAL PARK

Glacier National Park in Montana has the name, but North Cascades National Park in Washington has the glaciers. More than three hundred glaciers cleave to its pointy peaks, the most of any national park outside of Alaska. Visit today, because while these icy fields are visible from both roads and trails, they are retreating due to climate change. Bisecting the park is a long ribbon of highway and a national recreation area that allows for hydroelectric dams. It's not your usual national park fare, but the result includes two striking, milky-colored lakes far below the highway.

While a few lodging choices exist west of the park entrance, camping is really the way to go here. The Newhalem Campground, adjacent to the park visitor center, is the largest option, and sites can be reserved. Midweek visitors may opt for the lovely Colonial Creek Campground farther to the east. If these options don't pan out, try one of the many campgrounds near Baker Lake. While hiking is the main attraction, you can rent canoes and kayaks on Ross Lake, and Seattle City Light runs boat tours on Diablo Lake, as well as a powerhouse tour for kids ten and up.

And what a fine summit it is! Sauk Mountain is ringed on all sides with serrated mountains, as well as three volcanoes—Mount Baker, Glacier Peak, and Mount Rainier. On a very clear day, even the Olympic Mountains are visible. It makes you feel like you're standing on the dome of a volcano yourself. Enjoy the panorama, then retrace your steps to the trailhead.

37 NEWHALEM TRAILS: RIVER LOOP AND TRAIL OF CEDARS

BEFORE YOU GO
MAP Green Trails, Marblemount No. 47; area map available at visitor center
CONTACT North Cascades National Park
NOTES Dogs must be leashed; restrooms available
GPS N 48 41.427, W 121 05.874

ABOUT THE HIKE (RIVER LOOP)
SEASON Year-round
DIFFICULTY Easy to moderate
DISTANCE 1.8 miles loop
HIGH POINT 570 feet
ELEVATION GAIN 100 feet

ABOUT THE HIKE (TRAIL OF CEDARS)
SEASON Year-round
DIFFICULTY Easy
DISTANCE 0.7 mile loop
HIGH POINT 560 feet
ELEVATION GAIN 10 feet

GETTING THERE
From Interstate 5 in Burlington, take exit 230 and follow State Route 20 east 54 miles to the North Cascades Visitor Center. Turn right into the complex and follow signs to the large parking lot.

This view from the suspension bridge on Trail of Cedars shows how close a 2015 fire got to the Skagit River.

ON THE TRAIL

A network of short nature trails spins off from the North Cascades National Park Visitor Center and the company town of Newhalem next door. Since 2015, the trails have provided a window into the effects of a recent forest fire. During that summer, the visitor center, campground, and town almost succumbed to an intense fire that burned for weeks. Each of the nature trails was affected but largely spared the worst. If you are camping nearby, pick out a couple of short hikes in the area and don't miss Ladder Creek Falls and its colorful light show at night.

The **River Loop** is the longest of the area trails; it leaves from behind the North Cascades Visitor Center, skirts the campground, and loops by the Skagit River. Hike downhill through Douglas fir with deeply fissured trunks, losing 100 feet over 0.3 mile. Once in the flats, you will encounter several intersections. Follow the signs for "River Loop" so you don't end up in the campground. At 0.6 mile, reach the Skagit River. It is wide and swift moving, with the flow controlled by upstream dams. Hike for 0.25 mile along the river, then pull away into a forest charred by the 2015 blaze. Notice the varied impacts of the fire. Some trees are completely blackened, yet others were spared. Fireweed

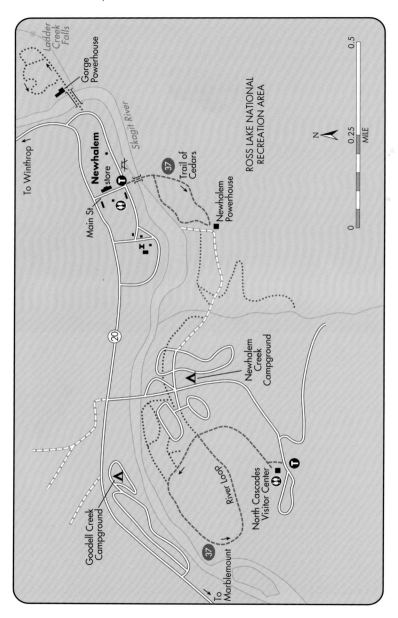

and bracken fern have quickly established themselves, making this place eerily beautiful. Soon, leave the burned forest behind, reaching a four-way intersection at 1.3 miles. Turn right and hike back uphill to the visitor center.

Another option in this area is **Trail of Cedars**—an ideal leg-stretcher on a long drive. At the end of Main Street in Newhalem, take a graceful suspension bridge across the Skagit River for this short interpretive loop. I suggest following it clockwise so you can enjoy the river on your return. Interpretive signs, mentioning the effects of a 1922 forest fire, seem a bit dated given the 2015 fire, which also skirted the edge of this area. Try to figure out which fire-blackened stumps are old and which are recent. At 0.3 mile, reach the Newhalem Powerhouse and read all about this original powerhouse, then curve back down to the river under the canopy of big cedars. This is the most pleasant part of the journey. Before you know it, you'll be standing on the suspension bridge again, gazing down into the clear green water.

Camping in the area? Then don't miss Seattle City Light's nightly light show at Ladder Creek Falls. A half-mile trail (150 feet elevation gain) leads up to the waterfall, illuminated in a cascade of colored lights each summer night. It's a weird place, created in 1925 by the City Light superintendent to showcase how anything was possible with electricity. You may want to have a flashlight to guide your way up multiple flights of steps to the falls, which tumble through the narrow gorge. The trailhead is next to the Gorge Powerhouse in Newhalem.

38 THUNDER KNOB

BEFORE YOU GO
MAP Green Trails, Diablo No. 48
CONTACT North Cascades National Park
NOTES Dogs must be leashed; privy available in campground
GPS N 48 41.427, W 121 05.874

ABOUT THE HIKE
SEASON March to November
DIFFICULTY Moderate to difficult
DISTANCE 3.8 miles roundtrip
HIGH POINT 1860 feet
ELEVATION GAIN 630 feet

GETTING THERE
From Interstate 5 in Burlington, take exit 230 and follow State Route 20 east 64 miles to Colonial Creek Campground. Park in the lot on the north side of the highway, outside the campground.

ON THE TRAIL
The North Cascades are known for their verticality. Many of the tallest peaks in the state are here, and this makes it difficult to find kid-friendly hikes. The easily scaled Thunder Knob is an exception, with a superhighway of a trail built at

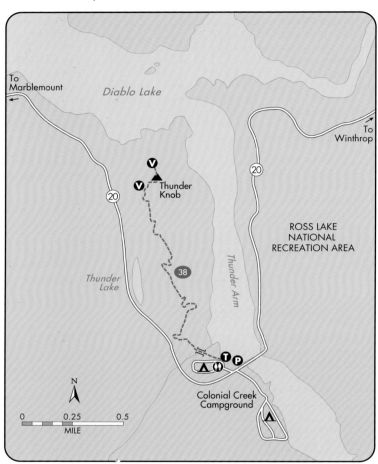

an even grade to its flattish top. In less than 2 miles of vigorous but well-paced hiking, you'll find yourself perched above turquoise Diablo Lake and ringed by a flank of seemingly impenetrable peaks.

Pass through the north section of the Colonial Creek Campground and follow signs for Thunder Knob. The trailhead is just beyond the parking area for sites 10 to 13. Walk over a series of bridges and notice how, after floods in 2003 devastated the area, Colonial Creek reclaimed a part of the campground, flowing over what used to be a road and burying a picnic table under rubble. Pass over the dry former creek bed, enter the trees, and start switchbacking up

Diablo Lake from Thunder Knob

the hillside. While the trail is never too steep, it is almost always uphill, gaining 400 feet over the first mile.

The first big viewpoint is at 1 mile, where 7771-foot tall Colonial Peak rises in commanding fashion, small glaciers clinging to its facade. Lodgepole pines, not often seen on the west slope of the Cascades, dot the hillside. The trail grade eases, then dips for 0.2 mile before making the final 0.4-mile push to the summit. Veer off the trail to the left to take in the aquamarine hue of Diablo Lake, the prominence of Colonial and Pyramid peaks, the ribbon of highway, and the textured green expanse of forest. In the distance are Davis Peak and the double steeples of McMillan Spires.

Back on the main trail, continue another 0.1 mile to its end. There are several places to take in a bird's-eye view of Diablo Lake—its twin coves and small islands. The hefty chunk of a mountain across the way is Sourdough Mountain. This spot is not as spectacular as the first overlook, but it carries a subtle beauty. Notice how the color of the lake changes depending on where you view it from and the time of day. When you are finished, return the way you came and enjoy the views that were at your back on the way up.

MOUNTAIN LOOP HIGHWAY

39 BOULDER RIVER

BEFORE YOU GO

MAP Green Trails, Mountain Loop Highway No. 111SX
CONTACT Mount Baker–Snoqualmie National Forest
NOTES Privy along road 3 miles from the trailhead
GPS N 48 15.040, W 121 49.013

ABOUT THE HIKE

SEASON Year-round
DIFFICULTY Easy to moderate
DISTANCE 2.5 miles roundtrip
HIGH POINT 1025 feet
ELEVATION GAIN 135 feet

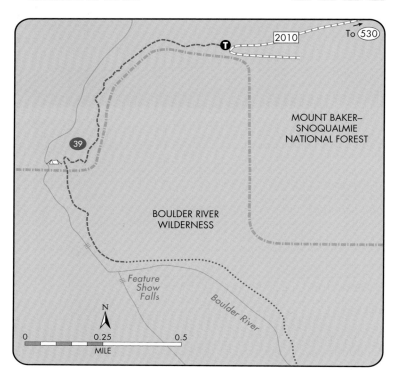

GETTING THERE

From Interstate 5 west of Arlington, take exit 208 and turn east onto State Route 530 (Arlington/Darrington). Follow SR 530 east through Arlington, as it briefly turns left onto SR 9, then immediately right to Darrington. Drive SR 530 approximately 20 miles, passing through the Oso slide area. Just after milepost 41, turn right on French Creek Road (Forest Road 2010) and take it to its end in 5.5 miles. This road is gravel and often potholed, but passable in a sedan. There is parking for about fifteen cars at the trailhead.

Trillium is one of the first flowers to bloom each season.

ON THE TRAIL

Lush wilderness, towering waterfalls, and an easy trail make Boulder River one of the best kid hikes around. What's more, this is one hike that might even be better on a rainy day. When the waterfalls are flush with rainwater, they are at their most spectacular.

The trail begins high above noisy Boulder River on the bed of a former railroad. The trail is wide and the walking is easy for even the smallest kids, but be aware that this first part has some steep drop-offs on the right side. Keep young kids close, and remind older ones to stay on the uphill side of the trail. This is not a good place for a misstep.

Stride past weeping basalt walls through a forest of cedars, Douglas firs, and alders as you climb gradually. At 1 mile, pass a campsite below and the Boulder River Wilderness sign. The trail will begin to descend and approach the raucous river. Notice the color; the milky green indicates that it is fed by glacial melt upstream.

The first waterfall—impressive during the winter and spring, wispy in the summer—is located here. A short, muddy trail leads to a gravel beach. Skip this side trip and go just a few more yards up the trail to Feature Show Falls at 1.25 miles. A double veil drops 259 feet directly into Boulder River. Another short, steep, rocky side trail leads to the river, where there are rocks to sit on. It's worth the effort, but can be tough for kids with short legs.

Most hikers choose to turn around at Feature Show Falls. However, the Boulder River Trail continues for another 3 miles, ascending moderately under deep old-growth forest cover. At the end of the trail are several campsites, making this an excellent overnight backpacking destination.

40 OLD SAUK

BEFORE YOU GO
MAP Green Trails, Mountain Loop Highway No. 111SX
CONTACT Mount Baker–Snoqualmie National Forest
NOTES Northwest Forest Pass required; privy available
GPS N 48 11.755, W 121 31.753

ABOUT THE HIKE
SEASON Year-round
DIFFICULTY Easy to moderate
DISTANCE 1.3 miles to 4.9 miles roundtrip
HIGH POINT 750 feet
ELEVATION GAIN 100 feet

GETTING THERE

From Interstate 5 just west of Arlington, take exit 208 and turn east onto State Route 530 (Arlington/Darrington). Follow SR 530 east through Arlington, as it briefly turns left onto SR 9, then immediately right. Follow SR 530 for 30 miles to Darrington. Turn right on the Mountain Loop Highway, and drive 5.7 miles

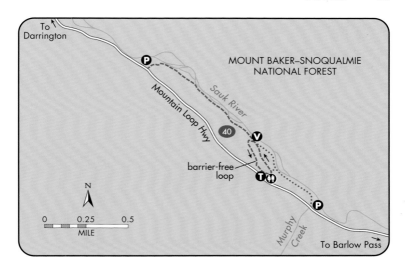

to the large trailhead on the left. This is the second of three entrances for the Old Sauk trail, and it is the most developed.

ON THE TRAIL

Rain or shine, the Old Sauk trail delivers a winning outing suitable for the whole family. Rarely crowded, this short 1.3-mile, barrier-free loop leads through a mossy forest of fir and alder to the banks of the Sauk River, where the trail continues in both directions. When the water is high, look for osprey and shorebirds from the bluff. When it is low, you can make your way to a cobblestone beach, where you may catch sight of a great blue heron or a salmon. The trail is low enough in elevation to be accessible year-round, but it is particularly delightful in the springtime for its woodland wildflowers and in October and November for its mushroom show. This is an ideal rainy-day hike.

From the information kiosk, follow the barrier-free loop in a counterclockwise direction on the gravel pathway. Just beyond the kiosk, reach an intersection. The right fork runs to the southern trailhead at Murphy Creek. Your route is to the left. At 0.5 mile, arrive at the banks of the Sauk River and another intersection. Follow the trail downstream to the left and reach a viewpoint. From here the barrier-free trail heads away into the forest on its return to the trailhead. You can certainly return on the loop for a roundtrip of 1.3 miles, but since you just reached the river, how about exploring a bit farther?

Although you leave the smooth gravel trail behind, it is still easy walking as you follow the dirt path downstream. Moss clings to old cedar branches and creates a kaleidoscope of green. The trees are tall but not that old, most of the area having been logged in the 1930s; telltale notches in the stumps indicate where springboards were installed so loggers could stand above the ground to

Pausing along the Sauk River

saw. In the fall, look under the canopy for mushrooms sprouting through the soil and moss. If it is spring, listen for frogs croaking in the rushes.

There are several places to view the river from above, and few access points to reach its banks. It's almost guaranteed that you will spot birds and waterfowl—American dippers (once called "water ouzels") and ducks. In the late summer and fall, you may also see salmon or steelhead as they swim upriver to spawn. From its departure from the barrier-free path, the trail goes 1.8 miles to the northern trailhead. If you reach a sign on the trail, you will have hiked 2.3 miles. Turn around, taking a right turn at the barrier-free trail, and follow it back to the trailhead.

41 INDEPENDENCE LAKE

BEFORE YOU GO
MAP Green Trails, Mountain Loop Highway No. 111SX
CONTACT Mount Baker–Snoqualmie National Forest
NOTES Northwest Forest Pass required; privy available
GPS N 48 07.018, W 121 31.344

ABOUT THE HIKE
SEASON July to October
DIFFICULTY Easy to moderate
DISTANCE 1.4 miles roundtrip
HIGH POINT 3725 feet
ELEVATION GAIN 175 feet

GETTING THERE
From Granite Falls, follow the Mountain Loop Highway 11 miles to the Verlot Public Service Center. In 14.8 miles, just past the entrance to the Big Four Ice Caves, turn left onto Coal Creek Road (Forest Road 4060). Take this sometimes bumpy gravel road 4.7 miles to the trailhead at the road's end.

ON THE TRAIL
Of all the easily accessible lakes along the Mountain Loop Highway, Independence Lake boasts the most vivid turquoise waters. It's hard to believe that this color is actually found in nature. You might consider bringing a baggie full of all the kids' blue-hued markers to test out which most closely resembles the color of the lake.

The trail starts out by climbing somewhat steeply on switchbacks through an old clear-cut now alive with fireweed, bracken fern, and younger trees. It doesn't take long, however, before it enters the sweet solitude of large Douglas fir, western red cedar, and western hemlock. Cross a seasonal creek bed on small rocks and continue up the trail. It may seem a bit steeper than it actually is, the result of exposed rocks and roots that are so characteristic of popular trails in the Mountain Loop area.

Fortunately, no one will have to work hard for very long before reaching their reward. At just 0.7 mile, come around a corner, and there it is! Gleaming blue water reflects the lake's namesake mountain, Independence Peak, as its precipitous slope drops almost straight into the east side of the lake. Scamper carefully over logs at the outlet of the lake to get a closer look, and then do a little exploring. The trail continues on a ridge along the west side where the color looks its richest. The north end of the lake has backcountry campsites and a privy, and the best access for wading. It's marshy here, but also an interesting place to poke around if the bugs aren't too bad. Note the extended gravel bar; it is almost like someone laid gravel paths through a flower garden. And if no one is camping, the campsites are fun to explore before heading back the way you came.

A young hiker bounds up the trail. (photo by Eugene Lee)

EXPLORING FURTHER

Another wild alpine lake lies less than 2.5 miles up the trail. But while the hike to Independence Lake was easy, the trail to North Lake is rugged, steep, and sometimes exposed. It is a 1250-foot elevation gain to reach a viewpoint of the lake, then another 750 feet down to the lake. Older kids could tackle this trail, especially as a day trip from a backcountry campsite at Independence Lake, but it's not a good choice for young hikers.

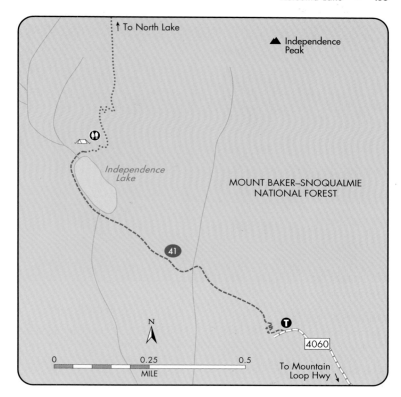

42 KELCEMA LAKE

BEFORE YOU GO

MAP Green Trails, Mountain Loop Highway No. 111SX
CONTACT Mount Baker–Snoqualmie National Forest
NOTES Privy available
GPS N 48 06.931, W 121 35.579

ABOUT THE HIKE

SEASON Late June to October
DIFFICULTY Easy
DISTANCE 1 mile roundtrip
HIGH POINT 3200 feet
ELEVATION GAIN 50 feet

Kelcema Lake

GETTING THERE

From Granite Falls, follow the Mountain Loop Highway 11 miles to the Verlot Public Service Center. From there, drive 12.2 miles and turn left onto Deer Creek Road (Forest Road 4052). Drive the rocky gravel road 4 miles to a wide bend in the road on the left.

ON THE TRAIL

Kelcema Lake has a different feel from the many other easy-to-reach lakes along the Mountain Loop Highway. Like its nearby cousins, the trail traverses old-growth forest to reach a sun-kissed cirque beneath formidable peaks. But the topography is less familiar, with long stretches of exposed bedrock underfoot. The trees are different too. Huge Alaska yellow cedars dot the trail and shoreline, giving hikers the impression that they've been transported to a high-elevation magical place.

A short and easy trail of 0.5 mile transports old and young alike to Kelcema Lake. The trail begins in a marshy area crowded with bog-loving plants like skunk cabbage and marsh marigolds that give way to summer treats like huckleberries and thimbleberries as you enter the Boulder River Wilderness.

It's your usual rock-and-dirt trail until you come to a big slab of rock that becomes the trail for 20 feet. As you walk, you'll encounter more exposed bedrock, interspersed with rickety boardwalks (watch little toes in the cracks!). Listen for the nearby creek and look for a fun, hollow tree among a grove of shaggy cedars.

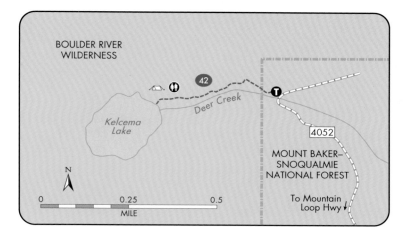

BOULDER RIVER
WILDERNESS

Kelcema
Lake

Deer Creek

42

4052

MOUNT BAKER–
SNOQUALMIE
NATIONAL FOREST

N

To Mountain
Loop Hwy

0   0.25   0.5
MILE

At 0.4 mile take a peek into a creek bed notable for its huge jigsaw puzzle of rocks and a seasonal waterfall. That will give you a good idea about what lies beneath a fairly thin layer of dirt all around. In moments, you'll arrive at the lake. There are several places to enjoy lunch while gazing up at Bald Mountain, and two locations where you can wade into the water for a swim. The water is warmed by summer temperatures and is quite refreshing on a hot day. A backcountry privy is a short distance up to the right.

A Boy Scout camp was located at Kelcema Lake until 1947. The big bare spot just off the shore was the site of a lodge. At that time the Mountain Loop Highway was complete only to Silverton, so supplies had to be brought in by pack mules. Exploring this area, you'll see why the Scouts so liked Kelcema Lake. There's a big rock that you can scamper up fairly safely for a bird's-eye view of the water, and several campsites good for beginning backpackers. Once you've had your fun, return the way you came.

Regular water breaks keep kids hydrated and happy. (photo by Jon Stier)

CAR CAMPING

One of the best ways to visit and hike in the more far-flung areas of the state is to go car camping. Sleeping outside, racing bikes around the campground, roasting hot dogs over a campfire, and waking up to birdsong are all highlights of summer in the outdoors for children—and adults.

With Washington's large and active population of outdoor lovers, however, it isn't always easy to get a campsite. Adding to the confusion is a byzantine collection of reservation and nonreservation policies. Plan ahead by zeroing in on where you want to go and following up online with the land management agency that operates the campground to see if and when you can reserve your site.

In general, campsites, cabins, and yurts in state parks can be reserved nine months in advance. Forest Service and national park campgrounds have varying policies about reservations. Those that accept reservations can be booked six months in advance. Forest Service campgrounds west of the Cascade crest are likely to accept reservations, while those to the east are less likely to take them. Most Forest Service and national park campgrounds on the Olympic Peninsula are first-come, first-served, with some exceptions.

If you don't have gear, look to your friends to borrow some, or rent from an outdoor equipment retailer. Sometimes trying out gear is the best way to determine what you really need. Do make sure you have a rain fly for the tent and raingear for the family to ensure that you stay warm and comfortable in all conditions.

Start a family car-camping tradition of exploring new corners of Washington.

43 BOARDMAN LAKE

BEFORE YOU GO

MAP Green Trails, Mountain Loop Highway No. 111SX
CONTACT Mount Baker–Snoqualmie National Forest
NOTES Northwest Forest Pass required; privy available at lake
GPS N 48 02.027, W 121 41.161

ABOUT THE HIKE

SEASON May to October
DIFFICULTY Easy
DISTANCE 1.7 miles roundtrip
HIGH POINT 3075 feet
ELEVATION GAIN 250 feet

GETTING THERE

From Granite Falls, follow the Mountain Loop Highway 11 miles to the Verlot Public Service Center. In 4.6 miles, turn right onto Schweitzer Creek Road (Forest Road 4020). It is signed for Boardman Lake and several other trailheads. Take this road 2.6 miles to a junction with FR 4021. Bear left and continue on FR 4020. In 2.2 more miles you will reach the trailhead parking on the right.

Boardman Lake

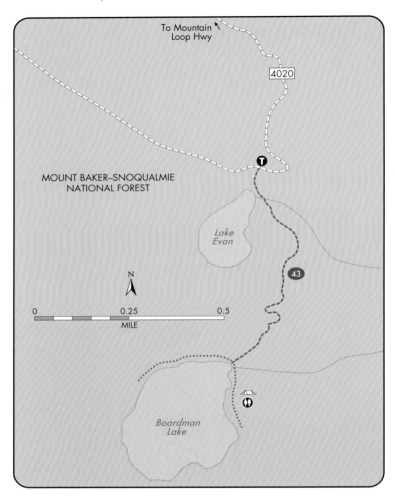

ON THE TRAIL

A grand alpine lake, one of the most accessible in the Cascades, awaits hikers of all ages along the Mountain Loop Highway. This is the place to go when it is hot and sticky in the city and you need to find a way to cool off and breathe some fresh mountain air. The trail climbs gently through cooling forest to a bountiful lake ideal for swimming. The entry slope is shallow, and the water is refreshing. It's also a good place to try out backpacking for the first time; five campsites are located along the east side of the lake. In the summer, go during midweek if at all possible, to avoid crowds.

Start your hike opposite the parking area and come almost immediately to Lake Evan. Although it may tempt you to linger, Boardman Lake is bigger, prettier, and has a much better shoreline. And it's only a mile away! The trail has a few of the usual roots and rocks to negotiate, but the grade is gentle, and the forest provides some ready distractions. Gaze up at truly massive cedars and look down at the green carpet of the forest. How many varieties of ferns can you count? While you walk, also keep a lookout for other denizens of the forest. We saw both grouse and rabbit when we were here.

Top a small crest at 0.7 mile and descend a short distance to the lake. The forest cozies up on all sides, and a rocky promontory on the far shore provides a reflective backdrop when the water is still. The trail approaches at the lake's outlet, and most visitors spread out a towel on the sitting stones and silver snags where the water is shallow. You may find some more solitude by taking one of the hiker paths that curve around the lake in either direction. A handful of campsites, a backcountry privy, and a small swimming cove can be found by crossing a logjam and climbing a set of old stairs. Or explore in the other direction and find your perfect spot to enjoy this big, spacious lake.

If it is too cold for swimming or wading, kids will enjoy throwing rocks in the water, watching dragonflies cavort across its surface, or even casting a fishing rod for some trout. It doesn't take long to get here, but you may find you will stay for a good part of the day. Plan accordingly, and when you are done, return the way you came.

44 OLD ROBE CANYON

BEFORE YOU GO
MAP Green Trails, Mountain Loop Highway No. 111SX
CONTACT Snohomish County Parks and Recreation
NOTES Do not pick up historical artifacts; be careful of uneven footing and downed logs; swift-moving river
GPS N 48 06.613, W 121 51.416

ABOUT THE HIKE
SEASON Year-round
DIFFICULTY Moderate
DISTANCE 2.4 miles roundtrip
HIGH POINT 1050 feet
ELEVATION GAIN 200 feet

GETTING THERE
From Granite Falls, follow the Mountain Loop Highway for 7 miles and park along the roadside directly across from Forest Road 41. A brick sign marks the trailhead.

Exploring some of the remnants of the region's logging and railroad past

ON THE TRAIL

I'm a big fan of hikes that showcase history. It adds an element of mystery and discovery beyond the bounty of nature that characterizes most hiking trails in Washington. At Old Robe Canyon, kids literally stumble over railroad ties and tracks, metal pipes, and bricks—remnants of the region's logging and railroad past. You will marvel that engineers thought it was a good idea to forge a railroad along the narrow canyon of the Stillaguamish River with its unstable, eroding slopes. Unfortunately, these same landslide-prone slopes that put an end to train traffic will halt your progress through this unique canyon, but not before delivering you to a satisfying place to enjoy the river where it narrows and intensifies.

Your destination is the old corridor of the Everett & Monte Cristo Railroad, abandoned more than a century ago. The railroad was built in 1892 to ferry gold and silver mined at Monte Cristo to Everett, but the decision to forge a path through Robe Canyon was a disaster. Time and again, storms flooded the Stillaguamish River, swamping tunnels, wiping out the grade, and causing landslides. The mineral deposits at Monte Cristo were disappointing too, and by 1915 the railroad had been completely abandoned. Nothing has really changed today. The river still floods and landslides still occur, making a mess of the railroad-turned-trail.

The hike begins at a brick sign, winds through level forest to the edge of a bluff, then proceeds downhill on three switchbacks. Please respect the efforts to keep hikers from making shortcuts; stick to the trail. At 0.5 mile, pass by a sign welcoming you to Old Robe Canyon Historic Park via a pretty maple glade. It's also quite swampy, so bring bug juice during the summer to ward off mosquitoes.

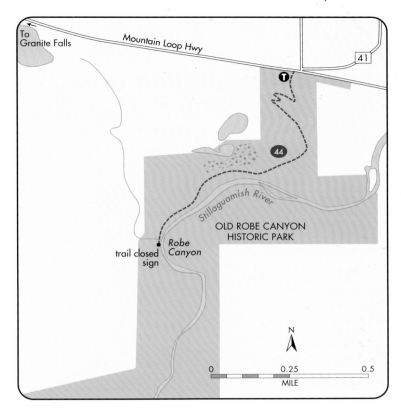

Your first encounter with the Stillaguamish River is at a wide and rocky section. It's hard to believe there used to be a train station near here, but there is still evidence in the form of rusty junk littering the forest floor. It's fun to make these discoveries, but please leave the relics for the next visitors to enjoy. In late summer, hikers can play in the rocks at the water's edge, but in springtime, this river can take on serious volume, making the shore unsafe.

The trail beyond is wide and flat, though there are obstacles that may be difficult for youngsters to overcome, most notably a logjam at 1 mile. But older kids love it. As they are whacking through bushes and crawling across logs, a world of discovery is at their feet: old train tracks, bricks, rotting wooden structures, and pipes. It is fun to theorize about what went on here and why they built in a wetland.

Beyond the logjam, the trail follows the railroad grade as it enters Robe Canyon. Notice how the river is suddenly constricted by more than half and changes appearance. Before you know it, a "trail closed" sign at 1.2 miles halts your journey. Landslides beyond the sign make it unsafe to pass, though you are likely to see others ignoring the warning. If the river level cooperates, carefully scramble down the smooth rock below the sign and find a dry pothole to relax in before returning the way you came.

STEVENS PASS WEST

45 WALLACE FALLS

BEFORE YOU GO
MAP Green Trails, Index No. 142
CONTACT Washington State Parks
NOTES Discover Pass required; restrooms and water available
GPS N 47 52.018, W 121 40.700

ABOUT THE HIKE
SEASON Year-round
DIFFICULTY Moderate to difficult
DISTANCE 3.6 miles roundtrip (to Lower Falls)
HIGH POINT 850 feet
ELEVATION GAIN 525 feet

GETTING THERE
From Everett, take US Highway 2 east 28 miles to Gold Bar. Turn left onto 1st Street (signed for Wallace Falls State Park), then right in 0.4 mile onto May Creek Road. Follow this main road for 1.3 miles to its end at Wallace Falls State Park. Parking is limited and not allowed on neighboring roads.

ON THE TRAIL
Depending on whom you ask, Wallace Falls consists of three waterfalls, nine, or even thirteen. While this is a point of debate, no one argues about the beauty of this iconic series of cascades that drop nearly 1000 feet over one very vertical mile. You can spot the long ribbon of white from the highway near Gold Bar, but it is far more satisfying to witness the power of the water up close. A word to the wise: This is an extremely popular trail, and if you want any chance of finding parking, you must visit on a weekday or arrive before 10:00 AM or after 4:00 PM on a weekend. Even then, you may have competition.

The trail begins under buzzy powerlines, but soon curves away into forest and the more pleasant sound of water. Follow the Woody Trail through a wooden stile, where you will get your first encounter with the Wallace River. This river may look inviting, but because of its strong current and many waterfalls, it should not be entered anywhere on the trail.

At 0.6 mile, begin to climb, somewhat steeply. The trail is well-engineered, but full of roots and rocks from so many boots, and this can slow those with

Middle Wallace Falls

short legs. There are several benches to catch your breath along the way. After climbing 300 feet over nearly a mile, descend to an impressive bridge over the North Fork Wallace River. It's now just a short and steep push to Lower Falls. Along the way, catch a surprising view of the Olympic Mountains, listen for the rumble of water, and finally feel the breeze of the waterfall. At 1.8 miles (850 feet), arrive at a covered picnic area and an overlook. From here, you can see Lower Falls, plus the tall drop of Middle Falls in the distance. Despite its popularity, there is plenty of space to settle in for a snack and be mesmerized by the water shooting over the falls. A small side trail leads down and behind

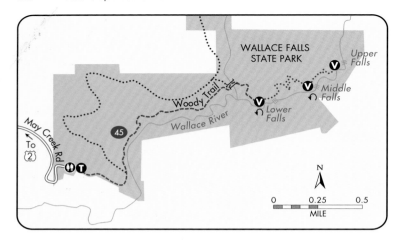

the pavilion for a vantage of some additional drops. Many people turn around at Lower Falls and retrace their steps, but if there is any gas left in the engine, it is well worth the additional effort to hike to Middle Falls (see below).

EXPLORING FURTHER

It's 0.3 mile and 250 feet of additional gain one-way—a huffer, to be sure, but not too far—to reach Middle Falls (1100 feet). The frothy white cascade crashes dramatically 265 feet into a narrow cleft, then twists and turns down to Lower Falls. A fenced-in viewpoint keeps everyone safely back from the steep drop, yet provides an excellent vantage. Upper Falls (1550 feet), is another 0.6 mile beyond Middle Falls. It is also tempting but is not quite as impressive as Middle Falls. However far you go, it's all good stuff. When the kids have reached their limit, turn around and return on the same path.

46 BRIDAL VEIL FALLS

BEFORE YOU GO
> **MAP** Green Trails, Alpine Lakes West Stevens Pass No. 176S
> **CONTACT** Mount Baker–Snoqualmie National Forest
> **NOTES** Northwest Forest Pass required; privy available
> **GPS** N 47 48.557, W 121 34.403

ABOUT THE HIKE
> **SEASON** April to November
> **DIFFICULTY** Difficult
> **DISTANCE** 4.1 miles roundtrip
> **HIGH POINT** 1585 feet
> **ELEVATION GAIN** 850 feet

GETTING THERE

From Everett, take US Highway 2 east through the towns of Sultan and Gold Bar. Seven miles east of Gold Bar, just before a bridge over the Skykomish River, turn right on Mount Index Road. Take this good gravel road for less than half a mile and veer right up a short spur road to the Lake Serene trailhead.

ON THE TRAIL

On my husband's first Father's Day as a dad, we packed up our son in the baby backpack and set forth on the popular Lake Serene Trail. Although we didn't make it to Lake Serene, we found that Bridal Veil Falls was a more than worthy destination. Our little guy delighted in the spray on his face, and we were thrilled to get an up-close-and-personal view of the waterfall that we had always seen cascading off Mount Index. We also learned that day to bring warm layers even on a hot afternoon. As much as the baby loved that spray, it chilled him quickly, and we had to beat a hasty retreat to get him warm again.

The hike to Bridal Veil Falls isn't particularly easy, especially if it is warm out. The trail goes through steamy salmonberry patches; these are great motivators when the berries are ripe—but when they are not and it is hot, they are

Downstream from Bridal Veil Falls

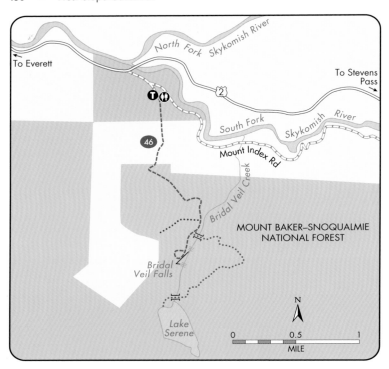

energy-sapping saunas. It ascends steadily, though not steeply, on an old road that has been converted to trail. Look for massive stumps logged long ago, some of them still embedded with loggers' nails. After leaving the roadbed and cresting a hill, descend slightly to the well-signed junction for Bridal Veil Falls at 1.6 miles (1185 feet). If you're quiet, you can hear the falls in the distance.

Take a good slug of water and grab a handful of gorp for the final 400 feet of elevation gain to reach the waterfall. The trail steepens, while exposed roots and rocks add to the difficulty. Clearly, you are not the first to beat this path to the waterfall. Thirteen sets of wooden stairs makes it a little easier, and the growing roar of the falls is a telltale sign you are getting closer.

A little loop at the top makes it possible to see Bridal Veil Falls from more than one vantage. I like going left, which allows you to first view the falls from below. Unless the wind is blowing mist in your face, pick your favorite spot and sit down to admire its shimmering flow over smooth rock. A knobby cedar stands sentinel over the falls, helping frame photos, though the midday glare makes it a challenge to digitally capture Bridal Veil Falls' beauty.

After enjoying the falls, return the way you came. Kids (and adults) need to be especially careful not to trip over the roots and rocks on the way down.

EXPLORING FURTHER

Most hikers on this trail are heading to the alpine splendor of Lake Serene. It's another 4 miles roundtrip and 1300 feet elevation gain to the lake from the junction with the trail to Bridal Veil Falls. Older kids may have the energy and fortitude to make it, but most little kids will not. From the trailhead it is 7.2 miles roundtrip and a 2500-foot elevation gain to the lake.

47 HEYBROOK LOOKOUT

BEFORE YOU GO
MAP Green Trails, Alpine Lakes West Stevens Pass No. 176S
CONTACT Mount Baker–Snoqualmie National Forest
GPS N 47 48.487, W 121 32.116

ABOUT THE HIKE
SEASON March to December
DIFFICULTY Moderate to difficult
DISTANCE 2.1 miles roundtrip
HIGH POINT 1700 feet
ELEVATION GAIN 900 feet

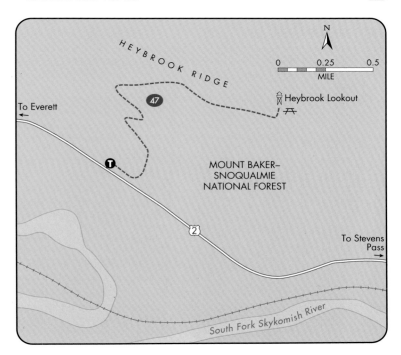

GETTING THERE

From Everett, take US Highway 2 east through the towns of Sultan and Gold Bar. Seven miles east of Gold Bar, cross over the Skykomish River on a steel bridge. In a little more than 2 miles, past milepost 37, look for a long, unsigned turnout on the left side of the road. This is the trailhead for Heybrook Lookout.

ON THE TRAIL

Despite the fact that this trail is steeper than nearby Bridal Veil Falls, it is an easier hike. Cooling forest and a mercifully short journey ease the way to a dandy of a reward—a 67-foot fire lookout tower that can be climbed to the top. From its lofty height is a view worthy of the effort: Baring Mountain, Mount Index, and a bird's-eye view of Bridal Veil Falls.

Begin your hike at the west end of the parking area and parallel the highway for a short distance before starting upward. The trail goes relentlessly uphill,

Climbing up Heybrook Lookout

but there are distractions along the way. On our most recent hike here we saw three hairy woodpeckers hammering away on trees right alongside the trail, completely ignoring our presence. Even if you're not fortunate enough to see a woodpecker, you can still look for the holes they drill on tree trunks. These woodpeckers are well-fed on the insects and larvae they find in the wood! After the first switchback, notice a scattering of big boulders in the woods. Where did they come from? At the second switchback, consider a rest stop near the damp, mossy wall. The kids will have fun exploring its nooks and crannies and will enjoy poking holes in rotten logs. After this spot, the forest opens up, with an understory of salal and a gentler grade. Washington Trails Association, whose volunteers lovingly help maintain many forest trails in this region, has made great improvements to the tread in recent years, installing puncheon and crib steps over especially rooty and rocky areas. Still, you may need to boost the kids up big steps along the trail.

The path breaks into the open at 1 mile. From here, you can see just how far you've climbed and spot the lookout tower. Kids who were dragging a moment ago will suddenly get a burst of energy to tackle the seven flights of stairs. While the stairway is narrow and steep, wire mesh lines the stairs to keep everyone safe and inside the tower. Open-air windows at the top provide a panoramic view above the treetops, and the eaves of the building are home to swallows. I especially like the lookout in spring and fall when snow clings to the cliffs of Mounts Baring and Index and the surrounding peaks. Take your time at the top; then once you're back at the base of the lookout, consider pulling out a lunch at the picnic table there before your return.

48 BARCLAY LAKE

BEFORE YOU GO
MAP Green Trails, Alpine Lakes West Stevens Pass No. 176S
CONTACT Mount Baker–Snoqualmie National Forest
NOTES Northwest Forest Pass required; privy available
GPS N 47 47.538, W 121 27.553

ABOUT THE HIKE
SEASON May to October
DIFFICULTY Moderate
DISTANCE 4.2 miles roundtrip
HIGH POINT 2475 feet
ELEVATION GAIN 250 feet

GETTING THERE
From Everett, drive US Highway 2 east for 40 miles to the townsite of Baring. Across from a convenience store, turn left on 635th Place NE. Cross the railroad tracks and proceed 0.3 mile to an intersection. Veer right onto Forest Road 6024 and drive the good gravel road 4.2 miles to the trailhead at the road's end.

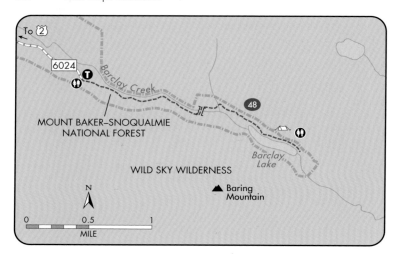

ON THE TRAIL

Baring Mountain makes a very impressive backdrop to glassy Barclay Lake on this kid-pleasing hike in the Cascades. Reached by a well-maintained trail that runs through mature forest and along pleasant Barclay Creek, this hike packs a lot of punch in an easy package. And if you've wanted to try backpacking, it makes an ideal destination, with a string of lakeside camps and excellent access for swimming.

The trail begins in scraggly woods, which thankfully transition in short order to a lovely hemlock forest. The trail gains just 250 feet over 2 miles, so kids have the energy to notice and explore their surroundings. At 0.8 mile, they may want to make their way to the banks of Barclay Creek, where the stream gently gurgles and pools invitingly for wading feet. In summertime, salmonberries and a few huckleberries provide irresistible snacks, and huge, moss-covered stumps and rocks demand to be climbed.

As you walk upstream, notice how the trail skirts big trees on narrow turnpike tread. Some of these trees have huge root systems, which require a bit of navigation for short legs. You may need to assist kids across the double-wide log stringer bridge over Barclay Creek at 1.3 miles. There's only one handrail, but as long as no one is horsing around, the bridge is wide enough to be safe.

Now the trail tilts upward ever so slightly, reaching a high point of 2475 feet just as Barclay Lake comes into view at 1.8 miles. The long, thin lake lies at the foot of imposing Baring Mountain, which looms over the lake 3600 feet below. Clouds cling to its perpendicular face, giving it a moody look, and snow lingers in crevasses long into the summer. Make your way another 0.25 mile along the north side of the lake to one of several small beaches and campsites. The farther you go, the more likely you will be to shed the crowds. This is a popular hike, especially on weekends. Wannabe campers are wise to arrive before

Kids will find many places to perch at Barclay Lake.

Saturday, when they may find the campsites occupied. Day hikers may wish they had a tent to spend the night, but will have to be satisfied by resting on one of the many fallen shoreline logs, swimming in the cold water, and grudgingly retracing their steps back to the trailhead.

49 LAKE DOROTHY

BEFORE YOU GO
MAP Green Trails, Alpine Lakes West Stevens Pass No. 176S
CONTACT Mount Baker–Snoqualmie National Forest
NOTES Northwest Forest Pass required; dogs must be leashed; privy available
GPS N 47 36.527, W 121 23.172

ABOUT THE HIKE
SEASON June to October
DIFFICULTY Moderate to difficult
DISTANCE 3 miles roundtrip
HIGH POINT 3060 feet
ELEVATION GAIN 850 feet

GETTING THERE
From Everett, drive US Highway 2 east for 45 miles. Turn right on Old Cascade Highway (signed for Money Creek Campground). Drive Old Cascade Highway for 1.1 miles and turn right onto graveled Miller River Road (Forest Road 6412). Follow Miller River Road 9.5 miles to the trailhead at the end.

ON THE TRAIL
Big, placid Lake Dorothy beckons a legion of hikers and backpackers who are drawn to its long shoreline, ample campsites, fishing, and swimming. The trail features fun boardwalks, a distinctive creek, tasty berries in season, and

Watch for slugs near your feet as you hike.

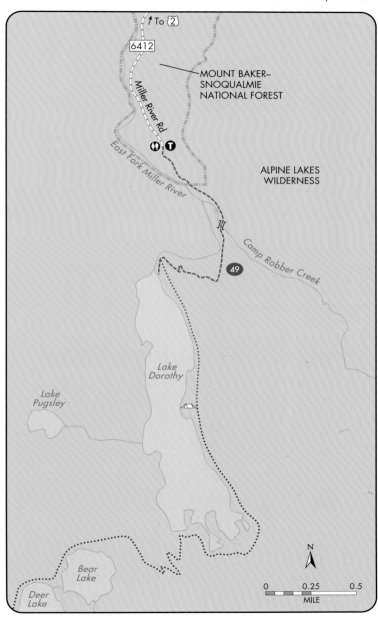

To ② ↑

6412

Miller River Rd

MOUNT BAKER–
SNOQUALMIE
NATIONAL FOREST

East Fork Miller River

ALPINE LAKES
WILDERNESS

Camp Robber Creek

49

Lake
Dorothy

Lake
Pugsley

Bear
Lake

Deer
Lake

N

0   0.25   0.5
MILE

a 2-mile-long shoreline. It's a quintessential example of why this area is called the Alpine Lakes Wilderness.

The trail is well-maintained but rocky and steep in places, which may make it difficult for little legs. Fortunately, it is just 1.5 miles to the lake. Travel through shady forest and enter the Alpine Lakes Wilderness at 0.4 mile. The trail follows the path of Camp Robber Creek, which noisily cascades and riffles downhill. A bridge at 0.7 mile spans the creek, where water seems to come from all directions and lazy riffles spill over smooth granite into a deep green pool.

The trail now climbs 500 feet over the next 0.8 mile. Tall steps built into the trail may be difficult for young kids to navigate, but they are interspersed with easier level stretches and boardwalk. Before you know it, the north end of Lake Dorothy (3060 feet) comes into view. Proceed straight to the outlet, where there is a nice place to rest, eat berries, and splash around in the water. Turn around here, or continue on for less than a mile; camping and the best swimming are available at the midpoint of the lake. The backcountry campsites fill on sunny weekends, so arrive early.

EXPLORING FURTHER

Beyond Lake Dorothy are three more sparkling alpine lakes: Bear, Deer, and Snoqualmie. The trail becomes much steeper and rougher after Lake Dorothy, and is often inaccessible due to snow, dicey creek crossings, and blowdowns early in the summer. It is nearly 4 miles from Lake Dorothy's outlet to Bear Lake.

50 DECEPTION FALLS NATURE TRAIL

BEFORE YOU GO
MAP Green Trails, Alpine Lakes West Stevens Pass No. 176S
CONTACT Mount Baker–Snoqualmie National Forest
NOTES Parking lot gated in winter and spring; privy available
GPS N 47 42.918, W 121 11.721

ABOUT THE HIKE
SEASON May to September
DIFFICULTY Easy
DISTANCE 0.7 mile loop
HIGH POINT 1850 feet
ELEVATION GAIN 50 feet

GETTING THERE

From Everett, drive US Highway 2 east to the town of Skykomish. Just past milepost 56, find the entrance to the Deception Falls picnic area on the north side of the highway. This picnic area is generally open May through September but is gated the rest of the year.

A picturesque bridge straddles Deception Falls.

ON THE TRAIL

We visit Deception Falls nearly every time we drive over Stevens Pass, and it never disappoints. A short, paved interpretive trail delivers hikers to the roiling whitewater of Deception Falls, which is particularly impressive when bursting with rainwater or snowmelt. But don't stop there. A short loop follows Deception Creek's frothy course to the Tye River, where it flows through a narrow gorge.

Follow the paved, barrier-free trail behind the parking lot a short distance to roaring Deception Falls. A cute bridge makes for good photo opps of the family getting a face full of spray from the falls as it drops directly beneath your feet. The highway is close by, but the constant drum of the water completely drowns out the sound.

Double back to the junction of the loop trail and take a right to follow it counterclockwise. Stop to read the informative information panels along the way. These signs provide great context for the forest and river environments. And make sure you visit each of the viewing platforms along the loop. The first one leads to another small waterfall. The second is my favorite: a unique

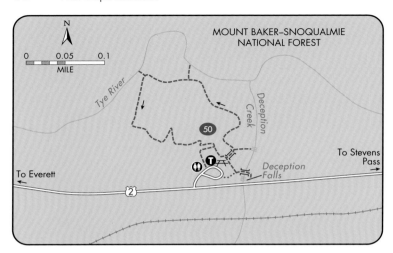

twist of geologic fate where the Tye River slams into a granite wall and makes a 90-degree turn. It's fun to ponder just how this phenomenon came to be. Was it a logjam? Soft rock? A fault line?

Finally the river bottoms out and calms down. A third short spur leads to the shore, where you can spread out a snack before returning uphill. The water is crystal clear and entices kids to throw in rocks and sticks, but this isn't a safe spot for wading; despite the quiet areas, the current moves fast. After a short break, continue on the path, listening for clues that you are returning to civilization: the sound of cars on the highway and trains on the busy rail corridor.

51 IRON GOAT LOOP

BEFORE YOU GO
   MAP Green Trails, Alpine Lakes West Stevens Pass No. 176S
   CONTACT Mount Baker–Snoqualmie National Forest
   NOTES Northwest Forest Pass required; stinging nettles; hike can be scaled for younger hikers; privy available
   GPS N 47 42.680, W 121 09.699

ABOUT THE HIKE (TUNNEL)
   SEASON Year-round
   DIFFICULTY Easy to moderate
   DISTANCE 2.5 miles roundtrip
   HIGH POINT 2260 feet
   ELEVATION GAIN 160 feet

ABOUT THE HIKE (LOOP)
   SEASON Year-round
   DIFFICULTY Moderate to difficult
   DISTANCE 6.1 miles loop
   HIGH POINT 2800 feet
   ELEVATION GAIN 700 feet

GETTING THERE

From Everett, drive 49 miles east on US Highway 2 to the town of Skykomish. Continue east another 9.5 miles to the signed Iron Goat Interpretive Site on the left side of the highway.

ON THE TRAIL

Follow the route of the Great Northern Railway as it once made its way up Stevens Pass on the side of a strikingly steep slope that required numerous tunnels and snowsheds to allow safe passage. The route was abandoned in 1929 in favor of the current tunnel that serves trains, but the lower and upper grades of a switchbacked section of the original route have been turned into a trail that is accessible for all. The wide, gentle lower grade is ideal for strollers and toddlers, while older kids will enjoy the more difficult loop option provided on the upper grade.

From the trailhead, climb on a paved trail until you reach the soft surface of the old rail line. The trail is wide and easy. In the spring, the way is carpeted in dainty wildflowers, including violets, bluebells, wild ginger, and trillium. Large mileposts along the way denote how far it is to St. Paul, Minnesota, where the Great Northern Railway originated.

It doesn't take long to reach the first destination of interest: a big retaining wall overhung with vine maple, the remains of a concrete snowshed. This snowshed runs for nearly a third of a mile, and once kept avalanches from burying the tracks. You'll want to stop and read the interpretive signs to enrich your understanding of how difficult it was to create a safe passage over the Cascades and the hardships of winter. My kids especially enjoyed the archival photos that bring the railroad alive again.

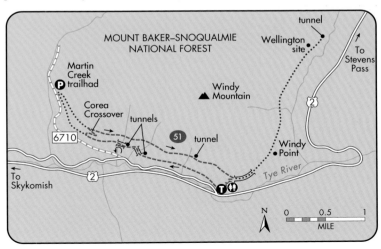

Old concrete snowshed on the Iron Goat Loop (photo by David Elderkin)

When you reach milepost 1719, you've hiked 1.2 miles. Just beyond is the first of a pair of tunnels that date to 1916. Like many of the tunnels along this stretch, sections of it have collapsed. It is unsafe to hike past the barrier, but you are allowed go a short distance inside to feel the cool breeze and observe the weeping walls. Families with small children may choose to turn around here, though the level and barrier-free trail continues another 1.8 miles to Martin Creek trailhead, where there is another parking area.

To do a loop hike, cross a rushing creek between the tunnel sections on a footbridge, staying far from the lush field of stinging nettles. Pass by another broken section of snowshed and over a pedestrian trestle before reaching an intersection with the Corea Crossover trail at 2.5 miles. Turn right and gain 150 feet in elevation to the upper grade of the Iron Goat Trail, where you will turn right again.

Now the trail becomes more rugged—no more wide, barrier-free grade. There are various hazards, like creeks to sidestep and concrete cliffs without railings. For older kids, it's great fun. You get to walk right up against a snowshed where water pours over in the springtime and poke your head into other decrepit tunnels. The views are better too, revealing Cathedral Rock and Surprise Mountain.

The final tunnel is at 5.3 miles. Shortly thereafter, reach a junction. The trail goes straight around Windy Point and to Wellington, the site of a 1910 avalanche disaster that sent two trains into the Tye River. You may want to check out the nearby half-mile snowshed that the Windy Point trail runs through. Or save it for another hike. To return to the trailhead, turn right, descending very steeply (700 feet over 0.8 mile) back down to the lower grade and trailhead.

SNOQUALMIE PASS CORRIDOR

52 CEDAR BUTTE

BEFORE YOU GO
MAP Green Trails, Rattlesnake Mountain No. 205S
CONTACT Washington State Parks
NOTES Discover Pass required; dogs must be leashed; drop-offs near summit; privy available
GPS N 47 25.946, W 121 45.995

ABOUT THE HIKE
SEASON Year-round
DIFFICULTY Moderate to difficult
DISTANCE 4 miles roundtrip
HIGH POINT 1880 feet
ELEVATION GAIN 950 feet

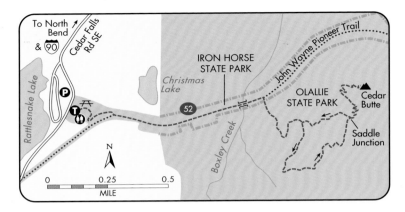

GETTING THERE

In North Bend, take Interstate 90 exit 32 (436th Avenue SE). Turn south and follow 436th Avenue SE, which merges into Cedar Falls Road SE, 3.1 miles to the Iron Horse State Park–Cedar Falls trailhead on the left, opposite the large Rattlesnake Lake parking area. Even when cars are parked all along the road, this large parking area may have space.

ON THE TRAIL

Across the road, but a world away from crowded Rattlesnake Lake and the Rattlesnake Ledges Trail, is relatively unknown, but sweet, Cedar Butte. The trail to the summit is shorter, easier, and safer than its popular neighbor—and offers remarkable solitude on the busy I-90 corridor. For kids, a US Geological Survey marker at the summit offers an irresistible misspelling.

Follow the signs for John Wayne Pioneer Trail/Iron Horse State Park, crossing access roads, until you reach a T-intersection at a converted railroad bed. Turn left onto the rail trail and walk on its wide pathway. The old sign for Cedar Falls marks a former depot where the Milwaukee Road deployed snowplows to keep the rails to the Snoqualmie Tunnel clear during winter months. Trains ran along this corridor until 1980, when efforts began to transform the abandoned railroad into a trail for hikers, bicyclists, and equestrians. The John Wayne Pioneer Trail, managed by Iron Horse State Park, now runs for 110 miles along the old Milwaukee Road, from the Columbia River to its terminus just beyond Rattlesnake Lake.

Watch for bicycles as you walk on the level tread 0.8 mile to Boxley Creek. The signed bridge is your reference point for the somewhat obscure turnoff for Cedar Butte. After crossing, look for a well-defined path about 150 yards up the trail on the right and a small wooden sign labeled "Cedar Butte" tacked onto a tree. Start climbing through a young forest, which was selectively logged as recently as the early 1990s. You can still easily spot enormous stumps, but the forest is regenerating nicely and offers shade on sunny days.

Read carefully to spot the misspellings.

At 1.2 miles reach a fork in the trail. The route to the left is the original trail, and it is short and steep. The newer route to the right is about a half mile longer and much more gradual. With kids in tow, take the easier right fork up and the steeper route down. The right fork swings wide to a ridge. Look for a depression through the trees—called the Boxley Blowout—where a leak from the City of Seattle's reservoir in 1918 exploded into Boxley Creek, washing out the tracks below and wiping out a small town 2 miles downstream.

Once you reach the ridge, turn left and walk through a little magical world of arching vine maples until you join up with the steep trail at Saddle Junction (2 miles, 1600 feet). Now begin your summit push. Eleven switchbacks ease the grade as you climb the final 280 feet over 0.3 mile. Keep kids close in this section, as there is a steep drop-off on the way to the summit.

At the top, soak in the views of Mount Si (left), the Middle Fork Snoqualmie Valley, and Mailbox Peak (right). After a rest, head back to Saddle Junction and turn right for the steep, short descent to the John Wayne Pioneer Trail and the trailhead.

53 TWIN FALLS

BEFORE YOU GO

MAP Green Trails, Mount Si NRCA No. 206S
CONTACT Washington State Parks
NOTES Discover Pass required; privy available
GPS N 47 27.182, W 121 42.339

ABOUT THE HIKE

SEASON Year-round
DIFFICULTY Easy to moderate
DISTANCE 2.7 miles roundtrip
HIGH POINT 920 feet
ELEVATION GAIN 350 feet

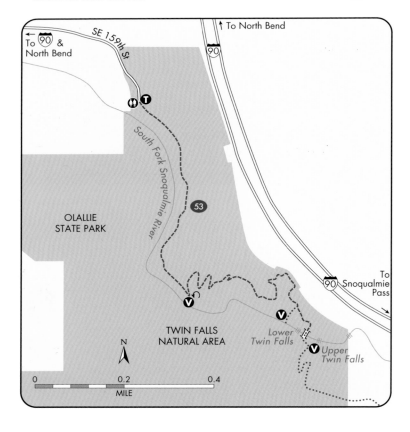

GETTING THERE

On the east side of North Bend, take Interstate 90 to exit 34. At the end of the exit ramp, turn south onto 468th Avenue SE. In 0.5 mile, just before crossing the South Fork Snoqualmie River, turn left on SE 159th Street, following it to its end in 0.5 mile.

Twin Falls

ON THE TRAIL

Twin Falls was the first trail my daughter hiked on her own two feet. She was not quite three years old, and it took us a long time. We took many breaks to admire the South Fork Snoqualmie River, to climb on benches and logs, and of course, to gaze at the impressive triple drop of the misnamed Twin Falls. Among the many trails along the I-90 corridor, this is one of the best for families. It provides just the right combination of length, elevation gain, and things to look at along the way.

Get started on the wide and level trail along the river, enjoying the dappled light, clear water, and pleasant sound it makes. There are plenty of places to wander down to the shore, including a big rocky beach at 0.4 mile. Just beyond the beach, a huge rock emerges out of the earth like the prow of a ship—a great place for a photo opp. Now the trail begins to climb above the river, switchbacking up a hillside to a viewpoint at 0.7 mile (850 feet). There are two high-backed benches with a view of the waterfall in the distance. Families with very young walkers might decide to turn around here, as the trail beyond loses elevation and then gains it again.

To proceed, descend 100 feet on a trail that has been impressively shored up and rerouted after a landslide closed it recently for two years. At the base of the hill, examine a huge Douglas fir that is at least 10 feet wide at its base, and then start to climb again. This is your last push to Twin Falls. Reach a staircase at 1.2 miles. Climbing down its 102 steps provides the best view of the waterfall, making it well worth the detour. Some of the stairs are quite steep, and kids may require a hand, but the effort pays off. Two viewing platforms hang over the river and provide an iconic view of Twin Falls, the water flowing like a feather over the rock.

Returning to the main trail, curve around a rocky outcrop and emerge onto a sturdy wooden bridge that straddles Twin Falls (1.3 miles, 920 feet). The frothy water flows through a narrow cleft, rests briefly, then plunges again and again for the final drop. From the far side of the bridge, you can see an upper falls as well. The trail beyond the bridge doesn't add much to the experience, so when you're done, retrace your journey back to the trailhead.

54 LITTLE SI

BEFORE YOU GO

MAP Green Trails, Mount Si NRCA No. 206S
CONTACT Washington Department of Natural Resources
NOTES Discover Pass required; privy available; drop-offs at summit
GPS N 47 29.267, W 121 45.340

ABOUT THE HIKE

SEASON Year-round
DIFFICULTY Difficult
DISTANCE 4.1 miles roundtrip
HIGH POINT 1576 feet
ELEVATION GAIN 1090 feet

GETTING THERE

In North Bend, take Interstate 90 to exit 32 (436th Avenue SE). Turn north on 436th Avenue SE, go 0.6 mile, and turn left on SE North Bend Way. In 0.3 mile, take a right onto SE Mount Si Road. Cross over the bridge and you will find the first of two parking areas on the left. This is an overflow lot and is connected by a trail to the main parking area 0.2 mile down the road. Note that these parking areas fill up quickly on weekends, and there is little street parking.

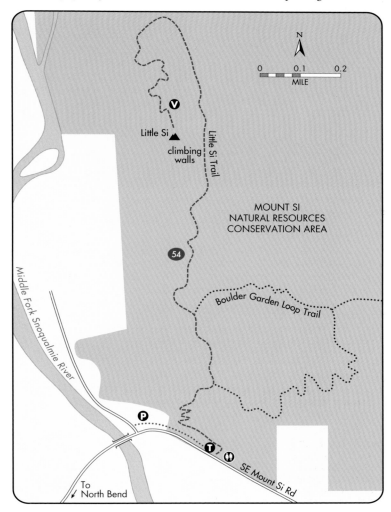

Less crowded and not as steep, Little Si is an attractive alternative to Mount Si for younger kids. (photo by Eugene Lee)

ON THE TRAIL

In the shadow of its well-known neighbor, Little Si offers a much more appropriate summit climb for kids. It's half as long and one-third as steep as Mount Si, and although it's still very popular, hikers will encounter far fewer people on their climb. Kids will have to work to reach the summit, but they will be proud of their accomplishment as they stand high above the Snoqualmie Valley.

From the main parking lot, the trail climbs steeply for the first quarter mile before it settles into a gentler ascent. Catch your breath at the first switchback by ducking off the trail to a viewpoint. What landmarks can you identify from here? Look for the interstate, the bridge you crossed, and Rattlesnake Mountain across the valley.

At 0.3 mile, reach the first junction. The 2.4-mile Boulder Garden Loop Trail veers to the right and is a flatter alternative to Little Si. For Little Si, go left and reach the turnoff to the summit on the left at 0.5 mile. This is my favorite section of the trail. The path approaches a big bluff—actually a flank of Little Si—where you may see climbers roped up and scaling the rock face. The forest canopy lets through dappled light that highlights vivid green moss on enormous boulders scattered haphazardly on either side of the trail.

Encourage your group to hike quietly. As the trail wends its way around the rock face to the north side of the mountain, it travels through a swale that has a unique acoustic quality. From here, the trail becomes steep, climbing 500 feet in just over a half mile on a rooty and rocky surface. This will get everyone breathless, and you may have to encourage little ones along the way. Just take your time, knowing that the reward is near.

Close to the top is an excellent viewpoint revealing the imposing bulk of Mount Si and a sneak peek of the Snoqualmie Valley. It is not much farther to the summit (1576 feet), with more views and plenty of rocks to rest on. Make sure you keep the kids close, as there are several places where the rocks drop off abruptly. Fortunately, kids should be too tired to goof off, and when they start to get restless you can pack up and head down the way you came.

55 MIDDLE FORK SNOQUALMIE RIVER

BEFORE YOU GO
MAP Green Trails, Middle Fork Snoqualmie No. 174SX
CONTACT Mount Baker–Snoqualmie National Forest
NOTES Northwest Forest Pass required; privy available
GPS N 47 32.883, W 121 32.228

ABOUT THE HIKE
SEASON Year-round
DIFFICULTY Easy to moderate
DISTANCE Up to 6.2 miles roundtrip
HIGH POINT Up to 1100 feet
ELEVATION GAIN 250 feet

Even though it is close to Seattle, you're unlikely to meet many hikers on the Middle Fork Snoqualmie trail. (photo by Jon Stier)

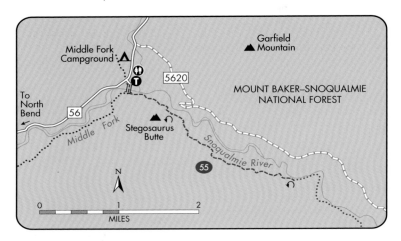

GETTING THERE

In North Bend, take Interstate 90 exit 34 (SE Edgewick Road). Turn north at the end of the exit ramp on 468th Avenue SE. Drive 0.6 mile and turn right on SE Middle Fork Road (Forest Road 56). At two successive intersections, stay left, remaining on Middle Fork Road. The large trailhead parking area is 11.6 miles up the road, on the right side.

ON THE TRAIL

Just outside of North Bend, the newly paved Middle Fork Road has made accessible a recreation area previously known only to those willing to brave one of the most potholed roads in Washington. New trails are being planned for this gorgeous corridor, but the gold standard is the Middle Fork Snoqualmie trail. Forging an upstream path parallel to its namesake river, the trail is most beloved for its architectural suspension bridge and the fanciful forest where it spends most of its time. There is no specific destination here—just a lovely walk in the woods with views of granite mountains and, in season, ample salmonberries to fuel the journey.

From the enormous parking area, head into the forest and cross a beautiful suspension bridge over the Middle Fork Snoqualmie River. Its construction in 1993 made access to this area possible, opening it up for hikers, equestrians, and mountain bikers, who may ride the trail on odd-numbered days. Pause to admire the olive-green water below and the arching beams of the bridge before heading upstream on the far side.

At 0.4 mile, peel away from the river into a magical mossy forest—every square foot a mélange of different plants. Slow down to count the different kinds of moss and ferns, and of course, to eat ripe berries. At 0.7 mile, the forest parts to reveal Garfield Mountain across the river. The trail then nestles up to the imposing 2000-foot face of imaginatively named Stegosaurus Butte.

This is a fine place to turn around, but if everyone is happy to keep rambling through the forest, press on. You'll cross creeks and debris chutes, pass big trees and a curious place where every tree is uniformly straight-trunked, planted after logging in this valley's previous era. If it is the wet season, keep your eye out for waterfalls. The last mile of trail descends gradually back to the riverside. There's a small place to sit and admire the ribbon of green water and imagine what lies on the other side of big Garfield Mountain. When you are well-rested, turn around and return the way you came.

56 TALAPUS AND OLALLIE LAKES

BEFORE YOU GO
MAP Green Trails, Snoqualmie Pass Gateway No. 207S
CONTACT Mount Baker–Snoqualmie National Forest
NOTES Northwest Forest Pass required; dogs must be leashed; privy available
GPS N 47 24.069, W 121 31.114

ABOUT THE HIKE (TALAPUS LAKE)
SEASON June to October
DIFFICULTY Moderate
DISTANCE 3.6 miles roundtrip
HIGH POINT 3300 feet
ELEVATION GAIN 660 feet

ABOUT THE HIKE (OLALLIE LAKE)
SEASON July to October
DIFFICULTY Difficult
DISTANCE 6 miles roundtrip
HIGH POINT 3800 feet
ELEVATION GAIN 1160 feet

GETTING THERE
From North Bend, take Interstate 90 east for 15 miles to exit 45. Turn left, driving under the freeway on Forest Road 9030. In less than a mile, reach an intersection. Go right on the gravel road (still FR 9030), traveling 2.4 miles to the trailhead at the end of the road.

ON THE TRAIL
Picturesque Alpine Lakes Wilderness is just a stone's throw from the I-90 corridor, but most of its many lakes involve long or steep approaches. Talapus and Olallie lakes are exceptions. These sweet lakes are among the most accessible in the region, making for a rewarding day hike, especially in late summer when it is warm enough to swim.

Pick up your free wilderness permit in the box at the trailhead and enter dense forest. There are no views on the climb, but the tree cover will keep you cool on hot days and dry on wet ones. The trail climbs steadily, but gradually, mostly out of earshot of the interstate. At 1.1 miles, reach Talapus Creek. This is a nice place to rest. Water-loving western red cedar and vine maple overhang the creek invitingly, as the water pinballs from boulder to boulder, resting momentarily in small pools before tumbling down to another rock. The trail levels out when it enters the Alpine Lakes Wilderness at 1.5 miles. Rustic bridges and boardwalks protect water-loving plants in a boggy area. Be careful on the uneven surface, as there are cracks and holes that can trap small feet.

Approaching Talapus Lake at 1.8 miles (3300 feet), the trail becomes more rooty, and you can really see the impact that people have had on this popular spot. Please heed any signs indicating that there is a restoration effort in effect. Talapus Lake glitters alluringly, nestled in a basin between Bandera and Pratt

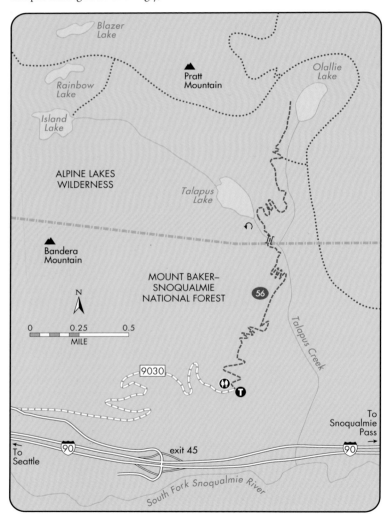

Listen for the distinct sounds made by woodpeckers, such as this red-breasted sapsucker, as you hike to Talapus and Olallie lakes. (photo by Jon Stier)

mountains. Unfortunately, a logjam at its outlet and forested shoreline make access a bit problematic. Still, there are some logs to sit on and spread out lunch. If swimming is on your agenda, look for paths farther down the trail that reach the lake and provide better access. You'll want to keep a close eye on your food, however, as the critters here are bold (please don't feed them!).

For many kids, this is as far as they'll get, but Olallie Lake (3800 feet) can be a more rewarding destination. It has much better access for swimming and dipping hot toes in cool water. The lake is small and intimate, and because it's at the end of its own spur trail, most of the hikers on the main trail bypass it on their way to other places. It is an additional 2.4 miles roundtrip from Talapus to Olallie Lake, but the trail gains only another 500 feet in elevation. In summer there may even be some tasty huckleberries to graze on along the way. To reach Olallie Lake, regain the trail and proceed 0.7 mile to the Talapus Cutoff Trail junction. Go left, and in just 0.5 mile reach the lake at the trail's end. Return the way you came.

57 ASAHEL CURTIS NATURE TRAIL

BEFORE YOU GO
MAP Green Trails, Snoqualmie Pass Gateway No. 207S
CONTACT Mount Baker–Snoqualmie National Forest
NOTES Northwest Forest Pass required; privy available
GPS N 47 23.568, W 121 28.462

ABOUT THE HIKE
SEASON June to November
DIFFICULTY Easy
DISTANCE 0.9 mile loop
HIGH POINT 2085 feet
ELEVATION GAIN 85 feet

GETTING THERE
From North Bend, take Interstate 90 eastbound 17 miles to exit 47 (Asahel Curtis/Denny Creek). Turn south (right), cross the South Fork Snoqualmie River, and reach a T-intersection. Turn left onto Forest Road 5590 (Asahel Curtis Road) and drive 0.4 mile on good gravel. Veer right at a fork in the road and turn immediately into the large parking area, shared with the Annette Lake trail, on the right.

ON THE TRAIL
When you really need to get the family outside for some fresh mountain air, but your kids have a limited attention span, the Asahel Curtis Nature Trail fits the bill. At just under a mile, it is easy enough for small children to enjoy an

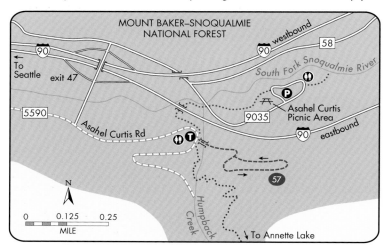

Look for tree trunks that host a variety of fungi. (photo by Jon Stier)

intimate dose of nature and later nap on the car ride home. To make it a longer family outing, hike the trail and then have a picnic at the nearby Asahel Curtis Picnic Area.

Asahel Curtis was one of Washington's most distinguished photographers and early mountaineers. Throughout the early 1900s, Curtis brought images of the state's wild places to people near and far. He was one of three founders of The Mountaineers and an early booster of the creation of Mount Rainier National Park. Fortunate for us, the forest that his namesake trail runs through remains much like what Curtis would have seen more than a century ago.

Stop first at the trail kiosk at the far end of the parking lot. This is an interpretive trail, and if you're lucky, there will be a pamphlet to carry with you describing the twelve numbered signs along the way. Climb up to two sturdy bridges crossing Humpback Creek and pause to listen to its raucous sound as it tumbles down from Annette Lake to the South Fork Snoqualmie River. At the junction, follow the trail numbers on the interpretive pamphlet and go right on a 0.5-mile loop.

Because this hike is so short, take the trail at a leisurely pace. It's a great demonstration garden for showing kids how life springs from dead trees, or nurse logs. Look for mosses, plants, and trees growing out of old stumps and rotting wood. In addition to searching for the "fun finds" listed here, linger among the marvelous giant trees on the far end of the loop. This "Parade of Giants" is one of a few stands of old-growth forest still remaining in the Snoqualmie Valley. Here you will find impressively big Douglas fir, western hemlock (Washington's state tree), and Pacific silver fir.

FUN FINDS ON THE ASAHEL CURTIS TRAIL

- Nurse logs
- A hemlock straddling a large boulder
- Enormous skunk cabbage
- Fungus growing on tree trunks
- Woodpecker holes
- Giant root balls
- Tree rings
- Hollow stump that kids can fit into

Soon you will be heading downhill again. At the junction, veer right to return to the trailhead. To reach the picnic area on foot, you can continue walking downhill, crossing under Interstate 90, for 0.5 mile to the picnic area along the river. To drive there, return to your car and cross over to the north side of I-90. When you reach the T-intersection on the other side, turn right. In 0.2 mile, at the intersection with Forest Road 58, veer right on FR 9035 and follow it to the picnic area.

58 FRANKLIN FALLS

BEFORE YOU GO
MAP Green Trails, Snoqualmie Pass Gateway No. 207S
CONTACT Mount Baker–Snoqualmie National Forest
NOTES Northwest Forest Pass required; privy available
GPS N 47 24.808, W 121 26.386

ABOUT THE HIKE
SEASON June to November
DIFFICULTY Easy to moderate
DISTANCE 2.3 miles loop
HIGH POINT 2610 feet
ELEVATION GAIN 270 feet

GETTING THERE
From North Bend, take Interstate 90 eastbound 17 miles to exit 47 (Asahel Curtis/Denny Creek). Turn north (left) and drive over the freeway. Turn right at the T-intersection, go 0.2 mile, and turn left on Denny Creek Road (Forest Road 58). Follow this road for 2.5 miles. Pass Denny Creek Campground and FR 5830, and look for the large new parking area on the right side of the road. Despite its size, the parking lot fills early on weekends.

ON THE TRAIL
Franklin Falls is a Snoqualmie Pass kids' classic: a pleasing, easy hike along a river to a graceful 109-foot waterfall. As of 2016, this trail is safer with the addition of bump-out viewpoints and a new observation area at the falls. And although Franklin Falls is no secret, there is a secret about Franklin Falls. You can do it as a loop by taking the popular Franklin Falls Trail up and the little-known historic Wagon Road Trail down.

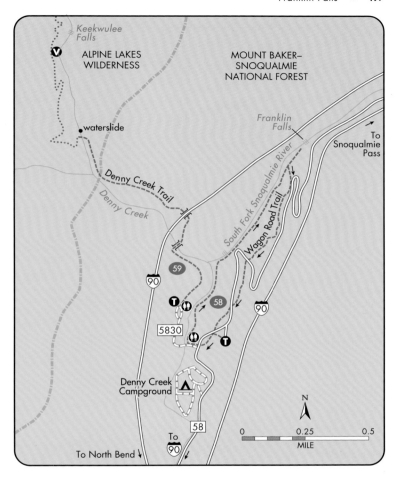

Locate the trail at the kiosk at the new parking area, following the trail 0.2 mile and crossing the road. This is the original trailhead and the location of a privy. Turn right into the woods and follow the South Fork Snoqualmie River upstream on a well-maintained path and past a few cabins on either side of the river. Parents will enjoy the thoughtful trail construction details—handrails near steep drop-offs and broad steps to avoid exposed roots and rocks. The riverside is inviting, with smooth sitting rocks and a pleasant burble. Occasionally, you'll encounter a monster tree. Search for one with three or four trunks of cedar and hemlock growing together. At 0.6 mile, the river narrows as Denny Camp Falls drops into a still green pool, then tumbles forth again.

Franklin Falls

The trail steepens until it tops out right before Franklin Falls (1.3 miles, 2610 feet). Franklin Falls is just beyond the westbound span of Interstate 90, but due to the roar of the water, the highway is not as obtrusive as you might imagine. A viewing area is available if conditions don't permit edging around the rocky entrance to the falls. For those who get up close, quite a bit of spray can come off the falls, and you may need to pull on a coat, even in the summer. Make sure that the kids never approach the base of the falls; the flow is strong and rocks can plummet from the top.

After enjoying the water show, look for a trail entering from the left soon after leaving the falls. This is the Wagon Road Trail. I like it for two reasons: it is quiet and peaceful, and the cushy duff is soft and easy on the knees. The only drawback is that the trail crosses Forest Road 58 three times on its descent. Make sure the kids know to stop at the road and wait for you (and traffic) before crossing. The trail on the far side of the road is marked with a reflector and is usually about 10 to 15 feet downhill.

This path generally corresponds with a historic route that crossed Snoqualmie Pass in the 1860s. A few ruts can be detected by those with a trained eye, and it is fun to imagine how the pioneers hauled their horse-drawn carriages through this forest. At the second road crossing, you'll be able to see the parking area, and you may decide to walk down the road. The trail, however, goes another 0.1 mile, crosses the road again, and rejoins the Franklin Falls Trail near the trailhead.

59 DENNY CREEK WATERSLIDE

BEFORE YOU GO

MAP Green Trails, Snoqualmie Pass Gateway No. 207S
CONTACT Mount Baker–Snoqualmie National Forest
NOTES Northwest Forest Pass required; dogs must be leashed; privy available; waterslide is slippery
GPS N 47 24.912, W 121 26.604

ABOUT THE HIKE

SEASON June to October
DIFFICULTY Moderate
DISTANCE 3 miles roundtrip
HIGH POINT 2800 feet
ELEVATION GAIN 450 feet

GETTING THERE

From North Bend, take Interstate 90 eastbound 17 miles to exit 47 (Asahel Curtis/Denny Creek). Turn north (left) and drive over the freeway. Turn right at the T-intersection and go 0.2 mile, and turn left on Denny Creek Road (Forest Road 58). Follow this road for 2.5 miles. Once you've passed Denny Creek Campground, turn left on FR 5830 and drive it to the trailhead at the end of the road. Parking is scarce, so arrive early.

It can get crowded at the Denny Creek waterslide during summer, even on weekdays.

ON THE TRAIL

There's nothing else in Washington quite like Denny Creek. A wide trail leads to a natural waterslide that can provide hours of splashy entertainment on summer days. Bring towels, water shoes, and a picnic—and be prepared for lots of company. This place is mobbed every sunny summer day. If you're aiming for more solitude, visit in September or October when the water level is low enough to not get wet, and the crowds have disappeared.

Hike up the well-trodden, forested trail alongside Denny Creek. The grade is gradual, and the creek is a pleasant companion that muffles the sounds of nearby Interstate 90. You're walking in the wedge of green space between two remarkably high and separate spans of the interstate. Leave the highway behind at 0.6 mile by crossing under the tall westbound span. Another 0.5 mile brings you to the boundary of the Alpine Lakes Wilderness. Now the trail begins to climb more steeply through mature forest, but the way is short, and before you know it you will find yourself at the waterslide, where water cascades in sheets over slick rock.

The waterslide can be a dangerous torrent in the spring, but by July conditions are ideal for scooting down the rocks on your bottom or splashing upstream through pools and water chutes. Be careful. Wet areas can be very slippery. But with a certain amount of caution, much fun can be had on the sunny, smooth rocks. Even if it appears crowded, the waterslide area is large enough to find a bit of real estate to call your own. Hang out for a couple of hours and then retrace your steps to your car.

EXPLORING FURTHER

Denny Creek drains the slopes of Low and Denny mountains, and there are two classic waterfalls upstream. If conditions don't permit water play or if your kids demand additional exercise, consider crossing the creek and hiking up to Keekwulee Falls. The trail beyond the waterslide is much rockier and steeper, as it breaks out of the trees onto hot, humid rock fields on the side of Low Mountain. Climb 350 feet over 0.8 mile to a viewpoint for Keekwulee Falls. It's an impressive waterfall, but from the path it can be seen only at a distance. The trail keeps going and eventually reaches picturesque and rocky Melakwa Lake at 5 miles and 4500 feet.

60 GOLD CREEK POND

BEFORE YOU GO

MAP Green Trails, Snoqualmie Pass Gateway No. 207S
CONTACT Okanagan–Wenatchee National Forest
NOTES Northwest Forest Pass required; privy available; picnic tables at the lake; no bikes, swimming, or fishing
GPS N 47 23.801, W 121 22.761

ABOUT THE HIKE

SEASON May to October
DIFFICULTY Easy
DISTANCE 1.4 miles loop
HIGH POINT 3000 feet
ELEVATION GAIN 25 feet

GETTING THERE

From Snoqualmie Pass, drive Interstate 90 eastbound 2 miles to exit 54 (Hyak). Turn left (north) and drive under the freeway to an intersection. Go right on Forest Road 4832 and parallel I-90 for 0.9 mile to Gold Creek Road. Turn left and drive 0.5 mile to the parking area.

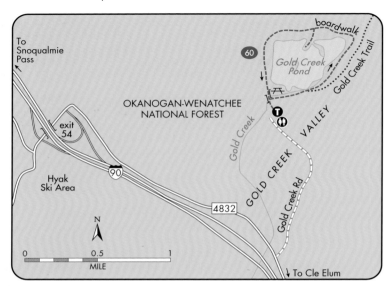

ON THE TRAIL

My favorite toddler hike in the I-90 corridor is Gold Creek Pond. Even the small-est tykes feel confident striding on a level paved pathway and wooden board-walks. Older children and adults will appreciate the pretty mountain views reflected in a tranquil pond. This is an excellent choice for one of those foggy Puget Sound summer days; you could shiver in the June gloom, but why not drive up Snoqualmie Pass and bask beyond the clouds in some summer sun?

Take the paved path to the left of the privy, soon coming to the loop trail. Head to the right, allowing the pond to slowly reveal itself. Travel alongside a babbling creek, through willows, flowers, and a young forest. You may notice that some terrain looks sculpted. In the 1970s and '80s, this quiet place was a gravel pit, serving the construction of Interstate 90. Huge cranes hoisted gravel into dump trucks until there was no more. In 1983, Washington Department of Transportation, in conjunction with the US Forest Service, began transform-ing this site into fish and wildlife habitat. I've been coming here for a decade, and each year the foliage looks wilder and more natural.

At 0.5 mile, reach a junction. The trail to the right takes hikers on a moder-ate ascent up the Gold Creek watershed. Continue left for the pond, just now coming into view, with clouds, trees, and mountains reflected brightly on its teal-colored surface. Below the boardwalk is a lush, marshy environment filled with ocean spray, bleeding hearts, yellow violets, and ferns.

Because this trail is so short, we have always slowed down to savor it. I've let the kids throw rocks into the water below the bridge, inspect the shaggy moss in the creek that feeds the pond, and come up with names for the two small

Enjoying Gold Creek Pond (photo by Jon Stier)

islands in the water. At 0.7 mile is a side trail. Take it! A little peninsula of green pushes far out into the pond, allowing kids the feeling of being in the center of a lake among jumping fish and skittering water bugs.

Having stretched out time as much as possible, press onward. At 1.1 mile, reach an expansive picnic area, complete with grills. The only thing it doesn't have is shade. If you're not spreading out a feast, cross over the creek again and head back to the trailhead.

61 MIRROR LAKE

BEFORE YOU GO
MAP Green Trails, Snoqualmie Pass Gateway No. 207S
CONTACT Okanogan–Wenatchee National Forest
NOTES No facilities
GPS N 47 20.527, W 121 25.328

ABOUT THE HIKE
SEASON July to October
DIFFICULTY Moderate
DISTANCE 2.5 miles roundtrip
HIGH POINT 4200 feet
ELEVATION GAIN 650 feet

GETTING THERE

From Snoqualmie Pass, take Interstate 90 eastbound 10 miles to exit 62 for Stampede Pass/Kachess Lake. Turn right onto Forest Road 54 and drive 1.1 miles, then turn right onto gravel FR 5480. At 5.6 miles, reach a three-way intersection at Lost Lake. Take the middle road (FR 5480) and drive another 1.9 miles on an increasingly brushy, potholed road until you reach a sign indicating the Mirror Lake Trail. Park here; the road ahead is impassable.

ON THE TRAIL

With its oval shape, blue hue, shoreline boulders, ring of conifers, and granite mountain, Mirror Lake is the epitome of an alpine lake. It's an exceedingly pleasant spot between Stampede and Snoqualmie passes and arguably the best lake destination on the south side of I-90. The trail is moderately graded, and if you time it just right, you can miss the mosquitoes and feast on berries.

Hike up the ridiculously rough road for 0.3 mile to the official trailhead, which may be difficult to locate. The entrance is on the left at the start of a sharp right bend in the road, and it may be helpfully marked with a cairn. Hike through an overgrown clear-cut and into more mature forest. If it has been wet, the trail may be a bit muddy with some tricky footing, but it is generally in decent shape. At 0.6 mile, cross a creek on stones, and in a short distance reach

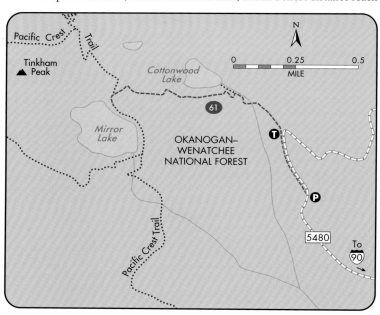

Mirror Lake

an intersection. The path to the right leads to Cottonwood Lake, a curious name for a shallow lake with no cottonwood trees in sight. It's worth a short visit if the bugs are not bad, but Mirror Lake is much nicer.

The route to Mirror Lake trends left above Cottonwood Lake on a hillside with hundreds of blueberry and huckleberry bushes. Timing your visit for August or early September is a delicious option. The trail continues to climb steadily another 0.5 mile to the intersection with the Pacific Crest Trail (PCT) (1.25 miles, 4200 feet). If you turn left and walk for more than 2000 miles, you will reach Mexico! If you go right, it is a shorter but still arduous trek to Canada. Fortunately, your destination is right in front of you.

Take a left on the PCT and make your way about 200 feet down the trail to a good spot to access the water. There are a few boulders to sit on and gaze across the sparkling water to Tinkham Peak. Swimmers can slip into the chilly water and splash around. When you are ready to return, follow your tracks back to the rough road and be thankful you didn't try to tackle it in an SUV.

HIGHWAY 410–MOUNT RAINIER NATIONAL PARK (SUNRISE)

62 FEDERATION FOREST

BEFORE YOU GO
MAP Green Trails, Greenwater No. 238
CONTACT Washington State Parks
NOTES Discover Pass required; dogs must be leashed; restroom available; park closed October to March
GPS N 47 09.114, W 121 41.310

ABOUT THE HIKE
SEASON April to September
DIFFICULTY Easy
DISTANCE 1.6 miles loop
HIGH POINT 1775 feet
ELEVATION GAIN 100 feet

GETTING THERE
From Enumclaw, drive east 18 miles on State Route 410. The entrance to Federation Forest State Park is on the right, just after milepost 41.

ON THE TRAIL
Wander through a magnificent stand of old-growth forest on an interpretive loop near the White River and bear witness to some of the largest trees you're likely to see in Washington. The forest is magical, especially in spring and early summer, when woodland wildflowers put on a delightful display, and in fall,

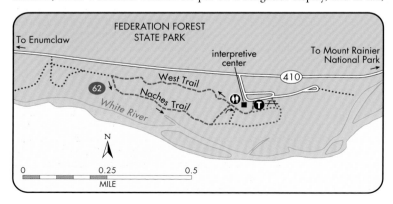

This huge Douglas fir has many like-sized friends in Federation Forest.

when the leaves of vine maples electrify the woods. Federation Forest State Park may not have a catchy name, but it is well worth a visit when driving to or from Mount Rainier National Park.

Several hiking routes are possible in the park, but some trails have suffered from a lack of maintenance and you may encounter downed trees or mud. The trails radiating from the interpretive center are in the best shape. To get a taste of both the giant trees and the roaring river, take the West Trail out and the Naches Trail on your return for a roundtrip of 1.6 miles. This loop is also called, confusingly, the Fred Cleator Interpretive Trails, the West Loop, and the Nature Trail. It appears trail names have changed over time, and signs and maps don't always match up. Never fear; all trails loop back to the interpretive center or out to the highway, so you can't get completely lost.

To get on the correct path, start at the interpretive center and, at each intersection, veer right so that you are on the outside loop, closest to the highway. You'll know you're in the right place when you reach a large kiosk with a map of the interpretive trails.

Slow your pace and enter a land of giants. Monster Douglas firs, enormous western red cedars, grand Sitka spruce, and impressive western hemlock (Washington's official state tree) stand tall in this delightful grove. Look closely at the bark for battle scars from windstorms, fire, and insects. Interpretive signs provide context to your journey, pointing out how to identify each tree. The understory is rather fabulous as well. In springtime it dances with shade-loving wildflowers: trillium, bleeding heart, bunchberry, and violets. In autumn, sunlight illuminates golden leaves of deciduous trees.

At 0.7 mile, reach an intersection signed Greenlees Grove and Nature Trail Return. To close the loop, go left toward the White River. Where the trail meets the river is a lovely spot from which to watch the milky water flow by. The White River starts in the glaciers of Mount Rainier, and its white color is due to "rock flour" generated by ice grinding against rock.

The trail now turns upriver along the historic Naches Trail. Native Americans used this track for generations as a trade route on either side of the Cascades. The first wagon train to successfully make the journey was the Longmire party in 1853. A metal-rimmed carriage wheel (that turns) commemorates this route at a junction that returns you to the trailhead. If you still have energy, you can continue for a short distance along the river. Make sure to visit the interpretive center (if open) and learn more about this interesting park and how it was saved by a dedicated group of women from the Washington State Federation of Women's Clubs.

63 SNOQUERA FALLS

BEFORE YOU GO
MAP Green Trails, Greenwater No. 238
CONTACT Mount Baker–Snoqualmie National Forest
NOTES Northwest Forest Pass required; privy available
GPS N 47 02.146, W 121 33.614

ABOUT THE HIKE
SEASON Late April to November
DIFFICULTY Moderate
DISTANCE 3.6 miles roundtrip
HIGH POINT 3100 feet
ELEVATION GAIN 680 feet

GETTING THERE
From Enumclaw, follow State Route 410 east for 28 miles to the Camp Sheppard trailhead. Turn left at the blue Camp Sheppard sign onto Forest Road 7155 and immediately turn right into the parking lot, shared with the Boy Scout camp.

ON THE TRAIL
Snoquera Falls shimmers and shines in spring and fall, a delicate wispy cascade fueled by snowmelt that plunges down a sheer rock face. Because snow melts early on this south-facing slope, it is a trail that can be hiked in springtime when nearby high-elevation trails are still snow-covered. The falls, however, dry to just a trickle during summer before the rains of fall fill it up again.

Begin your hike by passing beneath a maple archway, emerging into a Boy Scout amphitheater sheltered by massive Douglas fir and western red cedars. The trail is not signed, and it's a mistake to follow the most obvious path; that will put you on the Moss Lake Loop. Instead, skirt the amphitheater and

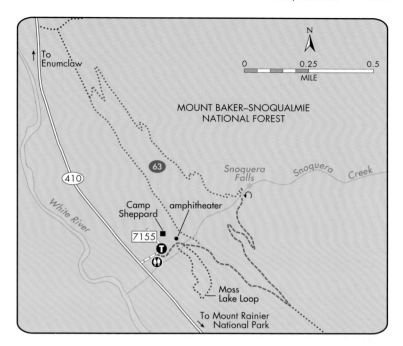

proceed up to the second row of benches on the right to locate the trail to Snoquera Falls.

Thankfully, the rest of the trail is well-signed. Proceed beyond the amphitheater a short distance to the White River/Snoquera Falls Trail. Choose the trail to the right, ascending through open forest dotted with enormous moss-covered boulders on a well-constructed and maintained dirt trail. At 0.6 mile, turn left and hike up two long switchbacks. It's fairly steep, but the distance is short.

Before you know it, you'll hear the distinct sound of falling water and break out into the open at 2 miles (3100 feet). Cross a rock field—deposited by a slide in 2008—to approach Snoquera Creek. Snoquera Falls plunges 287 feet down the craggy rock face of Dalles Ridge, then dances another 160 feet, crossing the trail. Watch the breeze carry a sheet of water through the air, or see if you can find faces or shapes in the tan and black rocks on the wall. Plants cling tenaciously to the cliff, and you can spot ferns, pink monkey flower, and even small bushes tucked into its cracks and crevices.

The outfall of the cascade runs over the trail. When it's at its fullest, you may not be able to cross safely to the other side, and even when it is running at a trickle it may be difficult for some kids to hopscotch the water. There is a steep

Ask the kids what could make this intriguing pattern.

and unstable trail to the base of the falls that runs along the far cliff face. Many people hoof it up the trail, but the best and safest perspective is from a distance before you return the way you came.

EXPLORING FURTHER

This hike can also be done as a loop, an excellent option for older kids. The loop is not much longer than hiking out and back, but it is brushy, crosses a rocky avalanche chute three times, and requires the use of hands for stability in a few locations. Weather can take a toll on this trail, sliding soccer ball–size rocks over the path, and it certainly is not a safe route when there is snow. Under good conditions, school-age kids may enjoy this challenge, but families with younger kids and those in baby backpacks should leave it for another year. To take the loop, cross the stream. When you reach the far cliff face, do a short switchback to the left, then to the right to reach the trail. This isn't obvious. Progress downward on switchbacks, past mammoth firs and rocky vistas.

GREAT GETAWAY: MOUNT RAINIER

Massive Mount Rainier beckons from far and wide, but it isn't very easy to visit. Like its snowy neighbor Mount St. Helens, Mount Rainier has several entrances and lacks a gateway town that provides lots of lodging. You have to make choices for your visit: do you head to the lofty flower fields of Paradise, the high ridges of Sunrise, or one of the lesser-known corners of the park? You can hardly go wrong, though you can go at the wrong time. If you visit Paradise in the summer, make sure you arrive early in the morning or late in the afternoon to get one of the limited parking spots.

To get a head start on the crowds, I like to camp in or near the park. Cougar Rock and Ohanapecosh are large campgrounds that can be reserved in advance. They provide good jumping-off points for Paradise and nearby areas. White River Campground on the east side of the park is just below Sunrise, and is first-come, first-served—to snag a site, it's often essential to arrive on Wednesday or Thursday. There are several Forest Service campgrounds along State Route 410 and US Highway 12 as well. The closest lodging options are in Packwood and Ashford, and in Mount Rainier National Park at Longmire and Paradise.

Eventually, the descent becomes gentler until you reach the White River Trail at 3 miles. Go left, passing the scout camp, until you reach a familiar intersection at 3.8 miles. Go right to make your way back to the trailhead.

64 SOURDOUGH RIDGE– SHADOW LAKE LOOP

BEFORE YOU GO
MAP Green Trails, Mount Rainier Wonderland No. 269S
CONTACT Mount Rainier National Park
NOTES National Park entrance fee; dogs prohibited; restrooms available
GPS N 46 54.874, W 121 38.508

ABOUT THE HIKE
SEASON Late July to mid-September
DIFFICULTY Moderate to difficult
DISTANCE 3.7 miles loop
HIGH POINT 6725 feet
ELEVATION GAIN 360 feet

GETTING THERE
From Enumclaw, drive State Route 410 east for 43 miles and reach the White River Entrance to Mount Rainier National Park. Turn right into the park, passing through the pay station. Take the Sunrise Road 16 miles to its end at the Sunrise Visitor Center. The Sunrise Road is open only seasonally, usually from early July to mid-September.

ON THE TRAIL

With intimate close-ups of Mount Rainier, glorious meadows of wildflowers, lingering summer snowfields, and a good chance to see wildlife, the Sunrise side of Mount Rainier National Park is a classic destination for families, with a half-dozen short hikes that radiate from the Sunrise Visitor Center. The loop described here is 3.7 miles, and I've noted how and where you can modify it to suit your family's interests and stamina.

Follow the main trail at Sunrise between the restrooms and snack bar up the broad stone steps to the first intersection. Go left, huffing and puffing up 250 feet to reach Sourdough Ridge. On a sunny summer day it can get downright hot, so make sure you have plenty of water, sunscreen, and a hat, plus bug repellent. Fortunately, once you reach the ridge, you've done most of the hard work!

Join up with the Sourdough Ridge Trail by heading left toward The Mountain. Traverse a long rock slope, admiring the stone handiwork that keeps sliding boulders from obliterating the trail. Every step takes you closer to Mount Rainier, its glacier-covered exterior gleaming in the near distance. In less than a mile, reach Frozen Lake, an icy roped-off reservoir that supplies water for the Sunrise facilities, and soon thereafter an intersection offering four choices. The trail to the right leads 1.3 miles and 460 feet to the Mount Fremont Lookout; straight ahead leads to Berkeley Park along the Wonderland Trail; and a soft left climbs up to the three Burroughs Mountains and even closer views of Rainier on a trail with a treacherous late-season snowfield. As long as the snows have melted, these alternatives may appeal to older kids who have more stamina and capacity for skilled footwork.

There's one more trail option. To the immediate left, the Wonderland Trail travels downhill and back toward the Sunrise area, creating a loop. Descend

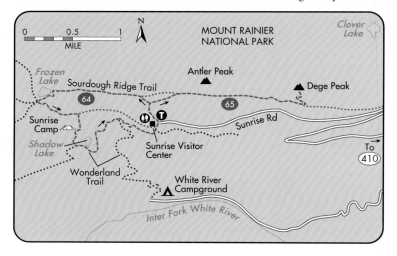

Frozen Lake is the water supply for the Sunrise Visitor Center complex.
(photo by Jon Stier)

into its heather meadows, pocked with a patchwork of snow and twinkling tarns. I'm pretty sure this is where fairies live. It's definitely habitat for marmots and other alpine denizens, so be alert for movement.

After 0.6 mile, reach a junction. The old road straight ahead is the most direct route back to Sunrise in just under a mile, making for a 2.5-mile loop. But why not idle beside an alpine lake, gaze at the immense (though shrinking) Emmons Glacier, or scout the walk-in campground? To do these, go right, remaining on the Wonderland Trail. Pass through more flowery meadows, shady firs, and the backcountry camp—a smaller, wilder version of a car campground that closed more than fifty years ago.

In a third of a mile, reach another intersection. The way right leads very steeply up to First Burroughs. To stay on your loop, go left and in a short distance pass side trails that lead to the banks of emerald-green Shadow Lake (sorry, no swimming). Continue on, curving all the way around the lake. Just beyond the junction where the Wonderland Trail peels off, there's a good spot to view the Emmons Glacier. Notice how the ribbon of river seems to appear out of nowhere. That is the toe of the Emmons Glacier and the headwaters of the White River. There's not far to go from here, but it is a tad uphill until you reach the parking area again.

65 DEGE PEAK

BEFORE YOU GO
MAP Green Trails, Mount Rainier Wonderland No. 269S
CONTACT Mount Rainier National Park
NOTES National Park entrance fee; dogs prohibited; restrooms available;
check at visitor center for snow conditions; steep drop-offs
GPS N 46 54.874, W 121 38.508

ABOUT THE HIKE
SEASON Late July to mid-September
DIFFICULTY Moderate to difficult
DISTANCE 4.2 miles roundtrip
HIGH POINT 7008 feet
ELEVATION GAIN 650 feet

GETTING THERE
From Enumclaw, drive State Route 410 east for 43 miles and reach the White
River Entrance to Mount Rainier National Park. Turn right into the park, pass-
ing through the pay station. Take the Sunrise Road 16 miles to its end at the
Sunrise Visitor Center. The Sunrise Road is open only seasonally, usually from
early July to mid-September.

Hiking from Sunrise to Dege Peak

ON THE TRAIL

It's a four-volcano hike! Mount Baker, Glacier Peak, Mount Rainier, and Mount Adams are all visible from the top of Dege Peak (pronounced "deg-ay"). When it comes to giving the kids a sense of accomplishment, you really can't do much better. They will work hard to get here, but the trail offers many distractions, and the ultimate payoff can't be beat.

Before going, check in at the visitor center for snow conditions. A snow cornice can hang over the ridge along the trail, making the way dangerous and impassable until it has melted. If it has melted out, you are in for a treat. Follow the main trail at Sunrise between the restrooms and snack bar up the broad stone steps to the first intersection. Go right, shedding the majority of your fellow hikers. This south-facing slope is a mixed blessing. In season, it offers up one of the finest subalpine wildflower displays in the park—fields of yellow glacier lilies, purple lupine, white bistort, lavender daisies, and scarlet paintbrush. But the flip side is unrelenting heat on sunny days. Make sure you've brought hats, sunscreen, and water.

The trail gains nearly 400 feet in the first 0.6 mile en route to the intersection with the Sourdough Ridge Trail but levels off for a mile of easy walking. At the junction, turn right on the ridge, but first take a break on the bench and enjoy the view. On a clear day you can see Mount Baker and Glacier Peak among the spires of the Cascades. Snow clings to the steep slopes below, and with the help of binoculars you might even spot mountain goats among the rocks. Tear yourself away, though, because the views will get more impressive.

The trail follows the ridge, first skirting Antler Peak and then reaching another pass. Make sure the kids do not approach the edge, especially if there is snow. Instead, stick to the trail and peer up at your destination: Dege Peak. At 1.8 miles, veer left on the trail to the summit and prepare to climb. Switchbacks ease the way on the 250-foot push to the top (7008 feet).

Before you know it, you are there, and WOW! Spin clockwise to take in the exquisite panorama: Mount Rainier and the Emmons Glacier; McNeely, Antler, and Marcus peaks nearby; many major peaks of the Cascades; shimmering Sunrise and Clover lakes; and Mount Adams and the pointy Cowlitz Chimneys. You can even spot the Olympics on a crystal clear day. Pull out a map and help the kids identify landmarks.

As you rest at the summit, you may be visited by a squirrel or two. They are undeniably cute, but because people have fed them, they have become little monsters. They will eat anything, including your maps, backpacks, and coats. Don't leave your belongings unattended for even a minute, or you will be sorry. Instead, guard your food and belongings, watch butterflies frolic in the breeze, and then head back the way you came.

EXPLORING FURTHER

Families traveling with two cars should consider stashing one vehicle at Sunrise Point, the parking area at the switchback on the Sunrise Road, for a one-way trip of just over 3 miles.

66 NACHES PEAK LOOP

BEFORE YOU GO
MAP Green Trails, Mount Rainier Wonderland No. 269S
CONTACT Mount Rainier National Park
NOTES Northwest Forest Pass required at Chinook Pass but not Tipsoo Lake;
   dogs prohibited; privy available
GPS N 46 52.194, W 121 31.189

ABOUT THE HIKE
SEASON Late July to September
DIFFICULTY Moderate
DISTANCE 3.5 miles loop
HIGH POINT 5850 feet
ELEVATION GAIN 600 feet

GETTING THERE
From the north, via Enumclaw, drive State Route 410 east approximately 47
miles to the intersection with SR 123 at Cayuse Pass. Continue on SR 410 by
veering left. Proceed 0.5 mile to the large Tipsoo Lake parking lot and picnic
area on your left. No permit is needed here. If the lot is full, there are two
additional parking areas 0.5 mile farther east, just past the Mount Rainier
National Park pedestrian overpass, where you can join the loop trail. A Northwest Forest Pass is required there.

ON THE TRAIL
Nonstop wildflowers, sparkling glacial tarns, and superlative views of Mount
Rainier earn the Naches Peak Loop a well-deserved mention on many hikers'
top ten lists. The best news is that this Shangri-la is attainable for families. The
trail is short, the elevation gain gradual, and there is much to tickle the senses.

The best way to enjoy views of Mount Rainier is to tackle the trail in a clockwise direction. There are a scattering of paths near Tipsoo Lake, but if you can
locate the Stephen Tyng Mather memorial plaque and keep to the left of the
lake, you will find signs directing you to the Naches Peak Loop.

In 0.25 mile, reach an alternative parking area at Chinook Pass. Here you
will join the Pacific Crest Trail for 1.5 miles of its 2650-mile run from Mexico
to Canada. We always look for speedy hikers with dirty packs and give them a
big hello. Cross over State Route 410 on a pedestrian overpass that announces
the entrance into Mount Rainier National Park and officially begin your
circumambulation of Naches Peak. Enter the William O. Douglas Wilderness
and shortly thereafter pull away from the road and enter a world of rolling hills,
wildflower meadows, rocky outcrops, and stands of trees. A jade-green tarn
is irresistible as a rest stop, but please be careful not to trample the meadows.

After the tarn, the trail climbs 200 feet in 0.5 mile to reach a scenic high
point overlooking Dewey Lake (1.7 miles, 5850 feet). The Pacific Crest Trail

There are views everywhere you look on the Naches Peak Loop.
(photo by Jon Stier)

splits off nearby, dropping 600 feet in 1.2 miles to the lake. Instead, loop hikers will continue right on the Naches Peak Loop, round a corner, and come face-to-face with Mount Rainier. "It looks like a painting," my daughter remarked, and indeed it does: immense and immoveable, almost floating in the background. It's hard to process the three dimensions.

In July and August you will want to linger among the colorful fields of lupine, paintbrush, daisies, and asters, as well as the reflective glacial tarn. Come fall, this stretch is equally picturesque in its golds and crimsons. Press on, glancing south at the sweeping vista of the Goat Rocks, Tatoosh Range, Mount

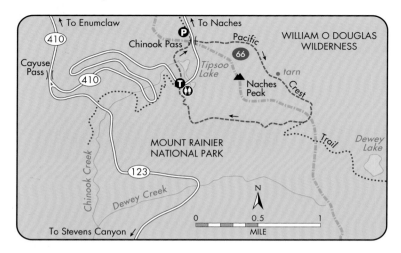

Adams, and broad valleys of the Gifford Pinchot National Forest while hiking the final 1.5 miles back to the trailhead. Reach the highway and carefully cross it. The safest bet is to join the trail around the south end of Tipsoo Lake to close the loop, but most hikers simply walk the road back to the parking lot.

MOUNT RAINIER NATIONAL PARK (PARADISE/STEVENS CANYON)

67 SILVER FALLS LOOP

BEFORE YOU GO

MAP Green Trails, Mount Rainier Wonderland No. 269S
CONTACT Mount Rainier National Park
NOTES Dogs prohibited; restrooms and water available
GPS N 46 44.166, W 121 33.950

ABOUT THE HIKE

SEASON June to October
DIFFICULTY Moderate
DISTANCE 3 miles loop
HIGH POINT 2300 feet
ELEVATION GAIN 400 feet

This Douglas fir on the path to Silver Lake has adapted to its sideways location.

GETTING THERE

From Enumclaw, drive State Route 410 east approximately 47 miles to the intersection with SR 123 at Cayuse Pass. Go straight, merging onto SR 123, and take it south 13 miles to the Ohanapecosh Campground. Turn right into the campground and park near the small visitor center. (From Packwood, drive US Highway 12 east 7.6 miles and turn left (north) on SR 123. In 3.6 miles turn left into the Ohanapecosh Campground.)

ON THE TRAIL

Campers at the popular Ohanapecosh Campground have many options for morning or evening hikes on the lush wooded side of Mount Rainier. Silver Falls is my favorite of the bunch. Hikers get big trees, a hot spring, frolicking whitewater, and an appealing waterfall, and it can be hiked directly from their

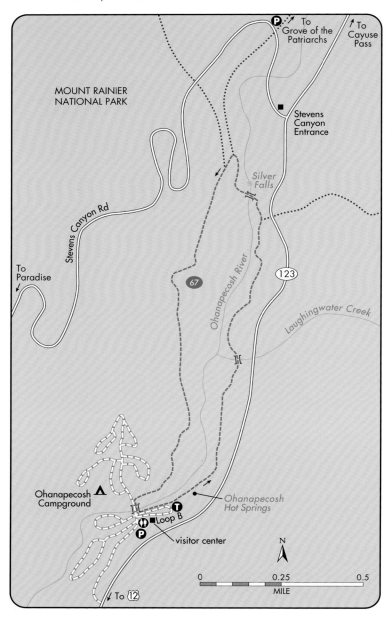

MOUNT RAINIER
NATIONAL PARK

P To
Grove of the
Patriarchs

To
Cayuse
Pass

Stevens
Canyon
Entrance

Silver
Falls

Stevens Canyon Rd

To
Paradise

67

Ohanapecosh River

123

Laughingwater Creek

Ohanapecosh
Campground

Ohanapecosh
Hot Springs

T

Loop B

H

P

visitor center

N

To 12

0   0.25   0.5
MILE

campsite. What's more, this trail offers solitude even in August, with far fewer hikers than the nearby Grove of the Patriarchs trail.

The trail can be accessed from the nature trail behind the visitor center or from the far end of Loop B. Almost immediately you arrive upon an unusual scene that invites closer inspection. Hot sulfurous water from Ohanapecosh Hot Springs flows through verdant green grasses downhill to the Ohanapecosh River. Let the kids kneel on the boardwalk, observe the plant life in its steaming environment, and, with permission, give the heated springwater a touch.

Carry on, with gentle ups and downs along the trail. The trail travels high above the Ohanapecosh River, which is often out of sight. The canopy is thick in places, making this place dark on cloudy days, but it is also enchanting, with a moss carpet that hosts a delicate understory.

At a trail junction at 1.3 miles, stay left for Silver Falls, which soon makes its appearance. Several viewpoints, with railings, bring you ever closer to the ribbon of white as it pours into an emerald pool. Cross over the river and watch the water funnel through a narrow cleft between mossy canyon walls. A short side trail approaches the falls. It's pretty dramatic to catch some cool spray on your face and breathe in its fresh scent, but keep the kids close by and at a safe distance from the waterfall.

Veer left at each of two successive trail junctions to remain on the loop—the first connects to the Grove of the Patriarchs trailhead in 0.5 mile; the second is an access point to the Wonderland Trail. The loop trail will track uphill, away from the river, until it tops out at 2300 feet before descending somewhat steeply to the campground at 2.8 miles. Follow the main path past tents and RVs until you see the bridge over the river. Turn left and reach the visitor center.

EXPLORING FURTHER

Nearby Grove of the Patriarchs is a 1.5-mile lollipop loop through an outstanding old-growth grove of cedars and Douglas firs over 300 feet tall. In addition to the ancient trees, a highlight is a swaying suspension bridge that crosses the Ohanapecosh River. This hike is one of the most popular in the park, and it is difficult to find a spot in the small parking lot on Stevens Canyon Road.

68 FARAWAY ROCK

BEFORE YOU GO

MAP Green Trails, Mount Rainier Wonderland No. 269S
CONTACT Mount Rainier National Park
NOTES National Park entrance fee; dogs prohibited; steep drop-offs; no facilities
GPS N 46 46.095, W 121 43.695

ABOUT THE HIKE

SEASON July to September
DIFFICULTY Moderate
DISTANCE 1.8 miles roundtrip
HIGH POINT 5250 feet
ELEVATION GAIN 400 feet

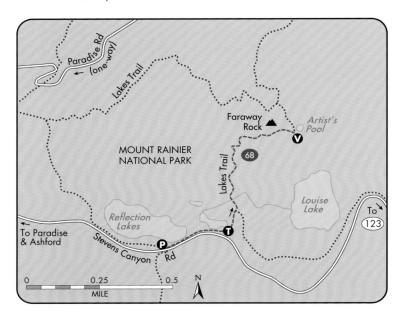

GETTING THERE

From Enumclaw, drive State Route 410 east approximately 47 miles to the intersection with SR 123 at Cayuse Pass. Continue straight, merging onto SR 123, and take this road 11 miles south to Stevens Canyon Road. Turn right, passing through the Stevens Canyon Entrance, and drive 17.5 miles to the small roadside parking area on the shore of Reflection Lakes.

From Packwood, drive US Highway 12 east 7.6 miles and turn left (north) on SR 123. Drive 5.4 miles to Stevens Canyon Road. Turn left and pass through the entrance to the park, then drive 17.5 miles to the small roadside parking area on the shore of Reflection Lakes.

From the Nisqually Entrance, drive SR 706 (the Longmire-Paradise Road) east 16 miles to the turnoff for Stevens Canyon Road. Go right, and travel 1.4 miles to the small parking lot on the shore of Reflection Lakes.

ON THE TRAIL

Faraway Rock isn't so far away, but it is a great way to escape the crowds at Paradise's Henry M. Jackson Visitor Center, to sit high above two sparkly mountain lakes, and to gain an appreciation for the craggy Tatoosh Mountains that usually play second fiddle to Mount Rainier. Wildflowers reign supreme in midsummer, berries burst forth in late summer, and the hillside turns crimson in fall.

Sit far from the edge while enjoying the views from Faraway Rock.

Gain your bearings by looking up toward Mount Rainier and a bit to the right. See the rocky outcrop? That's Faraway Rock, your destination. Finding the trailhead is a bit more difficult. It's located between Reflection Lakes and Louise Lake. Because the first 0.2 mile of trail is on a sidewalk that parallels the road, keep the kids close as you walk against the traffic. Find the sign for Lakes Trail and start climbing gently, then more steeply. Flowers are profuse along this stretch—bring a wildflower guide to identify columbine, tiger lilies, paintbrush, and spirea. There are also a good amount of blueberries and huckleberries in late summer.

Before you know it, you will reach Faraway Rock (0.9 mile, 5250 feet). Make sure the kids stay far back from the edge of the rock. This is a cliff, and if you have any concerns about your child's ability to stay safe, you should choose another hike. If everyone can respect the danger, they will have a fine time soaking in the view. Three lakes can be spotted from here: Louise Lake is a kaleidoscope of color immediately below, Reflection Lakes shimmer to the right near your car, and Bench Lake peeks out high above the road. Carefully trace the long path that Stevens Canyon Road takes east and pull out a map to try and identify the distinctive peaks across the way.

Just beyond the rock is Artist's Pool. Photographers can frame a fine photo by shooting across Artist's Pool with the Tatoosh Range as a backdrop. Turn around here or continue on for more adventures.

EXPLORING FURTHER

Complete a 3-mile loop by proceeding on the ridge above Reflection Lakes, following the signs for the Lakes Trail. Mount Rainier remains mostly hidden, but there isn't too much additional elevation gain and there are more wildflowers to see. The descent back down on the other side of Reflection Lakes is fairly steep, but it should be fine for most kids. Alternatively, hardy hikers can walk all the way to Paradise Inn (or from it).

69 SKYLINE–GOLDEN GATE LOOP

BEFORE YOU GO
MAP Green Trails, Mount Rainier Wonderland No. 269S
CONTACT Mount Rainier National Park
NOTES National Park entrance fee; dogs prohibited; trail can be scaled
to accommodate young hikers; restrooms available at visitor center
GPS N 46 47.190, W 121 44.192

ABOUT THE HIKE (MYRTLE FALLS)
SEASON July to mid-October
DIFFICULTY Easy to moderate
DISTANCE 0.8 mile roundtrip
HIGH POINT 5600 feet
ELEVATION GAIN 175 feet

ABOUT THE HIKE (LOOP)
SEASON July to mid-October
DIFFICULTY Difficult
DISTANCE 4 miles loop
HIGH POINT 6400 feet
ELEVATION GAIN 1000 feet

GETTING THERE

From Interstate 5, take exit 127 in Lakewood, driving east on State Route 512 for 2 miles. Go right/south on SR 7. Drive 35.5 miles to the town of Elbe, where you will stay straight onto SR 706. The Nisqually Entrance to Mount Rainier National Park is in 13.5 miles, and Paradise is in another 18 miles. There are several lots and parking along the road. Try to find a place as close to the Henry M. Jackson Visitor Center as possible.

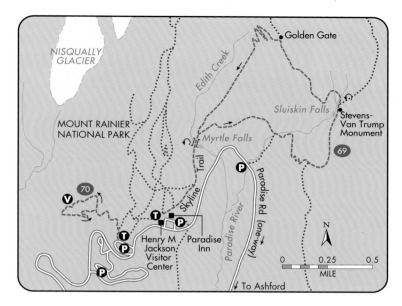

ON THE TRAIL

Find your own bit of paradise. What will that be? Glorious wildflowers or snow in July? Marmots or deer? Glaciers or waterfalls? Despite the insane parking situation, rarefied air, and straight-up trails, this loop can be scaled to fit your family's ability. Frolic past dancing wildflowers, spot cute critters, and be dazzled by The Mountain in all its glory. Whatever you do, arrive early, or you may find you must walk an additional mile or so from your car to the visitor center.

The Skyline–Golden Gate loop begins at the visitor center (5425 feet) and follows the Skyline Trail to the right on a paved trail. Pass above the historic Paradise Inn on a 0.4-mile jaunt to Myrtle Falls (5600 feet). Myrtle Falls cascades from shelf to shelf down a picturesque rocky cliff. You can view it from a bridge over Edith Creek or from below with Mount Rainier as an impressive backdrop.

This is a good place for families with toddlers to turn around, but it's also worthwhile to keep going. At 0.5 mile, reach a junction with the Golden Gate Trail. If you do the full loop, this will be your return. For now, stay to the right on the Skyline Trail. Views of the Tatoosh Range—The Castle, Pinnacle, and Plummer peaks—are stunning, as the trail maneuvers through stunted subalpine fir and a watery world of creeks, cascades, and snowmelt. The trail goes down, then up and gains 500 feet over less than a mile as it crests Mazama Ridge and comes to a nearly century-old stone bench full of inscriptions (1.8 miles, 6025 feet). The bench commemorates Hazard Stevens and P. B. Van Trump, who made the first known ascent of Mount Rainier in 1870. Look down from here to see Sluiskin Falls.

Wildflowers, snow, and one big mountain make the Paradise area fun to explore.
(photo by Jon Stier)

Some folks will turn around here, but it is worth going just another 0.1 mile to a cute little bridge over a creek choked with flowers—pink and yellow monkey flower, lupine, heather, and Indian paintbrush—and surrounded by itty-bitty conifers trying to survive in extreme conditions. Now it's decision time. Do you make the loop? From the bridge, it is another 0.6 mile and 375 feet of elevaton gain to Golden Gate (2.5 miles, 6400 feet).

Once you reach the Golden Gate junction, turn left and descend carefully on steep switchbacks for 0.5 mile to reach the Skyline Trail. Enjoy big views of Mount Rainier and glorious meadows of wildflowers. Look closely for marmots cavorting among the rocks. Satiated with beauty and cuteness, turn right to return to the visitor center for a 4-mile roundtrip.

70 NISQUALLY VISTA

BEFORE YOU GO
MAP Green Trails, Mount Rainier Wonderland No. 269S
CONTACT Mount Rainier National Park
NOTES National Park entrance fee; dogs prohibited; restrooms available at visitor center
GPS N 46 47.102, W 121 44.497

ABOUT THE HIKE
   SEASON July to mid-October
   DIFFICULTY Easy
   DISTANCE 1 mile loop
   HIGH POINT 5375 feet
   ELEVATION GAIN 50 feet

GETTING THERE

From Interstate 5, take exit 127 in Lakewood, driving east on State Route 512 for 2 miles. Go right/south on SR 7. Drive 35.5 miles to the town of Elbe, where you will stay straight onto SR 706. The Nisqually Entrance to Mount Rainier National Park is in 13.5 miles, and Paradise is in another 18 miles. There are several lots and parking along the road. Try to find a spot in the lower parking lot before you reach the Henry M. Jackson Visitor Center.

ON THE TRAIL

Mount Rainier's Paradise is a study in verticality. Trails depart straight up the broad shoulders of the mountain, attaining dizzying heights quickly. The newly redone Nisqually Vista Trail is an exception. The entire mile-long loop is smooth pavement, suitable for wheelchairs, strollers, and the youngest of walkers who want to look at one of the mountain's largest glaciers.

The trail begins at the far end of the lower parking lot, west of the visitor center. Look for the first photo opp almost immediately—a rock with a hole in the center and room for two. Just beyond, the trail takes off in a loop. Go right on a beeline for glacier vistas. At the half-mile mark there are four viewpoints for the Nisqually Glacier. The final one is the best. Check out the glacier's gray toe and the white veins of water thundering through the barren valley. Round a corner and close the loop at 0.8 mile, returning right for the trailhead. To learn more about Mount Rainier's glaciers, be sure to visit the upstairs portion of the nearby Henry M. Jackson Visitor Center.

The Paradise area is one of the best places to spot marmots.

GIFFORD PINCHOT NATIONAL FOREST

71 CURTAIN FALLS

BEFORE YOU GO
   MAP Green Trails, McCoy Peak No. 333; map at office
   CONTACT Gifford Pinchot National Forest
   NOTES Check in at Cispus Environmental Learning Center office
   GPS N 46 26.313, W 121 51.112

ABOUT THE HIKE
   SEASON April to November
   DIFFICULTY Moderate
   DISTANCE 2.6 miles roundtrip
   HIGH POINT 1835 feet
   ELEVATION GAIN 535 feet

GETTING THERE

From US Highway 12 in Randle, turn south on State Route 131. In 1 mile, veer left on Forest Road 23. Drive 8.1 miles and turn right on Cispus Road (FR 29). Follow Cispus Road for 1.3 miles. After it crosses the Cispus River, veer right to stay on the Cispus Road (now FR 76). Drive 0.7 mile and turn right into the signed entrance for the Cispus Environmental Learning Center. Check in at the office and park where they ask you to.

ON THE TRAIL

Adjacent to the Cispus Environmental Learning Center is a network of moderately used trails that lead to two waterfalls along Covel Creek. The most family-friendly of these, aptly named Curtain Falls, is an ideal outing for visitors camping nearby. What's more, part of the hike follows the Cispus Braille Trail, a yellow-roped loop for the vision-impaired. Following the scratchy rope is a great way to open up the conversation for how we use our senses when we hike, and what it would mean if we couldn't see the beauty around us.

The Cispus Environmental Learning Center is a year-round outdoor learning environment for Washington students, run by the Association of Washington School Principals. Your kids may one day attend a camp here. Be sure to ask for a map when you check in at the office. The trails can be confusing even with the map, but it helps. Start by crossing Cispus Road and enter the trees opposite the center's entrance, signed for Covel Creek. After 500 feet, reach an intersection with a yellow rope. This is part of the vision-impaired loop. Go right, and then right again, leaving the Braille Trail for now. There's another right ahead, then finally a left after crossing a bridge.

Climb gently uphill through a forest of firs and hemlocks interlaced with vine maple. At 0.5 mile, carefully cross a seasonal creek that has no bridge; the hill up and out can be tricky. Shortly thereafter, reach a Y-intersection. Left leads back to the Cispus Center (your return) and right leads to Curtain Falls. Leave the maze of trails behind, and encounter a second creek crossing without a bridge. It may be tricky at high water but is otherwise fine in summer. The trail steepens and climbs 300 feet over 0.3 mile. It won't be long before you see Covel Creek pouring and pooling below and hear the waterfall ahead. At 1.1 miles (1835 feet), reach a junction and proceed right a short distance to Curtain Falls (also known as Covel Falls).

Water showers off an overhang of rocks, constantly spraying the colorful mossy rocks below. It's pretty, especially in the spring or fall when the flow is heaviest. The neatest part of this waterfall is that you can walk behind it. The

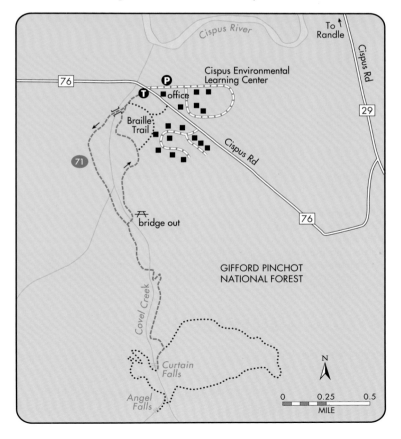

Hiking among the sword fern on the way to Curtain Falls

trail is a bit slippery from all of the water, so be aware of your footing and use the rope handrail if necessary.

Upon your return, take a slightly different route. Return to the intersection that points the way to the Cispus Center and go right, crossing the seasonal creek. Another bridge is missing here, but in summertime the creek bed is dry. There is a shelter on the other side that is perfect for setting out a picnic or escaping sprinkles. Walk toward the camp on a wide trail alongside the creek, encountering more intersections. You're back in the trail maze, but with camp buildings so close, it is hard to get lost. By keeping Covel Creek to your left, you will regain the Braille Trail and be able to follow your breadcrumbs back to the Cispus Center.

EXPLORING FURTHER

Looking for something else to do in the area? Explore Layser Cave, one of the area's most important archaeological sites. On a 0.4-mile interpretive trail visitors can climb into the cave and imagine living here 7000 years ago. Reach Layser Cave on your return to Randle. After turning left onto Forest Road 23, drive 2 miles to FR 83. Go right on the gravel road and find the trailhead in 1.5 miles.

72 LEWIS RIVER FALLS

BEFORE YOU GO
MAP Green Trails, Lone Butte No. 365
CONTACT Gifford Pinchot National Forest
NOTES Northwest Forest Pass required; privy available; stay back from edge near waterfall viewpoints
GPS N 46 09.960, W 121 52.100

ABOUT THE HIKE
　　SEASON March to November
　　DIFFICULTY Moderate
　　DISTANCE 3.1 miles roundtrip
　　HIGH POINT 1775 feet
　　ELEVATION GAIN 225 feet

GETTING THERE

From Interstate 5, take exit 21 in Woodland and drive east on State Route 503 for 29 miles to the town of Cougar. Beyond Cougar, SR 503 becomes Forest Road 90. Drive 18.4 miles to the intersection with FR 25. Veer right, staying on FR 90 and crossing over the Lewis River. Drive an additional 14 miles to the Lower Falls Campground, where you can find access to Lower Falls. Middle Falls trailhead is an additional 1 mile up the road on the right.

ON THE TRAIL

There are waterfalls in Washington that are taller and more forceful, but in my opinion there are none quite as stunning as the string of waterfalls along this short stretch of the Lewis River. In a 3-mile span, the Lewis River flows over

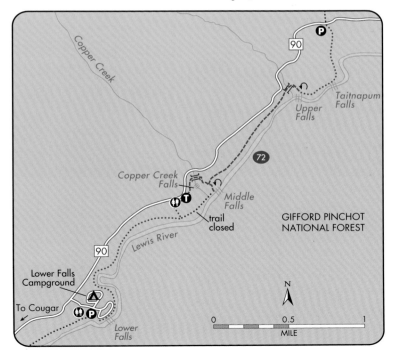

Copper Creek Falls is a charming bonus waterfall.

a series of giant steps carved out of basalt. The result is something you might see in a Hawaiian travel brochure—a fan of water pouring over horseshoes of ancient, smooth bedrock. This happens not once, but four times along a trail that can be accessed at several points or bitten off in one 6-mile hike.

The first thing to decide is where to begin. My recommendation is to hike to Middle and Upper Lewis River Falls, and then visit Lower Lewis Falls separately at the campground. From the Middle Falls parking area, walk 0.25 mile through forest that parallels the road before dropping down to a wooden bridge over charming Copper Creek Falls, which spouts from a narrow cleft to a small pool below. This is a bonus falls, and makes for excellent photographs from the trail ahead.

Hike another 0.25 mile to an intersection, where you can descend to Middle Falls on a switchback. Although Middle Falls isn't a long drop, it exudes a certain magic. In midsummer, you can walk out on onto a smooth bedrock slab and feel like you are a part of the waterfall. The falls pour gently over a broad area and down in two main chutes, reconnecting in a deep narrow green pool at the edge of the bedrock at your feet. Be careful here, as the rock can be slick and may be impassable in high water.

Return to the intersection and make a choice. Return to the trailhead for a 1.2-mile journey, or proceed right to Upper Falls for a 3.1-mile roundtrip. Beyond the junction the trail narrows, with some exposure, so tread carefully. Profuse ferns and mosses and vivid green water traversing the lava river give the hike its tropical feel.

In less than a mile, reach Upper Falls and observe this unusual and spectacular cataract. The basalt riverbed drops 58 feet, with water flowing in many different directions all at once. Some of the water fans over cliffs verdant with moss, but most of the river pours into a narrow side channel and down what resembles a natural fish ladder. A higher viewpoint for Upper Lewis River Falls is reached by hiking up another 100 feet, but I like the lower one better. If you aim to see all of the waterfalls, continue 0.2 mile beyond the upper viewpoint to Taitnapum Falls. When you are done, retrace your steps.

EXPLORING FURTHER

Don't miss Lower Lewis River Falls, located next to the campground. It's the most popular of the bunch and reachable just a few feet beyond the parking area on a universally accessible trail. New railings have been installed at all viewpoints to keep visitors safe. From Lower Lewis River Falls, you can also hike to both Middle and Upper Falls, which is an excellent option for older kids. Note that the riverside trail just before Middle Falls has permanently washed out, requiring a short detour up to the Middle Falls trailhead before returning to the river beyond the washout. The roundtrip from Lower to Upper Falls is approximately 6 miles.

73 STEAMBOAT MOUNTAIN

BEFORE YOU GO
MAP Green Trails, Mount Adams West No. 366
CONTACT Gifford Pinchot National Forest
NOTES No facilities; steep drop-offs atop mountain
GPS N 46 08.103, W 121 43.654

ABOUT THE HIKE
SEASON Mid-July to October
DIFFICULTY Moderate to difficult
DISTANCE 1.5 miles roundtrip
HIGH POINT 5413 feet
ELEVATION GAIN 620 feet

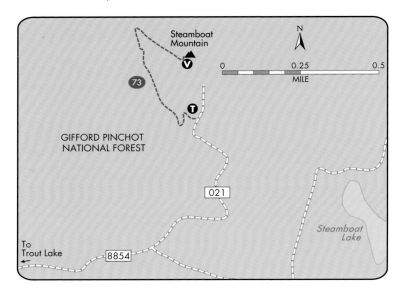

GETTING THERE

From Trout Lake, go west on State Route 141 for 1.4 miles. Turn right on Trout Lake Creek Road (Forest Road 88) and drive 12 miles to Tire Junction. Turn left onto FR 8851. In 3.2 miles, make a sharp switchback onto FR 8854. In a short distance, bear left on FR 021 and take it about 2.5 miles to its end at a large parking lot near a gravel quarry.

ON THE TRAIL

Driving through the dense green expanse of the Gifford Pinchot National Forest, it is hard to get a good perspective of where you are. It's high, forested country interrupted by two huge volcanoes. You want to see these volcanoes. Enter Steamboat Mountain. After less than a mile of steep climbing, you'll be standing at the site of an old fire lookout. On a clear day, views stretch out to the broad expanse of four Cascade volcanoes—Mount Adams, Mount St. Helens, Mount Hood, and Mount Rainier. Pull out a map to figure out where you are in the sea of green, but keep the kids nearby. The mountain has steep drop-offs.

From the parking lot, look up. That's where you are heading. And while it appears you will be going up an exposed slope, you're not. The trail leads through the trees and up a ridgeline to reach Steamboat Mountain. It's steep. You will gain more than 600 feet in 0.75 mile. But by then you will have summited and the hardship will be forgotten. As you traverse the west side of the mountain and switchback up to the ridgeline, the trailside is resplendent with wildflowers. Take your time and smell the tiger lilies, paintbrush, stonecrop, and columbine.

Just short of the summit at 0.7 mile is a killer view, perhaps better than the summit itself. Mount Hood is straight ahead to the south, and Mount Adams looms large in the east. From the viewpoint, you will be able to spot your vehicle in the parking area below. Be careful here, and stay well back from the edge.

A final push will land you atop Steamboat Mountain (5413 feet), where concrete footings of a former lookout remain. Peek through the stunted trees to identify Mount Rainier, the Goat Rocks, and Mount St. Helens. Count the lakes, and watch butterflies, swallows, and ravens cavort in the air. Finally, settle with a view of the star of the show: Mount Adams. There is nothing but forest between you and the volcano. Study its glaciers and magnificent breadth, and the scars on its slopes that tell stories of logging and recent wildfires. When you've had your fill on the summit, return the way you came, keeping the kids with you for safety.

Standing above a sea of green near the summit of Steamboat Mountain

74 PLACID AND CHENAMUS LAKES

BEFORE YOU GO
MAP Green Trails, Indian Heaven No. 365S
CONTACT Gifford Pinchot National Forest
NOTES No facilities
GPS N 46 02.929, W 121 48.550

ABOUT THE HIKE
SEASON Mid-July to October
DIFFICULTY Easy to moderate
DISTANCE 3.4 miles roundtrip
HIGH POINT 4250 feet
ELEVATION GAIN 200 feet

GETTING THERE
From Trout Lake, go west on State Route 141 for 1.4 miles. Turn right on Trout Lake Creek Road (Forest Road 88) and drive 12 miles to Tire Junction. Turn left onto FR 8851. In 3.2 miles, go straight onto FR 24 at a three-way intersection. Stay on FR 24 another 3.3 miles and turn right onto FR 30. In 5.5 miles, turn left onto gravel FR 420 (signed Placid Lake) and drive 1.2 miles. Park in the large, unsigned parking area on the left.

One of hundreds of tiny frogs hopping about the shores of Placid Lake

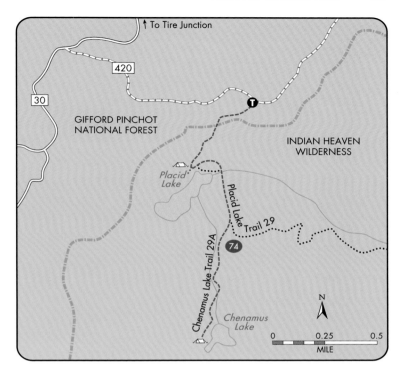

ON THE TRAIL

Absorb the charm of the Indian Heaven Wilderness on this less-traveled trail to two of the area's many little lakes. The lakes themselves are understated, yet pretty, ringed by green conifers that reflect in the still water. What makes this place special, however, is everything else: the echo-y silence of the forest, the bountiful harvest of berries, the colorful toadstools popping from the forest floor, and the wildlife. During our August visit, thousands of tiny frogs fanned out from Placid Lake and into the forest, providing a magical and unexpected experience that I was able to share with my daughter.

The trailhead is set back in the trees opposite the parking area, and from here, you'll pass almost immediately into the Indian Heaven Wilderness. Hike on the soft duff in this quiet forest. The elevation change is hardly noticeable. Mushrooms emerge from the forest floor after rains, and huckleberries line the trail. In just 0.6 mile, reach Placid Lake, where hellebore, bear grass, and lupine bloom in a marshy meadow. Mosquitoes are a defining feature of the Indian Heaven Wilderness, and you may find them in droves here; come prepared or wait for late August or September when they are not so bad.

Placid Lake, like its nearby cousin Chenamus Lake, is muddy-bottomed. You can soak your feet, but the lake is not ideal for swimming. Because you've hardly worked to get here, press on to Chenamus Lake. There are many social paths around Placid Lake that could be confusing. Return to the main trail and go right at the Y-intersection. The trail now climbs gently through a forest of gray tree trunks shrouded in lichen and an understory of tasty berries.

A little over a half-mile from Placid Lake, reach an intersection. Go right on Trail No. 29A and walk another 0.5 mile to Chenamus Lake (1.7 miles, 4250 feet). Chenamus Lake is a lot like Placid, but it offers more solitude and the best-tasting wild blueberries around. Notice, there is a theme here. This hike tastes good! There are a couple of campsites here and at Placid Lake if you wish to backpack. If not, retrace your steps to return to the trailhead.

MOUNT ST. HELENS

75 HUMMOCKS TRAIL

BEFORE YOU GO
MAP Green Trails, Mount St. Helens No. 332S
CONTACT Mount St. Helens National Volcanic Monument
NOTES Dogs prohibited; privies at Coldwater Lake Recreation Area
GPS N 46 17.194, W 122 16.308

ABOUT THE HIKE
SEASON March to November
DIFFICULTY Easy to moderate
DISTANCE 2.5 miles loop
HIGH POINT 2560 feet
ELEVATION GAIN 250 feet

GETTING THERE
From Interstate 5, take exit 49 in Castle Rock and drive east on State Route 504 for 45 miles. Pass the Coldwater Lake Recreation Area on the left and just beyond, turn right into a large parking area on the right side of the highway.

ON THE TRAIL
A delightful 2.5-mile loop meanders through meadows, ponds, and hills formed by debris piled high by a destructive lahar that raced from Mount St. Helens down the North Fork Toutle River in 1980. It's a fascinating walk through a landscape newly shaped and molded by forces beyond comprehension. Along the way, experience life bouncing back—colorful wildflowers, croaking frogs, young trees.

A hummock is a small knoll or hill—in this case, mounds of volcanic debris that are up to 500 feet high. Get your introduction by taking the loop left, in

Hiking toward Mount St. Helens on the Hummocks Trail (photo by Jon Stier)

a clockwise direction. The trail weaves over and around hills dotted with wild-flowers and stands of young red alder. Little ponds, created by rainfall or natural seeps, have formed in the depressions between hummocks.

At 0.7 mile, reach an intersection with the Boundary Trail and a good view of Mount St. Helens. The hills and vegetation provide scale and perspective to the volcano, so unlike the view at Johnston Ridge. Curve right, now heading toward the North Fork Toutle River, a ribbon of white through a valley still scarred by a torrent of debris unleashed decades ago. At 1.5 miles, reach a lower viewpoint for the Toutle where you can listen to the water and rest with a snack.

Curve away from the river and reach a series of beaver dams. You're unlikely to spot a beaver but may see swallows and warblers diving in and out among

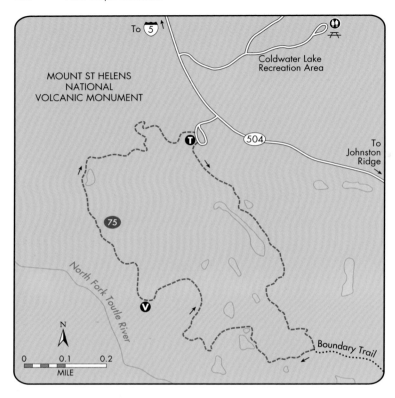

the grasses. The trail winds back past ponds and alder stands, regaining 250 feet of elevation that was lost on the journey. Take the uphill return slowly and steadily and soon arrive back at the parking area to complete the 2.5-mile loop. Head over to the Coldwater Lake Recreation Area for picnic tables and privies.

EXPLORING FURTHER

Consider also hiking the three major nature trails at Mount St. Helens. Start at the Johnston Ridge Observatory and take the paved 0.5-mile Eruption Trail from the visitor center to the far end of the parking area for spot-on views into the crater and across the barren plains. At Coldwater Lake Recreation Area, the short and sweet 0.6-mile Birth of a Lake Trail runs on a boardwalk over deep, cobalt-blue Coldwater Lake, a body of water that didn't exist prior to May 18, 1980. Finally, during summer when the Science and Learning Center is open, the 0.3-mile Winds of Change Trail boasts impressive views of the mountain and an intriguing look at the recovering landscape.

76 HARMONY TRAIL

BEFORE YOU GO
MAP Green Trails, Mount St. Helens No. 332S
CONTACT Mount St. Helens National Volcanic Monument
NOTES Northwest Forest Pass required; dogs prohibited; no facilities;
do not climb on floating logs
GPS N 46 16.465, W 122 06.268

ABOUT THE HIKE
SEASON July to October
DIFFICULTY Moderate to difficult
DISTANCE 2.4 miles roundtrip
HIGH POINT 4075 feet
ELEVATION GAIN 625 feet

GETTING THERE
From US Highway 12 in Randle, go south on State Route 131 for 2 miles, whereupon it turns into Forest Road 25. Continue on FR 25 for 17.8 miles and turn right on FR 99 for Windy Ridge. (From Cougar, drive east on Lewis River Road for 2.8 miles. It turns into FR 90. Drive FR 90 for 16 miles and bear left onto FR 25. Take FR 25 north to FR 99 and turn left.) Drive FR 99 13.3 miles to a small, signed pullout on the right. Many of these roads are closed seasonally.

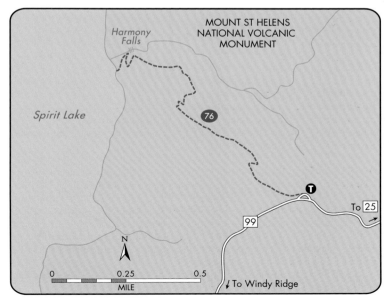

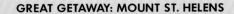

GREAT GETAWAY: MOUNT ST. HELENS

Before writing this book I had visited Johnston Ridge several times, but I had never explored the lava tubes of the Ape Cave or the airy rim of Windy Ridge. The captivating, wild, and extraordinary landscapes of all three approaches to Mount St. Helens took my breath away time and again and were some of the most satisfying surprises of my research.

Mount St. Helens is a difficult place to get to, and an even harder place to stay. The swath of destruction from the eruption in 1980 has left Mount St. Helens without campgrounds, cabins, or hotels. There are three access points to Mount St. Helens National Volcanic Monument. The most developed is Johnston Ridge, which can be reached from Interstate 5. There are several visitor centers on State Route 504, culminating at the Johnston Ridge Observatory in the heart of the blast zone. This is the best place to get an overview of the eruption and to trace its lahar of volcanic debris and water down the Toutle River. The least developed is Windy Ridge, high above Spirit Lake. From here you have the most intimate view of the crater and lava dome. The south side of the volcano, near the town of Cougar, was left largely untouched by the 1980 eruption, but was shaped by another eruption two thousand years ago.

A good plan is to establish a base camp at one of the access points and stay for a day or two. For Johnston Ridge, stay in Seaquest State Park or a motel near I-5 and SR 504, and then drive up to the monument for the day. For Windy Ridge, camp near Randle, just off of US Highway 12, or stay in a motel in Randle or Packwood. For the Ape Cave, lodge in the small town of Cougar or way back along I-5 in Woodland. Very little is close, but it is certainly worth the effort to explore this weird and wonderful world.

ON THE TRAIL

Once the center of a busy recreation area with six camps and lodges, Spirit Lake is now reached by just one trail. The 1980 eruption of Mount St. Helens transformed the lake into a sea of floating silver logs, and several viewpoints in the monument provide a vantage from above. But the lakeside view is something special. It seems right to see Mount St. Helens with a big, glistening lake in front of it.

Leave the road behind quickly, descending into a grove of greenery at the base of small north-facing cliffs. It provides shady relief even at midday, which will be welcome upon your return. Continue down 535 feet over 0.6 mile, passing a weeping wall and many varieties of flowers. The next 0.4 mile runs across a flat plain exposed to the sun and wind. It's an intimate immersion into how the 1980 blast rearranged the landscape. The lateral blast caused Spirit Lake to slosh more than 800 feet up the side of the mountain before you, creating a debris avalanche that stripped the mountainside clean and deposited the remains of up to a million trees into the lake.

Mount St. Helens makes its appearance rather suddenly. Round a corner, and there it rises, framed by a field of flowers. After a mile of walking, reach the

If you can find a place without logs, a dip in Spirit Lake is refreshing on a hot day.

final 100-foot, scenic descent to the lake. On the right, pass what's left of Harmony Falls, once an enticing destination, now reduced to a few riffles over red rock. Most of the original waterfall has been swallowed by Spirit Lake, which rose 200 feet after the blast.

At 1.2 miles (3440 feet), reach the shores of Spirit Lake. It's a mess of logs, so choose a safe resting spot that works for your family. You can clamber over the logs, but check to see if they move, and never step on a log that is in the lake. Now settle in, gaze at Mount St. Helens, and be quiet for a few moments. Here, all is silent but for the gentle lapping of water against logs and the silent stories told all around you of the massive disruption not that many years ago. Return the way you came.

77 WINDY RIDGE

BEFORE YOU GO
MAP Green Trails, Mt. St. Helens No. 332S
CONTACT Mount St. Helens National Volcanic Monument
NOTES Northwest Forest Pass required; dogs prohibited; privy available
GPS N 46 15.011, W 122 08.237

ABOUT THE HIKE
SEASON July to October
DIFFICULTY Easy to moderate
DISTANCE 0.6 to 1.6 miles roundtrip
HIGH POINT 4275 feet
ELEVATION GAIN 250 feet

GETTING THERE
From US Highway 12 in Randle, go south on State Route 131 for 2 miles, where-upon it turns into Forest Road 25. Continue on FR 25 for 17.8 miles and turn right on FR 99 for Windy Ridge. (From Cougar, drive east on Lewis River Road for 2.8 miles. It turns into FR 90. Drive FR 90 for 16 miles and bear left onto FR 25. Take FR 25 north to FR 99 and turn left.) Drive FR 99 16 miles to the end of the road at Windy Ridge. Note that many of these roads are closed seasonally.

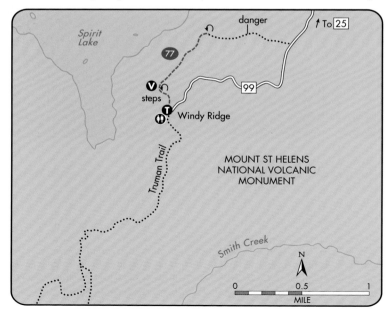

Hiking along Windy Ridge

ON THE TRAIL

Holy mackerel! After one of the most spectacular drives in the state, find yourself looking into the gaping maw of Mount St. Helens' enormous crater. Windy Ridge is as close as you can drive to the volcano, and most visitors are content to go no farther. But venture forth! There's much more to see, and there is no better way to understand the power of this volcanic eruption than by walking through the landscape it affected.

From the parking area, join the parade of visitors to the interpretive viewpoint. It's the ultimate stair climb. To ease the ascent, consider making a game of it by counting the number of steps. It's practically guaranteed that no two people will arrive at the same number, but it is somewhere around 440. Decades after Mount St. Helens erupted in 1980, it is humbling to witness how barren this landscape still is. There are clumps of flowers here and there, but only slopes that face away from the crater have any significant amount of green foliage. This stairway received the full brunt of the blast. Now it receives the full brunt of wind and sun.

Atop the ridge, at 0.3 mile (4275 feet), are comprehensive interpretive signs that describe intriguing facts and all of the weird geology on full display: Mount St. Helens' lava domes, Washington's youngest glacier, the pumice plain, hummocks, and the floating log mat on Spirit Lake. It's an impressive 360-degree view too, with even Mount Rainier visible to the north on a clear day. Note the astonishing number of floating logs in Spirit Lake. The blast sent a wave more than 800 feet high up the opposite ridge, which scoured the slope of up to a million trees that now drift on the surface. Be sure to gaze across the lake to the opposite slope. The Johnston Ridge Observatory is camouflaged among the rocks.

The trail continues beyond the viewpoint, but a scary warning sign dissuades hikers from proceeding. Indeed, there are sections where the trail drops suddenly, but you can easily stroll another 0.5 mile before encountering them. I like this section because the crowds disappear, the flowers bloom more profusely, and views of the lake become more expansive. When you reach the wall, it is time to turn around. The trail beyond is simply unsafe.

EXPLORING FURTHER
As an alternative or an add-on to your visit to Windy Ridge, consider hiking the Truman Trail from the opposite end of the parking area. The trail follows a road, open to bicycles, that rounds a ridge thick with alder, then opens up to ever-closer views of Mount St. Helens and fine looks at Mount Adams. This trail is less traveled than Windy Ridge and gains elevation gradually as it ascends 200 feet to a junction at 1.7 miles. Many hikers do a loop from here onto the otherworldly Plains of Abraham (8.8 miles, 1400 feet elevation gain), but you may find that this is as far as you need to go (for now).

78 TRAIL OF TWO FORESTS

BEFORE YOU GO
MAP Green Trails, Mount St. Helens No. 332S
CONTACT Mount St. Helens National Volcanic Monument
NOTES Northwest Forest Pass required; privy and picnic facilities available
GPS N 46 05.956, W 122 12.767

ABOUT THE HIKE
SEASON April to November
DIFFICULTY Easy
DISTANCE 0.25 mile loop
HIGH POINT 1950 feet
ELEVATION GAIN 10 feet

GETTING THERE

From Interstate 5 in Woodland, take exit 21 and follow State Route 503 east approximately 29 miles to Cougar. Continue on SR 503 (it becomes Forest Road 90 when you enter Skamania County) for 7 miles. Turn left on FR 83 and drive 1.7 miles to FR 8303. Turn left again and find the trailhead parking lot in 0.2 mile on the left.

ON THE TRAIL

It may be the shortest hike in this book, but do not skip the Trail of Two Forests in your haste to get to Ape Cave! On this short circuit, hikers are oriented to a weird and wonderful landscape transformed by Washington's most active

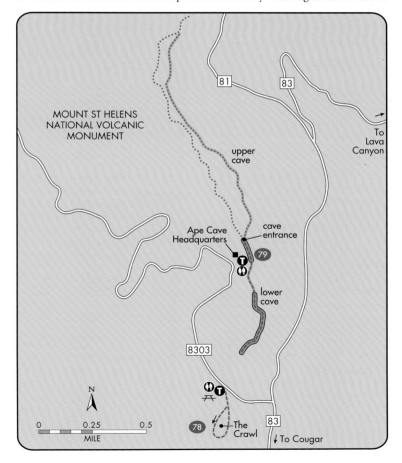

Climbing through the tree cast—a headlamp helps (photo by Jon Stier)

volcano, including an invitation to crawl on hands and knees through a tunnel shaped two thousand years ago by lava.

By walking the boardwalk trail in a counterclockwise direction you will detect immediately that this is no ordinary forest. Otherworldly round pits, some 8 to 10 feet deep, pock the forest floor. These are tree-casts formed when a river of lava engulfed the forest, creating a logjam of toppled trees and a pool of lava behind the dam. When the lava cooled, it left behind the three-dimensional impressions that you see today.

With the ancient forest frozen in time, a new forest has emerged. Moss, one of the first plants to recolonize the area, dominates the understory in a cloak of primeval green. Mighty Douglas fir and western red cedar have sprung from the basalt. Woodland wildflowers bloom in springtime. Life marches on in this volcanic environment.

On the far side of the loop is The Crawl, a 50-foot cast that hikers can crawl through. This isn't for everybody. My kids loved it—they went through three times each—but another five-year-old screamed and cried as her father urged her forward. It's a small, enclosed place—and dark. It helps to have a headlamp. It also helps to be small; adults may find their knees take a beating on the cold stone. But if you're not too claustrophobic, it is worth it to run your fingers over the impressions from the ancient tree bark. The experience makes you realize that some things haven't changed all that much in two thousand years.

79 APE CAVE

BEFORE YOU GO
MAP Green Trails, Mount St. Helens No. 332S
CONTACT Mount St. Helens National Volcanic Monument
NOTES Northwest Forest Pass required; dogs prohibited; privy available;
flashlights and coats necessary; lantern rental in summer
GPS N 46 06.503, W 122 12.692

ABOUT THE HIKE
SEASON May to November
DIFFICULTY Moderate
DISTANCE 1.5 miles roundtrip
HIGH POINT 2080 feet
ELEVATION GAIN 100 feet

GETTING THERE
From Interstate 5 in Woodland, take exit 21 and follow State Route 503 east approximately 29 miles to Cougar. Continue on SR 503 (it becomes Forest Road 90 when you enter Skamania County) for 7 miles. Turn left on FR 83 and drive 1.7 miles to FR 8303. Turn left again and find the trailhead parking lot in 0.9 mile on the right.

ON THE TRAIL
Grab a jacket, a flashlight, and some good shoes—let's go spelunking! How cool is this place? My kids must have said it was "very cool," "awesome," and "amazing" thirty times as we explored the lower lava tube. And, yes, it is chilly here too—a pretty constant 42°F year-round.

Exploring the Ape Cave should be on every family's bucket list. There simply is nothing else like it. At 13,042 feet long, Ape Cave is the longest continuous lava tube in the country, and the third longest in North America. It was created more than two thousand years ago when fluid lava coursed and surged down the south side of Mount St. Helens. Chunks on the surface hardened, but a river of molten lava continued to flow underneath for perhaps a year or more, carving out the tube you see today. A later event sent a mudflow through the main cave entrance and down the lower tube, scouring the cave of debris.

There are two routes through the Ape Cave, and unlike The Crawl on the Trail of Two Forests, in both routes you can walk upright! The lower route is 1.5 miles roundtrip through a surprisingly spacious chamber. There are a few steps to maneuver and the walking surface is uneven, but it is a pretty easy walk. The upper route is 3 miles roundtrip through the tube and an outside trail and is much more difficult; cavers must climb over twenty-seven boulder piles and scale an 8-foot lava wall. Older kids will undoubtedly want to do the upper cave, but families with younger children should start with the lower tube described here.

Hikers illuminate the "Meatball." (photo by Jon Stier)

Before leaving your vehicle, make sure you have everything you need to be safe and comfortable. Everyone should have their own light source—a headlamp or flashlight—plus extra batteries. In summer, you can rent large lanterns at the Forest Service's Ape Cave Headquarters, but personal flashlights are better. It's cold in the cave, so all hikers should don a fleece jacket or sweater. You may even want to bring along stocking caps and gloves. The final consideration is footwear. The cave can be done in tennis shoes, but the surface is uneven and hard. Your feet (and shoes) will hold up better with sturdy soles. Bring water, but leave behind food (you are not allowed to eat in the cave). Dogs are not allowed either.

Now that you are ready, proceed up the paved trail 500 feet to the cave entrance. Before plunging below the earth's surface, take time to read the information panels about how the cave was formed. Walk down two sets of stairs until you are on the floor of the lava tube. Those exploring the upper cave will go under the metal stairs and up the tube; for the lower tube, continue straight, going gently downhill.

You'll discover quickly that it is dark, damp, and a little musty in the cave. Despite this, I never felt claustrophobic. That's because it is simply so immense. There are places large enough for a freight train to rumble through. In fact, the "railroad tracks" are one of the primary features of the Lower Ape Cave: in one segment, which kids will identify immediately, the floor of the tube is raised like railroad tracks. The other fun feature is the "Meatball," a chunk of rock that dislodged from the ceiling and wedged in a narrow spot as lava flowed by.

As you explore, find a place where there are no other people and turn off your lights for one minute to experience total darkness. It's interesting to find out which family member wants to flick his or her light back on first. Three-quarters of a mile down the tube, it narrows and dead-ends. Despite the chill, you'll find that you will work harder on your return and may even break a sweat. When you return to the mouth of the cave, duck just beyond the metal stairway to the "Big Room," which is . . . big!

Finally, about the name "Ape Cave." No, it's not named after Bigfoot. It's named after a Boy Scout Troop called the Mount St. Helens Apes that extensively explored the cave in 1952 after it was discovered by a logger a few years earlier. They, and others, uncovered no evidence that it had been used in the past by humans (or apes).

80 LAVA CANYON

BEFORE YOU GO
MAP Green Trails, Mount St. Helens No. 332S
CONTACT Mount St. Helens National Volcanic Monument
NOTES Northwest Forest Pass required; dogs not recommended; privy available; stay on trail for safety
GPS N 46 09.942, W 122 05.311

ABOUT THE HIKE
SEASON May to November
DIFFICULTY Moderate
DISTANCE 1.4 miles roundtrip
HIGH POINT 2860 feet
ELEVATION GAIN 275 feet

GETTING THERE
From Interstate 5 in Woodland, take exit 21 and follow State Route 503 east approximately 29 miles to Cougar. Continue on SR 503 (it becomes Forest Road 90 when you enter Skamania County) for 7 miles. Turn left on FR 83 and drive 11.5 miles to road's end.

ON THE TRAIL
Hike through a steep-walled slickrock canyon that was scoured clear by a massive lahar during Mount St. Helens' eruption in 1980. The river serpentines like a whitewater theme park ride, tumbling over waterfalls on its path down the Muddy River. The water pools invitingly, but this is no theme park ride. There have been five fatal accidents on this trail, and four have involved fathers

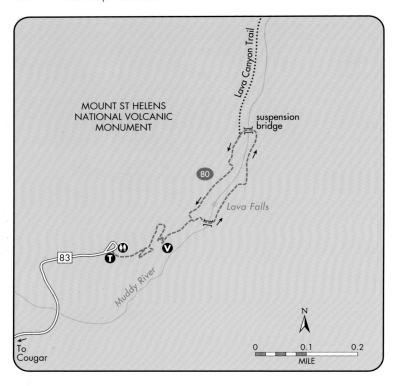

jumping into the river in pursuit of their kids. Lava Canyon is a magical place to visit, but please heed the signs and keep your family on the trail where they will be safe.

The hike begins on a barrier-free, but steep, paved trail that leads to an overlook of Lava Falls. As you walk, imagine the scene in May 1980 when 30 feet of ice from Mount St. Helens' Shoestring Glacier, combined with ash, rock, and pumice, raced down this canyon, consuming trees and vegetation in a 15-foot wave of muck. Across the Muddy River the "scour line" is clearly visible between tall conifers and shorter deciduous trees. Although devastating, the eruption did one thing right: it exposed the unique and hidden lava canyon that you are exploring.

At 0.4 mile, having lost 225 feet in elevation, reach an intersection. Go right, crossing the Muddy River on a sturdy metal bridge. You may see others dipping toes in the water and climbing over the rocks. Don't do it! The current is swift, and Lava Falls is just downstream. Instead, enjoy the cerulean-blue

Opposite: A high suspension bridge crosses the Muddy River.

tint of the water and the captivating way the ancient lava canyon twists and turns. The cliffs are fascinating as well, with rugged basalt columns that look like natural stairs.

The highlight of the hike is a 125-foot-high suspension bridge that takes hikers back across the river at 0.7 mile. It's bouncy and a tad bit scary, but high railings and fencing on both sides keep everyone safe. If you dare, linger in the middle and notice how fast the river plunges through this narrow gorge.

On the other side of the bridge, a trail leads to the right. This is an extremely difficult route that involves descending a 40-foot ladder and considerable exposure, and it is not recommended for children or those who aren't sure-footed. Instead, follow the main trail straight and begin ascending. You'll get a peek at the 132-foot Lava Falls before you join up with the paved trail for your return.

Opposite: *Summer physics workshop: rock stacking*

EAST SLOPE CASCADES

NORTH CASCADES HIGHWAY

81 RAINY LAKE

BEFORE YOU GO
MAP Green Trails, Washington Pass No. 50
CONTACT Okanogan–Wenatchee National Forest
NOTES Northwest Forest Pass required; privy available
GPS N 48 30.909, W 120 44.144

ABOUT THE HIKE
SEASON June to October
DIFFICULTY Easy
DISTANCE 1.8 miles roundtrip
HIGH POINT 4875 feet
ELEVATION GAIN 10 feet

GETTING THERE
From Marblemount, follow State Route 20 east for 52 miles to Rainy Pass. A large parking lot is on the right.

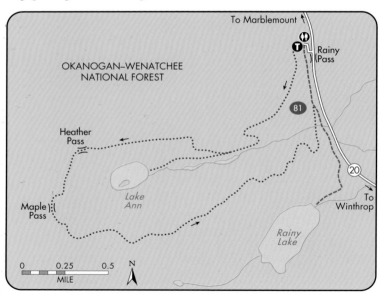

ON THE TRAIL

Here's a North Cascades hike with a photo-worthy destination that everyone can do! The trail is paved and level, with interpretive signs sprinkled throughout, and a jade-green lake twinkles in a rocky cirque at the end of the short trail. Its easily attained beauty is an exception to the rule that you must work hard to reap such a reward.

From the trailhead, head left on the paved trail, an ideal place for toddlers to try out their hiking feet. Because it is maintained by the Forest Service for wheelchair accessibility, there should be nothing on this path for them to trip over. The trail parallels the highway for 0.75 mile, and the occasional whir of vehicles is the price you pay for such a level hike. Interpretive signs identify trees like Engelmann spruce and Pacific silver fir. Our favorite sign describes a phenomenon called "pistol butt," where the pressure of snow moving downhill bends the trunks of young trees.

At 0.4 mile, pass a side trail to Maple Pass (more on this shortly), and at 0.75 mile curve away from road. Follow the sound of water for a few hundred more yards to a patio with two benches at Rainy Lake. The color and clarity of the lake is striking. You may even be able to spot fish. High, impassable cliffs surround the lake, and in June and July two distinct waterfalls pour loudly down the far side. If it is busy, a side trail leads beyond the patio to a couple of other vantages. When you are ready, retrace your steps to the parking area.

Jade-green water of Rainy Lake (photo by Jon Stier)

GREAT GETAWAY: METHOW VALLEY

Clomp the wooden boardwalks of Winthrop and imagine you are in an old-time western movie. The Old West charm isn't exactly authentic, but it is fun. The Methow Valley, from Twisp to Mazama, is a four-season destination that delights outdoor enthusiasts of all ages. It's one of those places where you can mix up hiking with many other activities to keep the kids happy. In addition to hiking, you can bike, horseback ride, fish, boat, swim, raft, and even balloon. And that's not even what the place is most famous for: in the winter, the Methow Valley transforms into a world-class cross-country ski destination.

There are ample lodging options and more than a dozen campgrounds to choose from. Some of the fanciest hotels and cabins book early, but I've found that I can usually snag a room on short notice in the summer. Campgrounds within state parks can be reserved, but Forest Service campgrounds are on a first-come, first-served basis. Some are fairly primitive and require you to bring your own water. Our family likes to begin with a few days of camping and then clean up in town with a night at a motel and a big ice-cream cone.

EXPLORING FURTHER

One of the premier hikes in the state, the Maple Pass Loop, leaves from the same trailhead. This 7.2-mile (2000 feet gain) trail is not to be missed in your lifetime. It traverses alpine meadows and ridges, with glorious shows of wildflowers and spectacular fall color, first ascending Heather Pass and then Maple Pass in a counterclockwise direction before dropping steeply to the Rainy Lake Trail. If that is too much to bite off with the kids, an easier alternative is Lake Ann, a 4-mile (600 feet gain) hike through forest and avalanche chutes to a shimmery alpine lake below Heather and Maple passes. This hike branches off from the Maple Pass Loop. If you do go to Lake Ann, make sure to bring bug spray; the mosquitoes are voracious.

82 BLUE LAKE (EAST)

BEFORE YOU GO
> **MAP** Green Trails, Washington Pass No. 50
> **CONTACT** Okanogan–Wenatchee National Forest
> **NOTES** Northwest Forest Pass required; privy available
> **GPS** N 48 31.132, W 120 40.456

ABOUT THE HIKE
> **SEASON** July to October
> **DIFFICULTY** Moderate to difficult
> **DISTANCE** 4.6 miles roundtrip
> **HIGH POINT** 6300 feet
> **ELEVATION GAIN** 900 feet

Peaceful Blue Lake

GETTING THERE
From Marblemount, follow State Route 20 east for 52 miles to Rainy Pass. Drive an additional 3 miles east to the signed parking area on the right.

ON THE TRAIL
Blue Lake—one of six lakes of the same name in Washington, and two in this book—boasts wildflowers in summer, golden larches in fall, and a healthy dose of alpine elixir. You have to work a bit to reach its boulder-strewn shore, but the trail is never too steep—just a steady grade through forests and rocky view-sheds on a well-maintained trail. The clear alpine water reflects Early Winters Spires in the afternoon, and you may even see a mountain goat making its way across its steep flanks.

The trail begins on a series of boardwalks, paralleling the highway on flat terrain for the first five to ten minutes. It then climbs slowly but steadily in woods until the trail emerges nearly a mile later in a sunny avalanche chute with a full-on view of distinctive Liberty Bell Mountain. In the summer, colorful displays of flowers are a treat. In the autumn, enjoy larches gleaming like electric lights on the mountain and the deep red foliage of huckleberry.

Continue on, gaining 400 feet over the next mile. Traverse another avalanche chute at 1.8 miles (6075 feet), after which the trail levels out a bit, with excellent views north to Whistler Mountain and Cutthroat Peak. Round the mountain and enter a delightful alpine wonderland of rocks, flowers, and a babbling brook—the outlet for Blue Lake. Once you skirt by a dilapidated cabin, find yourself at the edge of Blue Lake. Its teal waters are so clear that you can easily see fish swimming and jumping.

A big boulder above the lake makes a perfect location for lunch. When we visited, our neighbors kept talking about mountain goats, and when we turned

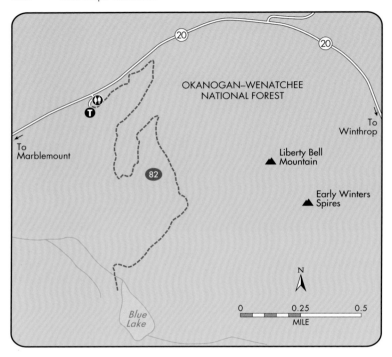

around, there was a billy goat standing sentinel on a rock high above the lake. My son had never seen one in the wild and was delighted by his brush with big wildlife. We made sure to keep our distance and hold our pee (goats are attracted to the salt in urine) until we had left the lake basin, returning the way we came.

83 CUTTHROAT LAKE

BEFORE YOU GO
MAP Green Trails, Washington Pass No. 50
CONTACT Okanogan–Wenatchee National Forest
NOTES Northwest Forest Pass required; privy available; watch for mountain bikes
GPS N 48 33.379, W 120 39.278

ABOUT THE HIKE
SEASON Late June to October
DIFFICULTY Moderate
DISTANCE 4 miles roundtrip
HIGH POINT 4950 feet
ELEVATION GAIN 500 feet

GETTING THERE

From Interstate 5, follow State Route 20 east across the North Cascades for 97 miles to Washington Pass. Descend the pass and after the hairpin turn look for Forest Road 400 on the left near milepost 167. Turn left and drive a short mile to the trailhead. (From Mazama, drive SR 20 west for 12.5 miles, turning right on FR 400.)

ON THE TRAIL

Ringed with flowering heather in the early summer and studded with golden larches in the fall, Cutthroat Lake is one of the most picturesque in the North Cascades, and optimally suited for children. The 2-mile trail gains elevation gradually, providing ample opportunity for berrypicking in August and sneak peeks to Cutthroat Creek and the mountains beyond. And then there is the lake basin, lovely as can be, wrapped in marshy grass and surrounded by an arc of mountains. The lake is also known for its good fishing and can be a refreshing place to cool off on a hot day.

Begin on the wide gravel path near the horse corral and cross Cutthroat Creek on a sturdy iron bridge. Anticipate encounters with horses and mountain bikes on this popular trail, stepping to the downhill side, if possible, to let them pass. As you climb gradually up the valley, notice trees not normally found on the western slope of the Cascades, including noble fir, subalpine fir, whitebark pine, western white pine, and western larch. Many are the size of Christmas trees, and the larches turn bright yellow in October before dropping all of their needles.

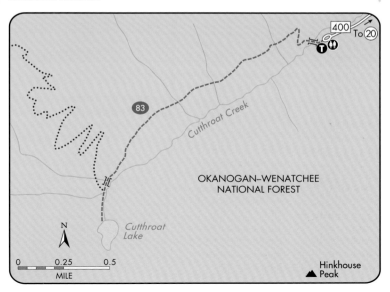

Cutthroat Lake sits in a dramatic cirque. (Aidan Stier)

At 1.7 miles, veer left at the fork in the trail. There are two somewhat precarious creek crossings before reaching the lake. The first is a single log stringer with no rails. The second is another single log, but this one is tilted. You may find it safer to hop across the creek on stones. Be careful where you step, however, as the meadow area has suffered from overuse.

The lake is a beauty, especially in fall when golden larches dot the mountainside. The pointy peak to the right is Cutthroat Peak; the massive mountain to the left is Hinkhouse Peak. If the water levels are low enough, the best place to sit is on the big boulders around the lake to the left. Swimmers should be prepared with water shoes. The bottom looks muddy, but sharp sticks lurk just beneath the muck. And even though this looks like an ideal place to camp, the Forest Service does not allow overnight use within a half mile of the lake. So when you're done with your daytime visit, return—however reluctantly—the way you came.

LAKE WENATCHEE– LEAVENWORTH–LAKE CHELAN

84 HIDDEN LAKE

BEFORE YOU GO
MAP Green Trails, Wenatchee Lake No. 145
CONTACT Okanogan–Wenatchee National Forest
NOTES Northwest Forest Pass required; privy and picnic tables available
GPS N 47 49.318, W 120 48.224

ABOUT THE HIKE
SEASON May to mid-November
DIFFICULTY Easy
DISTANCE 1.6 miles roundtrip
HIGH POINT 2275 feet
ELEVATION GAIN 175 feet

GETTING THERE

From Everett, travel 84 miles east on US Highway 2 to Coles Corner and State Route 207. (From Leavenworth, travel 15 miles west.) Turn left (north) on SR 207, drive 3.5 miles, and turn left on Cedar Brae Road (also signed "Lake Wenatchee State Park south entrance"). Follow Cedar Brae Road by taking an immediate left, away from the state park, along the south shore of Lake Wenatchee. The pavement ends after 3.7 miles, and the road becomes Forest Road 6750. Bear left in 0.4 mile and then turn left into the Hidden Lake trailhead after another 0.5 mile.

ON THE TRAIL

While camping at bustling Lake Wenatchee, don't miss this easy jaunt to a sweet mountain lake. It's the most family-friendly trail in the vicinity, perfect for a few hours' diversion from water sports, swimming, and campfires at the nearby state park.

Begin on the wide trail by the picnic table and enter a dense stand of cedars, firs, and hemlocks. There are several interesting things to observe as you walk through the forest. First, look for two cedar snags, hollowed out and blackened by a long-ago fire. Then inspect some of the other nearby snags. Crow-sized pileated woodpeckers have been busy excavating many enormous holes in search of beetles and bugs. Now gaze upward. Notice how many of the trees have been snapped in their mid- to upper reaches? A fierce, and localized, ice storm blew through the Lake Wenatchee area in December 2012, wreaking havoc on the trees. But despite fire, wind, bugs, and ice, this forest stands strong.

Checking out the work of woodpeckers

The trail is winding and gently sloped—a hardy two-year-old can make it on foot. At one point, the tree cover opens up, revealing Lake Wenatchee and humorously named Dirtyface Peak. In just 0.8 mile, top out at Hidden Lake (2275 feet). The best place to enjoy the lake is to the right, which requires carefully crossing the outlet stream on two old logs. Come to a well-used resting

GREAT GETAWAY: LEAVENWORTH

Where can you swim in a mountain lake, play miniature golf, eat a big juicy bratwurst, and sip a cup of hot cocoa at your creekside campsite—all in the same day? Right around Leavenworth! That's why it's my daughter's favorite place to go. She loves the variety, and if I let her play a round of mini golf, I have a much better chance of mushing her up the trail.

You can also float the Wenatchee River in an inner tube, ride horses, and sled, ski, or snowshoe the nearby slopes. Over the past fifty years, Leavenworth has intentionally positioned itself as an outdoor gateway community that has something for everyone. Some people zoom right through the Bavarian-themed town to hike in the lofty Enchantments, while others linger for the shopping and golf. Lodging choices abound, but none are cheap. The camping, however, is superlative, with a number of campgrounds located along the Icicle Creek Road and around nearby Lake Wenatchee.

spot under stately ponderosa pines. There are good stones and logs to relax on while the kids throw rocks or swim in the green-hued lake. More secluded resting spots can be found by following the social paths to the end of the lake. Note that mosquitoes can be particularly ferocious in early summer, so come prepared. Return as you came.

EXPLORING FURTHER

Continue the adventure by making your hike into a 2.5-mile loop. Directly behind the main resting area is the original trail to Hidden Lake. It drops into the forest and leads steeply to Glacier View Campground, 350 feet below. To return to your car, follow the gravel forest road uphill 0.7 mile back to the trailhead.

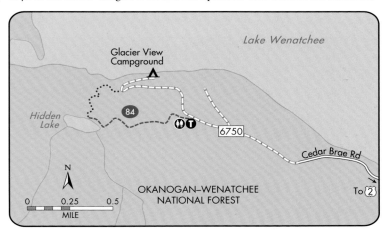

85 EIGHTMILE LAKE

BEFORE YOU GO
MAP Green Trails, Alpine Lakes East–Stuart Range No. 208SX
CONTACT Okanogan–Wenatchee National Forest
NOTES Northwest Forest Pass required; free wilderness day-use permit required
at trailhead; Enchantments Permit required for overnight visits; dogs prohibited;
privy available
GPS N 47 32.149, W 120 48.820

ABOUT THE HIKE
SEASON June to October
DIFFICULTY Difficult
DISTANCE 6.4 miles roundtrip
HIGH POINT 4650 feet
ELEVATION GAIN 1350 feet

GETTING THERE
From US Highway 2 on the west end of Leavenworth, take Icicle Creek Road
(Forest Road 76) 8.4 miles to Eightmile Road (FR 7601). Go left on FR 7601,
passing the Bridge Creek Campground, and travel 3 miles on washboard gravel
to the parking area opposite the trailhead on the left.

ON THE TRAIL
Eightmile Lake may be the hardest hike in the book, but it is the easiest trail
in the popular Enchantment Lakes Permit Area. Aside from its destination
lake, the hike is a living lesson in fire ecology. The trail burned in a massive
1994 wildfire, and then again in 2012. The entire area has been transformed
by these fires, and it is both fascinating and humbling to walk among the
charred remains. But fear not! This is no moonscape. The resilient landscape is

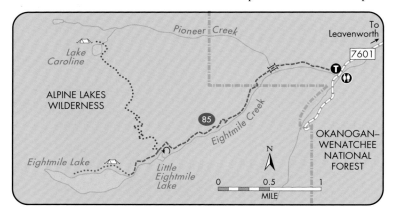

Eightmile Lake is the easiest lake to reach in the Enchantments zone.

bouncing back quickly, filling in with brilliant fireweed, plentiful thimbleberries, and fast-growing alder.

Because the trail is so exposed to the sun, get an early start, bring ample water, and apply sunscreen. It can get beastly hot in the summer. Find the trailhead opposite the parking area and begin ascending fairly steeply. Distract yourself with the views of regal Mount Stuart and swiftly moving Eightmile Creek. It won't take long to discover crispy, blackened ponderosa pines dotting the landscape.

After the initial climb, the trail's ascent becomes more gradual. Thimbleberries may encroach on the trail, but they are a tasty treat in midsummer. I credit them with getting my six-year-old to the lake, but also for slowing us to a near crawl. At 0.8 mile, cross Pioneer Creek on two log stringers, and at 1.2 miles pass into the Alpine Lakes Wilderness. The fire burned particularly hot here. The charred skeletal remains of once tall trees are so black they are almost blue. Their strange, ghostly shapes are particularly startling next to giant purple fireweed.

At 2.6 miles, top out at Little Eightmile Lake (4400 feet). A gracious and enormous Douglas fir welcomes you to sit under its shady lakeside branches. Somehow this beauty was spared the flames. Little Eightmile is pleasant, albeit a bit buggy. It's more of a pond than a lake, but it is a good spot to pull out the binoculars and check out the birds that call it home. Many families call it a day here. However, it is quite worth the extra effort to push the final half mile up to big Eightmile Lake. The terrain shifts, climbing through rusty-colored boulders that have tumbled off nearby Eightmile Mountain, and the trail nears the creek as it makes a final push to the lake at 3.2 miles (4650 feet).

Settle in and enjoy the view of Jack Ridge and the reflections of the mountains in still water. Strip off hiking shoes and socks and soak hot toes in the cold water. Older kids may want to fully jump in, and there are several good swimming spots to be found near backcountry campsites. During your exploration you may discover an old, partially collapsed stone dam that was used for irrigation in the Wenatchee Valley. It's a salient reminder that this wilderness isn't all that wild after all. When you are ready, return the way you came.

86 ICICLE GORGE

BEFORE YOU GO
MAP Green Trails, Alpine Lakes East–Stuart Range No. 208SX
CONTACT Okanogan–Wenatchee National Forest
NOTES Northwest Forest Pass required; privy available; this trail can be scaled for younger hikers
GPS N 47 36.525, W 120 53.572

ABOUT THE HIKE
SEASON May to October
DIFFICULTY Moderate
DISTANCE 4.4 miles loop
HIGH POINT 2775 feet
ELEVATION GAIN 200 feet

GETTING THERE
From US Highway 2 on the west end of Leavenworth, take Icicle Creek Road (Forest Road 76) 15.4 miles to the Icicle Gorge trailhead on the left. The final 3 miles are on good gravel. The parking lot is large enough for trailers to turn around in and park.

ON THE TRAIL
In a region known for its verticality, the Icicle Gorge Trail offers a gentle—and scalable—hike for the whole family. Its proximity to several excellent campgrounds and the town of Leavenworth make it an ideal three-season destination. Spring and early summer surprise with wildflowers and the remnants of snow and ice; summer brings cool breezes on warm days; and autumn delights with mushrooms and brilliant fall color. Icicle Creek is a nearly constant companion whether you decide to hike it to the overlook and back (1.6 miles), one-way to the Rock Island Campground (2.9 miles), or as a loop (4.4 miles).

Icicle Creek's name comes from the Native American term *nasikelt*, meaning "steep canyon or gorge." When white settlers arrived in the early 1900s, they mistook its pronunciation for "icicle" and recorded it that way on maps. While hiking the trail, my daughter and I had a long conversation about how they ever could have declared this a creek and not a river. It is simply so powerful and has such a great volume—fed by many mountain streams—that it feels much more like a river than a creek.

Taking a break along Icicle Creek (photo by Eugene Lee)

Start your hike near the privy and walk a short distance to the loop trail. You can walk either way, but I recommend following it downstream to the left. You'll descend gradually through forest, with an occasional interpretive sign, until you reach a sturdy bridge with high railings at 0.6 mile. Pause to observe the creek here. In spring and early summer, it is a frothy powerhouse as the water is funneled between the narrow gorge walls. In summer, as the flow decreases, white water rings become visible in smooth circular potholes where the water pools briefly before continuing downstream.

Cross the bridge and now follow Icicle Creek upstream where iron railings protect hikers from missteps. In less than a quarter mile, reach an overlook of Icicle Creek. The impressive stone masonry wall is an excellent place to pull out some snacks or lunch before either turning around or continuing on the loop.

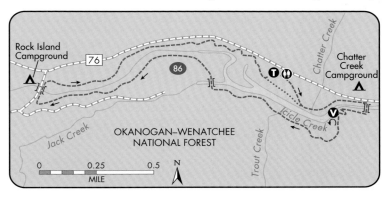

The trail pulls away from the river, meandering through a lush cedar swamp, past thimbleberries and huckleberries and across feeder creeks before rejoining Icicle Creek at 2 miles. Look for ways to keep the kids interested—admiring the big trees, tasting berries, and tossing sticks off the bridge on one side and racing to see where they go. At 2.9 miles, reach the Rock Island Campground. If you've parked a car here, your trip is done. If you're doing the loop, cross the bridge on the road and look for the Icicle Gorge Trail sign on the other side. In the summertime, you may want to follow the campers to the river where there is a swimming hole.

The north side of Icicle Creek has a different feel. See if the kids notice the change in the forest and understory. And cautiously take their hand on one of the many social trails to peer over the cliff to Icicle Creek before returning to the trailhead.

87 HORAN NATURAL AREA

BEFORE YOU GO
MAP Green Trails, Wenatchee/Mission Ridge No. 211S
CONTACT Washington State Parks
NOTES Discover Pass required; restrooms and water available within the campground, privy along the trail; wildlife closure December 1 to March 1
GPS N 47 27.616, W 120 19.823

ABOUT THE HIKE
SEASON March to November
DIFFICULTY Easy
DISTANCE 1.8 miles roundtrip
HIGH POINT 650 feet
ELEVATION GAIN None

GETTING THERE
From the west, follow US Highway 2 east toward Wenatchee. Where US 2 meets State Route 285, remain on US 2 as it makes a loop. At the first stoplight, turn right on Easy Street (signed for Wenatchee Confluence State Park). At the next stoplight, turn left on Penny Road and then take an immediate right onto Chester Kimm Road. At the T-intersection, turn left on Olds Station Road. After the railroad tracks, turn right on the access road into Wenatchee Confluence State Park. Park in the lot just outside the campground gate.

ON THE TRAIL
On the bustling industrial edge of Wenatchee lies a wildlife-rich oasis at the confluence of the Wenatchee and Columbia rivers. A former orchard and cattle pasture, the Horan Natural Area was transformed into a wetland estuary in the 1990s. Today, a level gravel path loops through cattails and cottonwoods, allowing hikers to walk within the preserve from March through November.

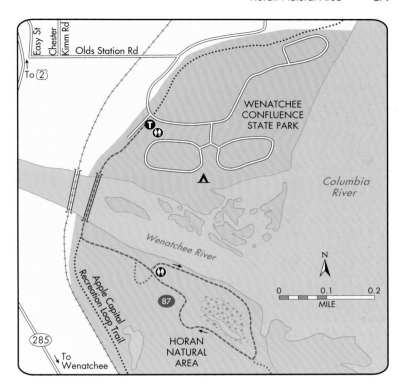

Wenatchee Confluence State Park, where the natural area is located, is a study in contrasts. On the north side of the Wenatchee River, a manicured campground attracts visitors year-round with green lawns, RV hookups, playgrounds, tennis courts, and a roped-off swimming area. On the south side of the river is the Horan Natural Area, managed for its wildlife habitat. Many families find this a winning combination: take a hike, play at the park.

Begin your visit at the parking area just outside the campground gate. Follow the paved Apple Capital Recreation Loop Trail to the right toward the Wenatchee River and a nifty concrete bridge with light blue railings. This is the Wenatchee River's last stretch before emptying into the capacious Columbia. From the bridge you can see where the two rivers intersect. I expected them to crash together, but instead the Columbia simply swallows its tributary.

Arrive at a kiosk full of information about the area wetlands and wildlife and proceed through the wooden gate onto the wide, flat gravel path. This is an interpretive trail with fifteen signs describing wildlife and plants that thrive here. Most of the signs are located at little bump-outs with benches. At an

In October, Horan Natural Area begins to explode in fall color.

intersection near the privy, take the trail to the left and walk beneath a grove of stately mature cottonwood. Peer through the bushes to the backwater river channel to discover wood ducks, painted turtles, river otters, and muskrats. Listen for the melody of birdsong; more than 230 species have been spotted in the park. Keep your eyes peeled for mule deer grazing in the grass. The quieter your party, the more likely you will see wildlife.

At the 1-mile mark, reach a junction. The trail continues straight another 0.3 mile to a gate at the paved bike trail. There is nothing new to experience in that short stretch. Instead, curve back around to the right on the other side of the wetlands. In spring and summer, red-winged blackbirds bob on cattails and frogs croak from the ponds. Look to the tops of the cottonwoods for bald eagles and osprey scoping their next meal. Soon enough, reach the gate and the bridge back to the campground for a sweet roundtrip of 1.8 miles.

EXPLORING FURTHER

Did you bring bikes? If so, try out the Apple Capital Recreation Loop Trail. The 10-mile paved path links a series of urban riverside parks on the west side of the Columbia River, then crosses the river and runs through wilder country on the east side. The Apple Capital Trail is also fun to cross-country ski or snow-shoe in winter months.

88 LITTLE BEAR

BEFORE YOU GO
    MAP Available online
    CONTACT Washington State Parks
    NOTES Discover Pass required; restrooms available
    GPS N 47 52.328, W 120 11.851

ABOUT THE HIKE
    SEASON March to October
    DIFFICULTY Easy to moderate
    DISTANCE 2.6 miles loop
    HIGH POINT 1380 feet
    ELEVATION GAIN 220 feet

GETTING THERE

From Chelan, drive on US Highway 97-Alt south (along the lake) approximately 3 miles to the three-way intersection with S Lakeshore Road (State Route 971). Veer right on S Lakeshore Road, driving 6 miles to Lake Chelan State Park on the right. (From US 2 in Wenatchee, exit at Euclid Avenue/US 97-Alt north and turn left. This road becomes US 97-Alt. Go 23 miles and turn right on SR 971. Drive 9 miles to S Lakeshore Road. Turn right and immediately left into Lake Chelan State Park.) Pass through the park entrance and ask the ranger to direct you to the Little Bear Trail across from campsite #10.

ON THE TRAIL

Fifty miles long, Lake Chelan is by far the largest and longest lake in Washington. The best hiking is in and around Stehekin, a small community at the northern end of the lake, reachable only by boat, foot, and float plane. Far more people, however, visit the southern end near the town of Chelan, where boating and camping reign supreme. You can break up the water play with a family-friendly hike in Lake Chelan State Park, where two circuits—a short interpretive loop and a longer scenic loop—lead from the campground.

Visit Little Bear in springtime for flowering lupine. (photo by Aidan Stier)

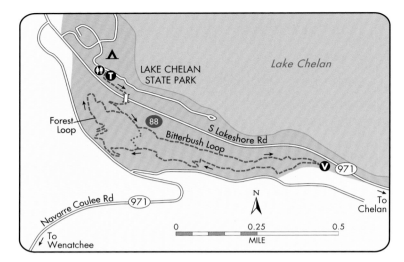

Begin your hike to the left of the restrooms. Duck into the woods, going through tree tunnels and a real underground tunnel beneath South Lakeshore Road on an interpretive journey that follows a small bear's imaginary adventures through the forest. At 0.3 mile reach a junction marked by a big wooden map. Choose your route. The interpretive trail goes to the right 0.9 mile on the Forest Loop. The longer Bitterbush Loop lies straight ahead. This 2-mile trail can be combined with the Forest Loop, leading to good views of the lake. It is an especially attractive option in the spring, when the hillside dances with lupine and balsamroot, and is the route I recommend.

Proceeding straight, ignore the next junction, and emerge out of the forest onto an open savannah of ponderosa pine, bitterbush, grasses, and balsamroot. A bench at 0.9 mile (1240 feet) provides a nice vantage to contemplate the lake and play with enormous ponderosa pinecones. Notice the semiarid golden hillsides dotted with trees, and the farms and houses on the other side of the lake.

Beyond the bench, the trail doubles back and reenters the trees. At 1.6 miles, rejoin the interpretive trail on the Forest Loop and begin to climb. The pines are impressive in here—ramrod straight with puzzle-like bark. Some are more than two hundred years old! After reaching a high point of 1380 feet, descend, crossing a stream and a meadow. Reenter the tunnel-like vegetation and finally reach the original junction at 2.3 miles. Go left, retracing yours steps to the campground.

EXPLORING FURTHER

If you're not camping at Lake Chelan State Park, plan some time to play here after your hike. There are playfields, a playground, and a beach for swimming.

TEANAWAY AND BLEWETT PASS

89 SWAUK FOREST DISCOVERY TRAIL

BEFORE YOU GO
MAP Green Trails, Wenatchee/Mission Ridge No. 211S
CONTACT Okanogan–Wenatchee National Forest
NOTES Northwest Forest Pass required; privy available; hike can be scaled for younger hikers
GPS N 47 19.915, W 120 34.728

ABOUT THE HIKE
SEASON June to October
DIFFICULTY Moderate
DISTANCE 2.7 miles loop
HIGH POINT 4525 feet
ELEVATION GAIN 275 feet

GETTING THERE
From Cle Elum, follow State Route 970 east for 10 miles until it merges with US Highway 97. On US 97, drive north an additional 14 miles to the top of Blewett Pass. Turn right on Forest Road 9716, and in 0.4 mile look for the large

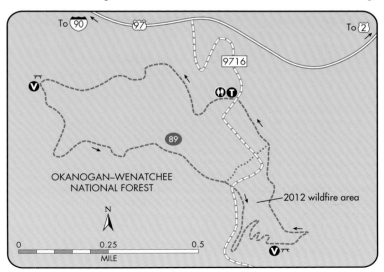

Golden larches dot the slopes of Diamond Head.

trailhead parking area on the right. (From the junction of US 2 and US 97 west of Wenatchee, follow US 97 south, 21 miles to Blewett Pass, and turn left on FR 9716.)

ON THE TRAIL

Swauk Forest Discovery Trail is a delightful, easy-to-reach hike that's educational too. It's a scenic interpretive loop, with two levels of instruction on forest ecology and management practices—the first, a twenty-five-stop route geared to teenagers and adults using an illustrative brochure; the second, a family-friendly route with signs that help identify trees typical of this environment. This is a great hike to learn how to tell the difference between a grand fir and a Douglas fir or a ponderosa pine and a western white pine.

The hike can be scaled as well, with a figure-eight loop that allows hikers to shorten or lengthen their outing. To get started, find the trail behind the interpretive kiosk in the large parking lot. For the first half mile or so, the trail parallels the highway through a wonderfully diverse stand of forest. Count how many different kinds of trees you see. The names of each will slowly be revealed during your journey.

At 0.7 mile, come to a bench near a ponderosa pine for an excellent view of Teanaway Ridge. From here, the trail curves away from the highway onto a more open slope. In spring and summer, look for a variety of wildflowers: trillium, Tweedy's lewisia, balsamroot, fairy slippers, clematis, and more. In fall, golden larches brighten the hillsides all around.

At 1.5 miles, reach a junction. Left steers hikers 0.5 mile back to the trailhead (a total elevation gain of 100 feet), but straight leads 1.2 miles along the best part of the hike. Cross a road and enter a forest that is regenerating after a 2012 wildfire. Notice how fickle fire can be. Some trees are blackened to a crisp; others seem to have escaped the flames altogether. There are places where the fire burned underground, leaving tunnels and root holes, so do stick to the trail. All around, new life is sprouting in the form of baby trees, grasses, and wildflowers.

The trail climbs higher, revealing more mountains and vistas until it tops out at a scenic bench at 1.9 miles (4525 feet). The fire changed course here, for the path ahead leads through stands of healthy larches, white pine, and ponderosa pine. On a clear day, you can see forever. Mount Stuart, the second-highest nonvolcanic peak in the Cascades, rises to the west, next to the glorious Enchantments, which are hidden behind the wall of Wenatchee Ridge. To the south are Mount Rainier and Teanaway Ridge. Directly east are Diamond Head and Tronsen Ridge.

When you've had your fill, descend into a larch forest. In fall, the needles make a soft yellow carpet underfoot. In 0.5 mile, the shortcut trail joins with the main trail for the quick jaunt back to the parking area.

90 RED TOP LOOKOUT

BEFORE YOU GO
MAP Green Trails, Alpine Lakes East–Stuart Range No. 208SX
CONTACT Okanogan–Wenatchee National Forest
NOTES Northwest Forest Pass required; privy available; drop-offs near lookout
GPS N 47 17.803, W 120 45.561

ABOUT THE HIKE
SEASON June to October
DIFFICULTY Moderate
DISTANCE 1 mile roundtrip
HIGH POINT 5361 feet
ELEVATION GAIN 350 feet

GETTING THERE
From Cle Elum, follow State Route 970 east for 10 miles until it merges with US Highway 97. On US 97, drive north an additional 6.7 miles to the Mineral Springs Campground. Just beyond the campground, turn left onto gravel Forest Road 9738. In 2.6 miles, turn left on FR 9702, signed "Red Top." In another 3.7 miles, stay straight and drive less than a half mile to the Red Top parking area.

ON THE TRAIL

Oh, the things you can see! I love lookouts because of the unfettered views in all directions. At Red Top Lookout, you're on top of the world and looking straight into the heart of the Alpine Lakes Wilderness. Regal, 9415-foot Mount Stuart and the impenetrable Stuart Range lie to the north, while Mount Rainier and Mount Adams poke up on the horizon to the south. It's a great place to observe raptors swooping on the air currents and identify wildflowers blooming on the mountainside. To top it off, the hike is ridiculously short.

However, the trail isn't for everyone. Parents with small children will find the cliffside location and sharp rocks around the lookout nerve-racking. The weather matters too: on windy days, it may feel like you could be blown away, yet on a calm afternoon with calm kids, you can focus on the vista—and it's really spectacular.

From the parking area, walk up the road to the turnaround to the trailhead and spot the lookout. It's perched on stilts in a most dramatic fashion. At the

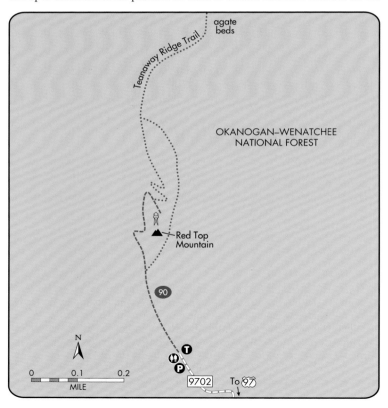

Red Top Lookout is easier to reach than it looks from the trailhead.

trail junction, take the left fork for the very short ascent to the summit. There's no doubt the trail is steep, and because you are over a mile high, everyone is likely to be huffing and puffing. Just take it slowly, admiring the wildflowers—larkspur, glacier lilies, violets, lupine, and trillium—and looking up occasionally to see what new mountain has come into view on the horizon.

When you arrive at a cute A-frame outhouse, you are almost there. Hold smaller children's hands as you round the switchback. If you're lucky, Red Top Lookout will be open and staffed by a volunteer, and you can visit within its relative safety. If not, find a rock and sit down. It's fun to search the panorama for rivers, snow, ridgelines, and to pretend you are a fire lookout and scan the horizon for smoke. In addition to the identifiable mega-peaks of Stuart,

Rainier, and Adams, look for the city of Ellensburg and the deep valley that goes up Snoqualmie Pass. Closer at hand is the Wenatchee range. In October, brilliant swaths of golden larches brighten its hillsides. When you've had your fill, families with small children will want to return the way you came.

EXPLORING FURTHER

Families with older kids may wish to extend their trip and visit the agate beds along Teanaway Ridge. This area is known as one of the best places to look for geodes, thunder eggs, and agates, and it is a popular destination for amateur rock hounds. People spend full days digging holes in hopes of finding a semi-precious gem, but unfortunately, many people have left craters in their wake. It's sobering to walk through this minefield. You may join in too, but it takes patience, perseverance, and it is essential to leave the area as you found it.

To reach Teanaway Ridge, either retreat from the lookout the way you came and choose the other trail at the junction, or drop off the steep backside of the lookout trail near the solar panels. Do the latter only if there is no snow or ice, and only if your kids have solid footwork. It's steep for a short distance before it enters a cool, forested ridge. Once you reach the rock hounding etiquette sign on the Teanaway Ridge Trail, follow it along the ridgeline, up to a mile. Even if you don't dig for agates, it's pleasant walking, especially in spring and early summer when the wildflowers are blooming.

CLE ELUM–ELLENSBURG AREA

91 HYAS LAKE

BEFORE YOU GO
MAP Green Trails, Alpine Lakes West Stevens Pass No. 176S
CONTACT Okanogan–Wenatchee National Forest
NOTES Northwest Forest Pass required; privy available
GPS N 47 32.696, W 121 05.889

ABOUT THE HIKE
SEASON July to October
DIFFICULTY Moderate
DISTANCE 4 miles roundtrip
HIGH POINT 3500 feet
ELEVATION GAIN 100 feet

GETTING THERE

From Snoqualmie Pass, drive Interstate 90 eastbound 27 miles to exit 80 (Roslyn/Salmon La Sac). Turn left onto Bullfrog Road. Drive 2.8 miles to the traffic circle with State Route 903 and turn left toward Roslyn. Stay on SR 903/Salmon La Sac Road for 16 miles until you reach the Salmon La Sac Campground. At the Y-intersection, veer right onto Cle Elum Valley Road (Forest Road 4330) and drive the gravel road 12.2 miles to its end. Most of the road is well graded, but the crossing of Scatter Creek may require high clearance.

ON THE TRAIL
Take the "fruitway" to Hyas Lake where wild blueberries, huckleberries, thimbleberries, and salmonberries line the trail all the way to a classic alpine basin. Because it isn't particularly deep, Hyas Lake offers warmish swimming on a hot day and a place to rinse off sticky purple fingers. It's also a good place to camp, with a handful of lakeside campsites strung out along the shore.

Don't be discouraged by the number of cars in the parking lot. This trailhead is a prime entry point for exploring the Alpine Lakes Wilderness, and

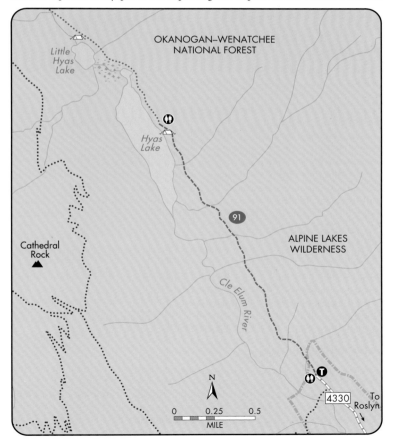

The trail to Hyas Lake is ripe with berries in August. (photo by Jon Stier)

most hikers on their way to loftier destinations don't linger at Hyas Lake. The berry fruitway begins immediately on the mostly level trail. I can't imagine how frustrating it would be to hike here when they aren't ripe. Late July and August is their prime time. This trail is a pie-maker's dream. Note the best patches during your hike, then do your picking as you return.

Soon after beginning your journey, cross into the Alpine Lakes Wilderness. Pass above a grassy wetland and step across several creeks. Occasionally the trail opens up to reveal the remote valley and surrounding peaks. Because the trail is so gentle, the 2-mile trek to Hyas Lake gets you there quickly. Reach the lakeside by walking through one of the half-dozen campsites. One of the best spots is opposite the backcountry privy.

The long, shimmery lake is surrounded by trees and the sentinels of Cathedral Rock and Mount Daniel. It's quiet here but for the rustling of the breeze through alders, the lapping of the lake, and the distant thrum of a waterfall. If you've brought water shoes, test the water for a swim. Because the lake isn't deep, the temperature may be tolerable and could be a welcome escape from biting insects. It wouldn't be a bad place to cast a fishing line either. Return the way you came, filling up a hard-sided container with tender fruits.

EXPLORING FURTHER

If you're backpacking or looking for a little more adventure, press on to Little Hyas Lake. It's technically one body of water, but grassy water plants have pinched the lake into two parts. It is an additional 0.8 mile to a fine campsite at the upper lake where you can wander out on a little peninsula and feel like you're in the middle of the water. Beyond the lake, the trail ascends steeply to the Pacific Crest Trail and Tuck and Robin lakes.

92 GINKGO PETRIFIED FOREST

BEFORE YOU GO
  MAP Available online
  CONTACT Washington State Parks
  NOTES Discover Pass required; dogs must be leashed; privy available;
    rattlesnake country
  GPS N 46 56.864, W 120 02.174

ABOUT THE HIKE
  SEASON March to November
  DIFFICULTY Easy to moderate
  DISTANCE 1.4 miles loop
  HIGH POINT 1310 feet
  ELEVATION GAIN 250 feet

GETTING THERE
From Ellensburg, take Interstate 90 eastbound 29 miles to exit 136 (Vantage), the final exit before crossing the Columbia River. Turn left on Main Street/ Vantage Highway and follow it 2.7 miles to the trailhead on the right side of the road.

ON THE TRAIL
Yes, there can be a forest without any trees. At the Ginkgo Petrified Forest the trees are under your feet, buried in basalt millions of years ago by a cataclysmic volcanic event that sent floods of lava streaming across the landscape and burying a lush tropical forest that then thrived here. Ginkgo, walnut, sycamore, chestnut, and oak trees were among the diverse array of plants that had flourished among swamps and lakes. It would all be gone today but for one quirk of

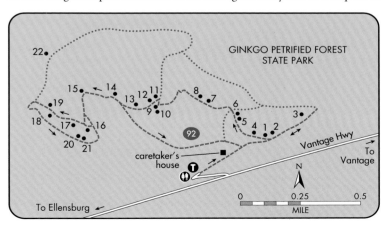

The petrified specimens are in cages to protect them from vandalism.

fate: the trees were so waterlogged that a chemical process called petrifaction took place, turning the trees to stone.

The ancient forest was discovered in the 1930s and turned into a state park. Today, you can take a 1.4-mile loop trail past twenty-one specimens from nine different species. The only trees aboveground are those surrounding the caretaker's house, so this trail can get beastly hot. Bring water and a hat! And note that this is rattlesnake country. Stay on the trails and be alert for sunning reptiles.

Start your exploration by passing beneath the cool stone overhang of the house, which was constructed by the Civilian Conservation Corps in 1936. Follow the lumpy paved trail and number signs to your first two petrified specimens: a maple and a Douglas fir, imprisoned in locked cages. Yes, this is disappointing. However, it is necessary to prevent plundering and vandalism. Use it as a teachable moment. If we each took a memento home with us, there wouldn't be anything left to visit.

The paved trail runs until the third specimen. The trail that continues beyond goes high above the other petrified trees and isn't as interesting, so to see more trees you'll need to backtrack to #1 and take a right. On a gravel trail you'll pass spruce, walnut, elm and the namesake ginkgo (#11), which is a nice place to stop and rest after climbing 200 feet in 0.5 mile. From here you can see a wedge of the Columbia River and the distant glint of cars driving on I-90. If it is early spring, wildflowers are an added bonus.

There are two points (after #6 and #13) where you can cut your loop short and return downhill toward the caretaker's house. But if you want to see all of the petrified trees, continue following the numbers. After #13, the trail leads right, uphill, in a lollipop loop, where you will add sweetgum (#16) and horse chestnut (#18) to your list. Redwood (#22) can be found on a short optional spur trail after #19. It is an impressive assortment of tree species, especially considering how arid the climate is now.

After passing #21, choose the trail on the right at each remaining intersection to return to the trailhead. If you haven't already, drive 2 miles east to the Ginkgo Petrified Forest State Park headquarters. A small interpretive center is generally open weekends and holidays. Even if it is closed, it is worth feeling the smooth polished petrified wood outside, gazing at the Columbia River, and viewing pictographs that were salvaged from the Wanapum Dam construction and moved here.

93 UMTANUM CREEK CANYON

BEFORE YOU GO
MAP Washington Department of Natural Resources–Yakima
CONTACT Bureau of Land Management–Oregon/Washington
NOTES Bureau of Land Management parking fee May 15 to September 15; federal Interagency Pass accepted; privy available; watch for rattlesnakes
GPS N 46 51.336, W 120 29.006

ABOUT THE HIKE
SEASON March to November
DIFFICULTY Moderate
DISTANCE 3.5 miles or more roundtrip
HIGH POINT 1750 feet
ELEVATION GAIN 400 feet

GETTING THERE
From Interstate 90 in Ellensburg, take exit 109. Turn left onto Canyon Road/State Route 821 and drive south 11.8 miles to the Umtanum Creek Recreation Area. Turn right into the recreation area and park in the lot near the suspension bridge and campground.

ON THE TRAIL
Umtanum Creek Canyon pulsates with life. From chattering kingfishers and orioles to scurrying creatures in the underbrush, it is immediately evident that you are not alone on this trail. A ribbon of green penetrates the desert environment, acting as a magnet for dozens of species of birds, mammals, and reptiles. This hike is excellent for wildlife sightings, especially in spring and fall.

Begin your hike by crossing a wooden-decked suspension bridge over the Yakima River. After crossing under the railroad tracks, come upon a junction. Left leads to Umtanum Ridge, which offers excellent views of the Stewart Range and a sublime spring wildflower display—on a trail with significant elevation gain. Right takes you along Umtanum Creek for a more intimate nature experience on a more kid-friendly trail.

It's not always an easy trail, however. In several places, the trail braids into two paths and then one peters out in a thicket. When that happens, backtrack and try a different way. It's an adventure! And you can't truly get lost with the creek by your side.

Spring and fall are the best times to visit Umtanum Creek Canyon.

The first 0.5 mile, fortunately, is straightforward, as the trail weaves in and out of sagebrush and cottonwood on the south side of the creek. Stop occasionally to check in with your senses. Observe how the cottonwood leaves shimmer in the breeze, smell the sagebrush, and listen to the birds. Notice how your very presence flushes the wildlife. And speaking of wildlife, this is rattlesnake country. When weather turns warm, the likelihood of encountering a rattler increases. If that is something you want to avoid, visit in the fall after they hibernate.

At 0.75 mile, pass through an old gate to the remnants of a former homestead. A few apple trees still remain, and concrete footings of buildings can be found if you hunt around. Shortly after the fence posts, the trail braids; you should choose the right trail even though it is the fainter one. This will lead to a place where you can cross the creek on rocks or logs. Look around this area for beaver activity. They've been busy knocking down trees and constructing elaborate dams.

As the canyon narrows, the trail alternates between rocky flower-filled meadows, black basalt talus, and outcrops of aspen and cottonwood that provide respite on sunny afternoons. Train your eyes—or better yet, binoculars—on the canyon walls for grazing bighorn sheep. A herd comes into the canyon

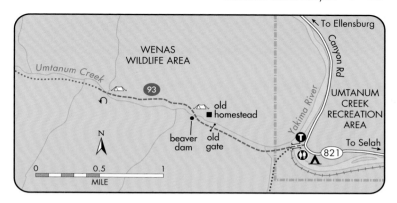

each winter and lingers on the hillsides into spring. Look also to the skies. On a recent visit we saw a pair of turkey vultures guarding their cliffside lair, a protective osprey patrolling the skies for danger, and dozens of songbirds flitting in the bushes.

Near 1.7 miles, the trail crosses the creek a second time. This makes a fine turnaround point. If you proceed, the trail continues to follow the creek until it gets more and more choked out by vegetation at 3 miles. On your return, look for things you didn't see before. Did you miss the beaver dam? Can you actually spot the birds you hear? Can you identify any scat or footprints? Chances are you will see something new.

EXPLORING FURTHER

Umtanum Creek Canyon makes an easy overnight backpacking destination. Campsites can be found near both of the creek crossings.

HIKING IN CENTRAL AND EASTERN WASHINGTON

Don't overlook hiking in Central and Eastern Washington. You'll find wide-open spaces, wildflowers and cactus, and quiet forests in this part of the state. If you enjoy hikes like Umtanum and Cowiche canyons, then you'll want to venture out farther in Central Washington. The best seasons to visit are spring and fall, when the animals are most active and the temperatures pleasant. If you're in search of solitude and off-the-beaten-track rambling, be sure to explore the Okanogan Highlands and the Colville National Forest of Northeast Washington or the Blue Mountains of Southeast Washington.

There are two guidebooks to the region: *Day Hiking: Eastern Washington* by Rich Landers and Craig Romano and *Best Desert Hikes: Washington* by Alan Bauer and Dan Nelson. These two books comprehensively cover the wide range of trails that crisscross this less-traveled part of the state. Many of the hikes are short and ideal for kids.

YAKIMA AREA

94 COWICHE CANYON

BEFORE YOU GO
MAP Conservancy map available online
CONTACT Cowiche Canyon Conservancy
NOTES Porta-potty available; open to horses and bikes; rattlesnakes in summer
GPS N 47 52.018, W 121 40.700

ABOUT THE HIKE
SEASON March to November
DIFFICULTY Easy to moderate
DISTANCE 3.6 miles roundtrip
HIGH POINT 1490 feet
ELEVATION GAIN 150 feet

GETTING THERE

From Interstate 82 in Yakima, take exit 33 onto Yakima Avenue. Drive 1.6 miles and turn right on Summitview Avenue. Follow Summitview Avenue out of town. After 9 miles, look for a large log home at the bottom of a hill. Turn right immediately after the house onto Weikel Road. In 0.5 mile, turn right at a white building at a curve in the road and park in the parking area 500 feet ahead.

ON THE TRAIL

Minutes from downtown Yakima is a basalt canyon that begs to be explored. Lazy Cowiche Creek, lined with red osier dogwoods, runs through the canyon,

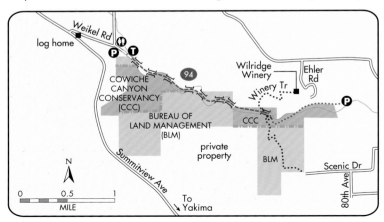

Turkey vultures fly over Cowiche Canyon. (photo by Jon Stier)

and alongside it is an easy trail on an abandoned railroad corridor. Raptors, most notably turkey vultures, and ravens circle overhead, and grasshoppers buzz in the sagebrush. With four trailheads and a winery, there is plenty to explore here. Take this hike for starters, then come back again and begin at a different trailhead.

Cowiche Canyon is best explored in the spring and fall when the weather is cool and the foliage most colorful. It can get extremely hot during summer, and there is little shade. The trailhead is past the homes at the end of the road, where you will pass through a gate onto an old railroad trestle over Cowiche Creek. This is the first of eight restored trestles crisscrossing the creek over 1.8 miles. The railway used to serve fruit warehouses nearby, and you can still find rusty spikes and railroad ties along your journey. Please, however, leave anything you discover for future visitors to see.

The canyon walls narrow as you go—dominated by reddish basalt, but also with sedimentary rock that in some places looks like layers of phyllo dough. Dark crevices and small caves high on the walls harbor birds and mammals. Scan the skies for turkey vultures, which look long and lean when flying, but squat and thick-necked when perched. They soar and circle in groups looking for their next meal. If you visit in the spring, flowers and new growth brighten the hillsides. In the fall and early winter, the creekside is aflame with the bare stems of red osier dogwood. An occasional tall ponderosa pine stands alone amid the sagebrush.

Mosey along on the wide trail, enjoying scenery and scents so different from most trails in Washington. At 1.5 miles, pass around some rockfall, as well as memorial rocks placed by the Cowiche Canyon Conservancy, the land trust responsible for preserving and maintaining this canyon. Hikers can proceed a full 3 miles to the east trailhead along Cowiche Creek, or up to the Wilridge Winery. However, a nice turnaround is at the intersection with the Winery Trail (1.8 miles). There's a sturdy trestle just beyond it where you can gaze at the creek before returning the way you came.

95 BOULDER CAVE

BEFORE YOU GO
MAP Green Trails, Old Scab Mountain No. 272
CONTACT Okanogan–Wenatchee National Forest
NOTES Northwest Forest Pass required; dogs must be leashed; privy available; trail closed late October to late May to protect bat habitat; bring flashlights
GPS N 46 57.639, W 121 05.140

ABOUT THE HIKE
SEASON Late May to October
DIFFICULTY Easy to moderate
DISTANCE 1.4 miles roundtrip
HIGH POINT 2700 feet
ELEVATION GAIN 250 feet

GETTING THERE
From Interstate 82 in Yakima, take exit 31 toward US Highway 12 West/Naches. Follow US 12 for 17 miles, through Naches, to the junction with State Route 410. Stay straight, merging onto SR 410, and drive another 21 miles. Just after the town of Cliffdell, turn left on Forest Road 1704, signed "Old River Road—Boulder Cave Recreation Area." Cross the river and at the T-intersection turn right and drive to the road's end.

ON THE TRAIL
There's something mysterious about a dark, cool cave that triggers the imagination. And while Boulder Cave is more of a tunnel than a cave, it is the winter home of the Townsend's big-eared bat, which heightens the mystique. If this kind of thing makes your heart skip a beat, note that your time in the cave is short. You're also unlikely to be alone; the Boulder Cave Recreation Area is a popular destination for weekend picnickers and aspiring spelunkers from Yakima.

At the trailhead, read the informative signs about the bats. These sensitive creatures mate and hibernate in Boulder Cave during the fall and winter,

Boulder Cave is a popular summer weekend destination. (photo by Jon Stier)

necessitating the cave's closure from October to May. Biologists are also extremely concerned that white-nose syndrome, which has devastated bat populations in the east, could be spread here. Out of consideration for the bats, please follow a few simple rules: be quiet, using whispers to communicate; don't shine the flashlight at the ceiling; refrain from touching cave walls; and remain on the trail. If you have been in other caves, make sure your shoes, clothes, and other equipment have been decontaminated to prevent potential spread of the fungus.

In early summer, wildflowers along the wide trail dance in the breeze. Big ponderosa pines lend a fresh scent and shade on a short ascent to an overlook of Devil Creek. The creek slows to a trickle by summer's end, but interpretive signs along the trail describe how thousands of years ago this stream was responsible for carving out Boulder Cave.

After a quick 0.5-mile hike, reach the cave entrance. Follow the directional loop by heading right through the big basalt overhang. This is a good place to put on an extra layer of clothing and break out the flashlights or headlamps. Optimally, everyone will have a flashlight, but your party should have at least two. The trail is rocky and rough—and it is pitch dark. Try turning off your lights to see just how dark it can get. If anyone is scared, don't worry; you'll see a strip of light very soon. The stretch of trail in the cave is only 400 feet long.

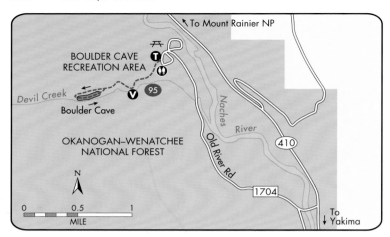

As you make your way, listen to the tinkling sound of Devil Creek, which flows through the cave. Emerge into the light, casting your eyes from the ceiling to the floor. Imagine fitting the rocks under your feet into the giant jigsaw puzzle above. With all of its jagged niches, it's easy to understand why bats would choose to roost in this cave.

The climb back to the main trail has two platforms that offer different perspectives on Boulder Cave and the dramatic chartreuse and rust-colored lichen on the black basalt walls. As you reach the main trail, be prepared for the kids to cajole you into making another loop through the cave before returning to the trailhead.

Opposite: *Dodging the waves at Third Beach* (photo by Jon Stier)

OLYMPIC
PENINSULA

HOOD CANAL

96 RANGER HOLE

BEFORE YOU GO
MAP Green Trails, Olympic Mountains East No. 168S
CONTACT Olympic National Forest
NOTES Northwest Forest Pass required; privy, water, and picnic table available; drop-offs at river
GPS N 47 40.896, W 122 59.654

ABOUT THE HIKE
SEASON Year-round
DIFFICULTY Easy to moderate
DISTANCE 1.9 miles roundtrip
HIGH POINT 325 feet
ELEVATION GAIN 200 feet

GETTING THERE
From Quilcene, drive on US Highway 101 south for 15 miles. (From Hoodsport, drive US 101 north for 22 miles.) Turn left (west) on Duckabush Road (signed "Duckabush Recreation Area") and proceed 3.6 miles to the Interrorem Cabin on the left.

The Interrorem Cabin can be rented for overnight visits.

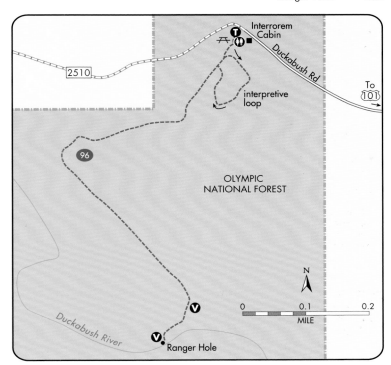

ON THE TRAIL

Trace the steps of one of Olympic National Forest's first rangers, Emery Finch, from his log cabin at the trailhead to a viewpoint over the Duckabush River near where he would fish for his supper. The log cabin can now be rented from the Forest Service, and a well-traveled path leads through maples, hemlocks, and firs to a dramatic chasm through which the river roars, especially after a big rain.

Before leaving on your hike, take a look at the century-old Interrorem Cabin, being considerate of any renters. Built in 1907, this was the first administrative site for Olympic National Forest and operated in various official capacities until 1986. A quarter-mile interpretive spur, just beyond the trailhead, gives greater context to the various activities of Ranger Finch, Depression-era works programs, and its logging history. The logging past can also be observed in the monster-sized stumps of trees felled during those early years at this once-remote outpost.

Exiting the interpretive loop, head left on a fairly direct route to the Duckabush River. Notice how the forest changes as you go, and how the murmur of the river comes and goes. After cresting a hump, the trail trends mostly downhill.

At 0.9 mile, the descent becomes significantly steeper, dropping 100 feet in the next 0.1 mile to a series of river views. The Duckabush races through a narrow section below, milky green from glacial silt high above. It's mesmerizing to watch, especially when the river is swollen with rain or snowmelt.

Make sure kids stay far back from the cliff's edge for safety, and when you are ready, return the way you came, bypassing the interpretive loop. If the kids still have energy, consider combining this trail with Murhut Falls (Hike 97).

97 MURHUT FALLS

BEFORE YOU GO
    MAP Green Trails, Olympic Mountains East No. 168S
    CONTACT Olympic National Forest
    NOTES No services available; unstable footing near falls
    GPS N 47 40.592, W 123 02.313

ABOUT THE HIKE
    SEASON March to November
    DIFFICULTY Easy to moderate
    DISTANCE 1.5 miles roundtrip
    HIGH POINT 1040 feet
    ELEVATION GAIN 240 feet

GETTING THERE

From Quilcene, drive on US Highway 101 south for 15 miles. (From Hoodsport, drive on US 101 north for 22 miles.) Turn left (west) on Duckabush Road (signed "Duckabush Recreation Area") and proceed 3.6 miles until the pavement ends at the Collins Campground. Continue on a good gravel road another 2.7 miles to a Y-intersection. Choose the right fork and drive 1.2

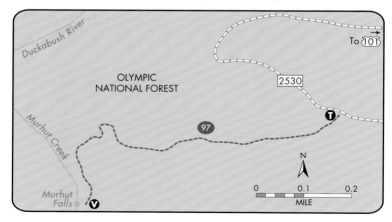

Light filters through cedar branches on the trail to Murhut Falls.

miles on Forest Road 2530 to the small pullout on the left side of the road for Murhut Falls.

ON THE TRAIL

Waterfall fans: here's a graceful, two-tiered cascade on a lesser-known trail not far from several popular campgrounds. At just 1.5 miles roundtrip, it's a trail that nearly anyone can hike and offers a fine diversion for families looking for a bite-sized adventure on the eastern side of the Olympics. Families with older or energetic kids may want to combine it with the nearby Ranger Hole trail (Hike 96) for a longer outing.

The trail begins opposite the small parking area on the right side of the gravel road. You'll be walking up a decommissioned Forest Service road, cleverly disguised by well-planned trail building. Still, there are signs of its previous use: new trees, culverts, and straight sections. It's ironic that the very existence of this trail (and many others) is due to the extraction of the resource we long to see—big trees. But what's this? At 0.6 mile, the trail veers away from the old road, and the trees get much bigger. Descend gradually into a steep-walled ravine, the roar of the falls becoming more and more audible. Watch your footing as you approach Murhut Falls (0.75 mile, 1040 feet). Many hikers have left the trail here to climb down to the base of the waterfall, and their descent has eroded the trail. As tempting as it may be to do the same, resist; the slope is extremely steep and unstable.

Instead, enjoy viewing the falls from the end of the trail where it pours 117 feet sideways, then changes direction for another 36-foot drop into a small pool crisscrossed by two stripped logs. From there, the water speeds down Murhut Creek, under the cover of huge western red cedars, before eventually dumping into the Duckabush River.

Retrace your steps for your return, noticing imposing Mount Jupiter beyond the curtain of trees. If it is early summer, you may also be treated to the pink blossoms of native rhododendrons.

98 DOSEWALLIPS STATE PARK

BEFORE YOU GO
   MAP Green Trails, Olympic Mountains East No. 168S
   CONTACT Washington State Parks
   NOTES Discover Pass required; dogs must be leashed; restrooms, water, and picnic tables available; hike can be scaled for younger hikers
   GPS N 47 41.279, W 122 54.160

ABOUT THE HIKE
   SEASON Year-round
   DIFFICULTY Moderate
   DISTANCE 3.2 miles loop
   HIGH POINT 450 feet
   ELEVATION GAIN 400 feet

GETTING THERE
From Quilcene, drive US Highway 101 south for 12.2 miles. (From Hoodsport, drive on US 101 north for 24.5 miles.) Turn left (east) into the day-use area for Dosewallips State Park. The trailhead is on the other side of US 101 near the campground.

Chances are you won't slip here.

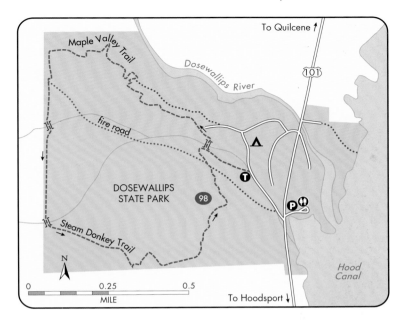

ON THE TRAIL

Just beyond the manicured lawns of the Dosewallips State Park campground is a magical world of thick moss, profuse ferns, tinkling creeks, and in spring a frilly carpet of wildflowers. The forest is ever changing, with big Douglas firs giving way to big-leaf maples and river views. One large 3.2-mile loop connects the Steam Donkey and Maple Valley trails. This can be shortened by following a fire road back to the campground, providing options for families with smaller kids—or for those who are awaiting low tide to dig for clams in Hood Canal.

Begin your hike by crossing US 101 and following the park road 0.2 mile toward the campground. The trailhead is to the left of a bridge just before the park entrance station. When you reach a signed junction, go right on the Rhody Cut-off trail, climbing to the top of a ridge above the campground amphitheater. In springtime, the blooms of pink rhododendrons add color to the greens of the forest.

Descend to an intersection with the Maple Valley Trail at 0.9 mile. The trail to the right leads back to the campground, but you will turn left and parallel the Dosewallips River for a short distance before climbing up a mossy slope. The shade of mature forest gives way to an alder-choked clear-cut at the western edge of the state park.

At 1.3 miles (205 feet), reach a two-track fire road on the left. Following this road back to the trailhead will cut 0.8 mile and 200 feet of elevation gain off of your hike. Up for a bit more? Then proceed straight on the Steam Donkey

Trail. Cross Phantom Creek and start climbing up to the high point of the trail at 1.9 miles (450 feet). The trail will become somewhat swampy, but your feet will remain dry on a log boardwalk and a bridge signed with a slightly naughty name. As you descend, the forest opens up, letting in more light. Look for rhodies, red huckleberries, cottonwoods, and finally, a maple glade verdant with sword ferns.

Pass a stagnant pond, ringed by two giant trees. Here is where the Steam Donkey Trail got its name. "Steam donkey" is the nickname for a steam-powered logging engine that relied on water, and this pool once was the water source. Just beyond, reach the fire road. Make a left, then a quick right. A few feet beyond, go left at an interpretive sign that describes how logs were removed from this forest and sent to a sawmill in Seabeck. Reaching the Rhody Cut-off junction at 3 miles, bear right to return to the campground road.

99 LENA LAKE

BEFORE YOU GO
MAP Green Trails, Olympic Mountains East No. 168S
CONTACT Olympic National Forest
NOTES Northwest Forest Pass required; privy available
GPS N 47 35.985, W 123 09.073

ABOUT THE HIKE
SEASON March to November
DIFFICULTY Difficult
DISTANCE 6.4 miles roundtrip
HIGH POINT 1950 feet
ELEVATION GAIN 1300 feet

GETTING THERE
From Quilcene, drive on US Highway 101 south for 23 miles. (From Hoodsport, drive on US 101 north for 14 miles.) Turn left (west) on the Hamma Hamma River Road (Forest Road 25). Follow the paved road for 7.6 miles to the trailhead.

ON THE TRAIL
Lena Lake's popularity is legendary, and sadly, the impacts of too many hikers behaving badly have tarnished this lovely trail and destination. But the destination is popular for a reason, and it is hard to resist the pull of a big mountain lake that is so accessible and capacious. Dipping hot toes into Lena Lake's cool blue water after more than 3 miles of hiking is heavenly. And if you've brought a tent and sleeping bags, this trail makes an excellent backpacking trip. When you visit, however, be sure to model good hiker behavior by not cutting switchbacks and by packing out all of your waste.

The trail gets to work immediately, switchbacking up the hillside while gaining 500 feet over the first mile. This is the most difficult part of the hike,

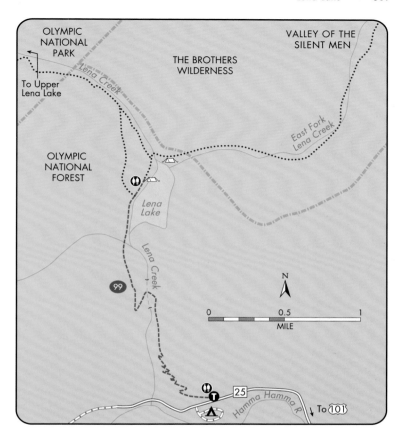

and everyone will fare best if you begin your start in the cool of the morning. The trail is rooty and rocky, so wear sturdy footwear and watch your step.

As the trail ascends, it passes through larger trees; as you near Lena Creek at 1.7 miles (1560 feet), one monster snag is hard to miss. What you may miss is the creek. Pause for a moment on the bridge over the dry, rocky streambed. Lena Creek is visible and quite audible below, and it drains from Lena Lake above. Where is the water? In fact, it flows silently underground, emerging below the trail to resume its raucous course downhill. Nifty!

Now on the opposite side of the creek, follow the contour of the mountainside, climbing more gradually. At 2.6 miles (1850 feet), reach a creek and a junction. Although a side trail leads down to the lake's outlet, it is not a good place to enjoy the lake. Instead, keep straight on the main trail, climbing above the lake for a pleasant view at 3 miles (1950 feet), then dip down to its shore and

Lena Lake

numerous campsites at 3.2 miles. Behold the sparkly basin, ringed by green. If you can find a spot away from others, listen to the sounds of nature: the gentle lapping of the lake, the beating percussion of water on logs, the breeze through cedars, and the chorus of birds. After relaxing at the lake, retrace your steps. Please refrain from cutting the switchbacks in your hurry to return; this wouldn't save you much time, but it would do lasting damage to the forest.

EXPLORING FURTHER

You can lug a backpack and plan to stay the night in one of the twenty-eight campsites at the lake. These fill on summer weekends and holidays, so plan accordingly and go midweek or in spring and fall if you can. Please use only the existing fire rings and the outhouses that are provided. If your kids are strong hikers, consider a day hike from your base camp at Lower Lena Lake to its alpine sister, Upper Lena Lake. Upper Lena Lake (no dogs allowed) is an additional 4.1 miles one-way and a difficult 2700-foot elevation gain. If that is too much, wander through the old-growth forest up the Valley of the Silent Men, also known as The Brothers Trail.

100 STAIRCASE RAPIDS

BEFORE YOU GO

MAP Green Trails, Olympic Mountains East No. 168S
CONTACT Olympic National Park
NOTES National Park entry fee; dogs prohibited; privy available; off-trail water hazard
GPS N 47 30.933, W 123 19.782

ABOUT THE HIKE

SEASON Year-round
DIFFICULTY Easy to moderate
DISTANCE 2.2 miles loop
HIGH POINT 910 feet
ELEVATION GAIN 130 feet

GETTING THERE

From Shelton, take US Highway 101 north for 12 miles to Hoodsport. Turn left on Lake Cushman Road, following it for 9.3 miles. At a T-intersection, turn left on Forest Road 24. Drive FR 24 6.6 miles (after 1.6 miles the pavement will give way to an often potholed gravel road) to the Staircase Entrance to Olympic National Park. Enter the park and drive 1.2 miles to the trailhead parking across from the campground near the ranger station. Note that the road into Olympic National Park may be gated and closed in winter.

ON THE TRAIL

Enormous trees, frothy whitewater, and a massive suspension bridge over the North Fork Skokomish River make this hike a winner for even the most reluctant hiker. The rapids are impressive in all seasons, but are especially turbulent in the spring when they are full of snowmelt and in the fall after a big rain. The ancient Douglas firs and western red cedars provide ample shade on sunny summer afternoons and cover on drippy mornings. There really is no wrong time to walk in this primordial world.

Begin your hike by crossing the North Fork Skokomish River on a concrete bridge beyond the road's end and proceed straight along the river. Immediately

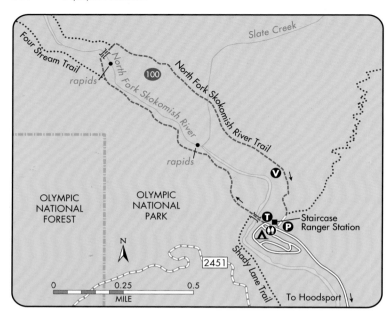

enter the old-growth forest. It's hard not to be impressed by the size of the ancient trees that grow here and how they have been weathered by the ravages of time. Bugs, birds, moss, and more have shaped and scarred their trunks. At 0.2 mile is a short side trail to an enormous cedar, now lying on its side after succumbing to a storm in the 1990s.

Resuming your hike, take note of the increasingly raucous rapids. The river ping-pongs between big boulders, loudly racing downstream through churning whitewater. When the river slows, the water is so clear and green that you can see different-colored rocks below the surface. Pause for a closer look, but make sure everyone stays back from the edge.

At 0.9 mile, reach a junction. The loop route turns right over a very impressive—and sturdy—cable suspension bridge. The former bridge on this site was wiped out by floods in the late 1990s, and the loop option for this hike was impossible until 2013 when this span was completed. At least 10 feet higher than its predecessor, and anchored by thick cable, this bridge is built to withstand the worst conditions. Enjoy your bird's-eye view of the rapids below before picking up the North Fork Skokomish River Trail for your return.

On leaving the bridge, proceed straight and reach another junction. This trail runs from the trailhead to the Duckabush Trail more than 15 miles away. Turn right for your journey back to civilization. The trail pulls away from the river a bit, under shade. At 1.4 miles, cross Slate Creek on single log stringers. Late in the season, it may be possible to hop across on rocks.

There are enormous Douglas firs and cedars in the Staircase area.

Now the trail will climb up to a view above the river at 2 miles. Notice how a landslide took out an old segment of trail, plunging it into the river. Stay away from the cliff and take the alternate route around it. Regaining the main trail, it is just a short distance back to the trailhead parking lot behind the ranger station.

EXPLORING FURTHER

The best extension to this hike is to postpone the loop route via the suspension bridge and proceed straight on Four Stream Trail on the west side of the river. The river mellows out, and the summer crowds thin. The trail continues another mile or so through forest shaped by the vagaries of wildfire to more old growth and places where you may dip your toes in the water. It's possible to camp at Four Stream.

Another option is the Shady Lane Trail, which meanders a mile downstream from the concrete bridge, opposite the park campground. If you thought the trees at Staircase Rapids were big, these will blow your mind. The trail runs 1 mile to Forest Road 2451.

NORTH PENINSULA

101 FORT FLAGLER STATE PARK

BEFORE YOU GO
MAP Available online
CONTACT Washington State Parks
NOTES Discover Pass required; dogs must be leashed; restrooms
and water available; use caution when exploring batteries
GPS N 48 05.615, W 122 43.289

ABOUT THE HIKE
SEASON Year-round
DIFFICULTY Moderate
DISTANCE 4.1 miles loop
HIGH POINT 130 feet
ELEVATION GAIN 130 feet

GETTING THERE
From Hood Canal Bridge, drive west on State Route 104 for 5.2 miles. Turn right on SR 19 and follow it north 9 miles to the town of Chimacum. Turn right on Chimacum Road and drive 1.6 miles to the intersection with SR 116. Turn right on SR 116. (From Port Townsend, follow SR 20 west approximately 4 miles to the intersection with SR 19. Bear left on SR 19 for another 3.4 miles and turn left on SR 116.) Follow SR 116 as it wends its way more than 10 miles to Marrowstone Island and Fort Flagler State Park. Once in the park, turn left

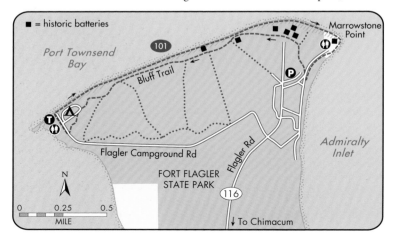

Exploring Fort Flagler's historic batteries (photo by David Elderkin)

on Flagler Campground Road and drive 1.2 miles to the day-use parking area and trailhead near the beach.

ON THE TRAIL

Hike beach and bluff in a loop with two personalities: Puget Sound beach stroll and military history labyrinth. The first part offers a 2-mile walk along Port Townsend Bay, with water and mountain views, crab shells, and parts of military buildings that have fallen off the cliff above. The second part is kid heaven, with a succession of bluff-top batteries that are open for exploration. With parking areas on each end, the hike can be scaled for a shorter visit or a particularly high tide, but it is fun to scout both beach and batteries on one long loop.

From the end of the road, clamber over driftwood and survey the scene: Port Townsend across the bay, ferries plying their way toward the bluffs of Whidbey Island, distant Mount Baker, and a long ribbon of beach. The 2-mile walk up the beach is often in shade, protected from the sun by the tall bluff. There is excellent beachcombing, fascinating metamorphic rocks layered in colors and patterns, and military debris fallen from the eroding bluff.

At 1.6 miles, begin to round Marrowstone Point for a surprise view of Washington's least-visited volcano, Glacier Peak. And in 2 miles, reach the end of this stretch of beach at a fisheries research center. This is an excellent spot to break out lunch and relax before part two.

Make your way up the park road to the top of the bluff (where there is alternate parking). At the end of the fence, exit the road and double back, right, onto the Bluff Trail. Here you'll encounter a cluster of historic batteries where kids can play some serious hide-and-seek. Fort Flagler is one of four

GREAT GETAWAY: OLYMPIC NATIONAL PARK

The Olympic Peninsula is one of Washington's best four-season destinations. Most hikes at lower elevations can be tackled year-round, offering pleasures in every season. Go for wild rhododendrons in the late spring or bugling elk in fall, summertime camping or winter visits to the saltwater shoreline or oceanside beach. The highest drive in Olympic National Park, Hurricane Ridge, is even open in the winter, with skiing and tubing opportunities. But hiking isn't the only thing you can do here. You can rent a boat on Lake Crescent, visit a lavender farm near Sequim, ride bikes on more than 70 miles of the multi-use Olympic Discovery Trail, and shop and eat in Port Angeles.

Port Angeles offers a variety of centrally located lodging options, though they do fill up on summer weekends. The largest campground is Heart o' the Hills at the entrance to Hurricane Ridge, but note that campsites there, as well as in most national park and forest campgrounds on the Olympic Peninsula, are available on a first-come, first-served basis (with the exception of Kalaloch during summer months). If certainty is more to your liking, the campgrounds at Fort Worden and Fort Flagler state parks and the Salt Creek Recreation Area are recommended and can be reserved.

artillery forts on the Olympic Peninsula and Whidbey Island that were established at the turn of the twentieth century to protect Puget Sound from invaders. Despite the heavy fortification, they never saw action, and they were converted to state parks in the 1950s. Today, they are tended by volunteers who help maintain and keep open the buildings so that we may take a walk through history.

It's great fun to explore the warren of rooms, climb ladders, and scamper over catwalks. Younger kids will need close supervision, however. There are many edges without railings, where a fall could be dangerous, and it is possible to get scared in the dark spaces of the batteries.

Continue along the bluff, going slowly downhill and passing several side trails. About midway back is my favorite spot: Battery Calwell, which features benches with views. At 3.4 miles, bear right at the V-intersection, going downhill to the campground, where you will make your way back to the day-use parking area.

102 DUNGENESS SPIT

BEFORE YOU GO
MAP Available at refuge website
CONTACT Dungeness National Wildlife Refuge
NOTES Refuge fee required; dogs prohibited; restrooms and water available; some parts of refuge closed seasonally; closed at sunset
GPS N 48 08.486, W 123 11.431

ABOUT THE HIKE
SEASON Year-round
DIFFICULTY Easy to difficult
DISTANCE 1 to 11 miles roundtrip
HIGH POINT 125 feet
ELEVATION GAIN 120 feet

GETTING THERE

From Sequim, take US Highway 101 west for 4.4 miles and turn right on Kitchen-Dick Road (from Port Angeles, drive on US 101 east for 10 miles and turn left on Kitchen-Dick Road). Drive 3.2 miles on Kitchen-Dick Road to a sharp right-hand turn where it becomes Lotzgesell Road. Take Lotzgesell Road just 0.25 mile and turn left on Voice of America Road (signed "Dungeness National Wildlife Refuge, Dungeness Recreation Area"). Drive approximately 1 mile through Dungeness County Park to the trailhead at road's end.

ON THE TRAIL

Jutting 5 miles out into the Strait of Juan de Fuca is the nation's longest natural sand spit. The curving spit and wildlife-rich bay are part of the Dungeness National Wildlife Refuge, home to brants and widgeons, seals and eagles—all of which thrive in its protected waters. Hikers can walk the entire length of the spit—an 11-mile roundtrip—to a lighthouse at the very end, or simply take the

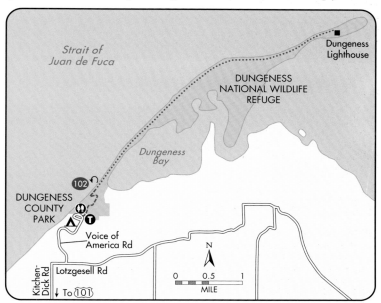

Playing in the driftwood at Dungeness Spit (photo by Eugene Lee)

half-mile trail to the shore to play on the rocky spit, climb the driftwood, and take in the mountain backdrop.

A paved trail leads into a coastal forest, punctuated by western hemlock, western red cedar, salal, and ocean spray. It makes you work just hard enough to feel like you deserve the long beach and wildlife sanctuary at trail's end. In just 0.4 mile reach an overlook with interpretive signs where you can see the sweep of the spit and the historic lighthouse at the very end, with Mount Baker looming behind. From here, it is a short, but steep descent down the bluff to the beach.

Now what? For many, this is about as far as they go. There is a playground of driftwood to poke around in, excellent sand for castle-making, and waters inviting for waders. There is also the lure of the lighthouse, which is open to the public year-round, 5 miles farther down the spit. If you're visiting during low tide, the walking will be easier, but it is a long trek.

There's likely some happy medium for your family. Our adventures are usually slowed by a distinctive piece of driftwood with a hole at its base that simply begs to be scaled. If you can motivate the crew, continue on. Shorebirds are best spotted by walking about 2 miles down the beach. Even if your presence spooks the birds, if you sit quietly, they may return. Bring a field guide and binoculars to help identify what you see. Many of the birds are here only briefly, on a stopover during long annual migrations. If you do make it all the way to the lighthouse, you'll find picnic tables and toilets. You may even be able to scale the lighthouse tower.

During your visit, please heed all signs. Some areas are closed permanently or seasonally to the public for wildlife feeding, resting, and nesting, and the bluffs are dangerous and unstable to climb on. Please also note that this is a wildlife refuge, and ball-throwing, kite-flying, and campfires are not allowed. When you're ready to return, check for all of your belongings and head back the way you came.

103 SUNRISE POINT

BEFORE YOU GO
MAP Green Trails, Elwha North–Hurricane Ridge No. 134S
CONTACT Olympic National Park
NOTES National Park entrance fee; dogs prohibited; restrooms available
GPS N 47 58.203, W 123 29.701

ABOUT THE HIKE
SEASON June to October
DIFFICULTY Easy to moderate
DISTANCE 1.2 miles loop
HIGH POINT 5450 feet
ELEVATION GAIN 250 feet

GETTING THERE
From US Highway 101 in Port Angeles, turn on S Race Street and follow it south 1.1 miles to Hurricane Ridge Road and the Heart o' the Hills Entrance to Olympic National Park. Pass through the entrance booth, proceed 17 miles, and park in the large lot just before you reach the Hurricane Ridge Visitor Center.

ON THE TRAIL
The meadow trails above the Hurricane Ridge Visitor Center are a pure delight in an easy package. Many of the trails are paved, making them ideal for strollers, and you can choose from a variety of loop options to create your own adventure. Hike through dancing wildflowers, playful butterflies, and stunted "Christmas" trees to views of a panorama ranging from Mount Olympus out to the Strait of Juan de Fuca.

This recommended loop takes hikers off the pavement to lofty Sunrise Point, and its nifty 360-degree view, before it returns to the blacktop along the Cirque Rim Trail. Start at the east end (downhill side) of the visitor center parking lot on the paved Cirque Rim Trail. Quickly reach a junction and go right on the High Ridge Trail. Catch your breath at a bench at a quarter mile and orient yourselves at the helpful interpretive sign. On a clear day, you can see all the way to Glacier Peak in the Cascades.

Continue upward, ignoring side trails, to the Sunrise Point summit at a half mile (5450 feet). We had fun spotting the ferry that travels from Port Angeles to Victoria and looking through binoculars to see if there were any mountain goats on Mount Angeles. Keep your food and packs close by to prevent thievery from roving chipmunks and squirrels.

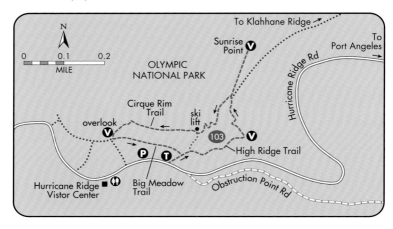

Once you've had your fill of the Olympic panorama, return to the trail junction below. A sharp left is the trail to Klahhane Ridge, a great choice for older kids and a fine way to lose the crowds. For the short, kid-friendly loop, turn right and descend fairly steeply until you level out under a ski lift. Hold on. A ski lift? Olympic National Park hosts one of only two ski areas within a national park. Tucked away at this location are two rope tows and a T-bar lift for winter play.

The trail junction at the ski lift offers two options: go left to close the loop by shortcutting to the High Ridge Trail and returning to the trailhead, or go right

Look for butterflies cavorting in the wind at Sunrise Point.

on the Cirque Rim Trail for more meadows, flowers, views, and a patchwork of lingering snowfields. I recommend choosing the meadow route where you can walk among green false hellebore, purple lupine, and grassy snowy sedge. Notice how, just as the snow melts, the plants take the opportunity to bloom and seed during short summers.

At 1 mile, reach a large overlook and crossroads. From here you can get one final view of the water and read up on the effects of a 2003 fire in the park. Turn around and check out an intriguing visual perspective where people on the horizon actually appear larger than the mountains. Then walk toward that horizon to return to your car. Straight leads to the visitor center, and the Big Meadow Trail leads back to the trailhead.

104 HURRICANE HILL

BEFORE YOU GO

MAP Green Trails, Elwha North–Hurricane Ridge No. 134S
CONTACT Olympic National Park
NOTES National Park entrance fee; dogs prohibited; restrooms available at visitor center and picnic areas
GPS N 47 58.570, W 123 31.051

ABOUT THE HIKE

SEASON June to October
DIFFICULTY Moderate to difficult
DISTANCE 3.4 miles roundtrip
HIGH POINT 5757 feet
ELEVATION GAIN 700 feet

GETTING THERE

From US Highway 101 in Port Angeles, turn on S Race Street and follow it south 1.1 miles to Hurricane Ridge Road and the Heart o' the Hills Entrance to Olympic National Park. Pass through the entrance booth and proceed 17.5 miles to the Hurricane Ridge Visitor Center. To reach the trailhead, continue another 1.5 miles to the large parking area at road's end.

ON THE TRAIL

Hurricane Hill is an Olympic classic. Legions of hikers trek across high alpine meadows to this hill's panoramic summit each year. It's a favorite for locals and foreign travelers, the very young and very old. From lofty Hurricane Ridge, hikers can roam the far reaches of the ridge and climb to a small summit with views from the Olympic Range to the Strait of Juan de Fuca and Canada.

The trail is more difficult than it looks, and you might find that younger kids run out of gas along the way. Because the trail is paved for most of its length, it's possible to bring a stroller along, and there is plenty to see even if you need to turn back short of the destination. I have enticed my crew with the lure of spotting wildlife. On a recent visit, we saw marmots, deer, grouse,

DON'T FEED WILDLIFE

Please, please, please do not feed wildlife. When you feed a chipmunk a peanut or allow a gray jay to nab a piece of bread from your hand, you are not helping it fatten up for winter; you are hindering its ability to survive without begging from humans. When an animal becomes habituated to human food, it is more likely to let its guard down with predators and to be weakened by food that it isn't well adapted to digest.

What's more, feeding the wildlife makes them into little monsters. In Olympic National Park, I've had to shoo a mama doe and her baby away from our picnic table. At Mount Rainier National Park, a ground squirrel insistently tried to break into my backpack. When that didn't work, it chewed a hole in my map when I turned my back to take a photo. Most hikers are familiar with gray jays, who gather in trees and dive-bomb when the snacks are brought out. These are all real problems that humans have caused. Please don't make it worse. Eat your food and let the wildlife find theirs. They don't need any "help."

Chipmunks and ground squirrels have become problems in Olympic and Mount Rainier national parks. Please do not feed them.

Hiking the paved trail to Hurricane Hill (photo by David Elderkin)

hawks, butterflies, and chipmunks. The wildlife in Olympic National Park is ridiculously tame, which delights the kids, but also is an indication that they are being fed far too often by humans.

The first 0.5 mile is easy. Start on the far side of the parking area and follow the conga line of hikers along the asphalt path. The trail straddles the ridge, allowing for dramatic views both north and south, before steepening and traversing an open south-facing slope draped in wildflowers and grasses. This section can also be hot, and plentiful water and a brimmed hat can make a difference. Go slowly, encouraging the kids to examine the wildflowers, seedpods, and bugs along the way. A pair of binoculars provides a good distraction.

When you reach the junction with the Elwha Trail at 1.4 miles (5625 feet), you're almost there. Ahead are two viewpoints with signs labeling every peak near and far. My kids especially enjoyed looking north, where they could see into Canada, spot the town of Port Angeles, and wonder about the fire that made the trees on Unicorn Peak and Unicorn Horn all silvery. We even pulled up a marine app on our phone and were able to identify two vessels cruising the water.

The panoramic signs are well worth the stop, but you haven't yet reached the summit. Scamper up the hill to reach the site of a former lookout tower (1.7 miles, 5757 feet). From the 1930s to the 1960s, people spent their summers

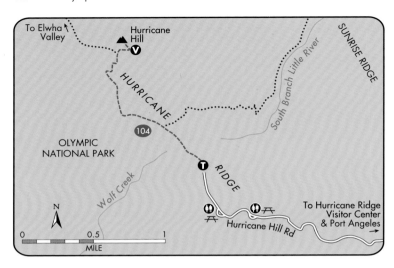

living here and watching for fires. In the 1940s it served the dual purpose of scanning the strait for enemy ships during World War II as well. When you are done, return the way you came.

105 SMOKEY BOTTOM

BEFORE YOU GO
MAP Green Trails, Elwha North–Hurricane Ridge No. 134S
CONTACT Olympic National Park
NOTES National Park entrance fee; dogs prohibited; privy available at Glines Canyon Spillway Overlook
GPS N 48 00.114, W 123 36.265

ABOUT THE HIKE
SEASON Year-round
DIFFICULTY Moderate
DISTANCE 3.6 miles roundtrip
HIGH POINT 750 feet
ELEVATION GAIN 150 feet

GETTING THERE
From Port Angeles, follow US Highway 101 west for 9 miles. Just before the El-wha River Bridge, turn left onto Olympic Hot Springs Road (also signed Elwha Valley). Drive 5.5 miles, past the entrance station to Olympic National Park, and arrive at the Glines Canyon Spillway Overlook. Immediately beyond the overlook, bear left onto a gravel road and take it 0.2 mile to a small parking lot.

ON THE TRAIL

Witness the rebirth of the Elwha River on a lovely woodland trail that reaches into the heart of the Elwha Valley. Smokey Bottom is the old Lake Mills Trail, a name change necessitated because Lake Mills doesn't exist anymore. In 2014, the final piece of the dam that created manmade Lake Mills was removed, draining the reservoir once and for all. Hikers now travel the same trail, but look out onto a transformed landscape as the Elwha River regains its natural, free-flowing course.

The history of the Elwha and its dams is similar to that of so many western rivers, but the largest dam removal project in United States history has rewritten its future. The Elwha River once boasted one of the most productive fisheries outside of Alaska. More than ten anadromous fish runs filled this river so full that it was said to look smokey (hence the new trail name). The native Klallam people relied on the fish for their subsistence, and tales are told of gargantuan salmon weighing in excess of 100 pounds. All of that came to an end in 1913 when the first of two dams was constructed to produce power for the

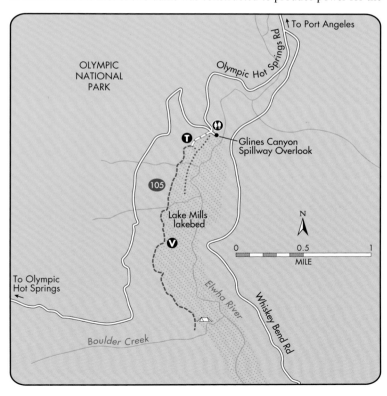

With the removal of the Glines Canyon Dam, the Elwha River flows freely once more.

booming logging industry in Port Angeles. Without fish ladders, salmon were unable to return to their native habitat, and without fish, Native Americans were cut off from a vital resource for their subsistence and culture.

Fortunately, attitudes changed over the years, and after two decades of planning and mitigation, the dams came down, and salmon are once more returning to their original waters. The Smokey Bottom Trail traverses the west side of the river, through alders, firs, and big-leaf maples, on an upland route that provides opportunities to observe the concrete supports of the old dam site, the bathtub rings of Lake Mills, and the unrestrained river braiding its way down the valley. The gravelly gray lakebed will fill in with native trees, bushes, and flowers, changing year-by-year until the former Lake Mills is a distant memory.

The trail goes gently up and down, across side creeks, on a sometimes narrow tread. Younger children could have problems navigating one of the bridges and the steep side slope of the trail without help, but for the most part it is a fairly moderate hike. At 0.9 mile reach a grove of peely-barked madronas at a curve in the trail. Peer over your shoulder to find a camera and solar panels that record the progress of the river environment.

Descend a bit, proceeding through some muddy patches to a peaceful camping spot at 1.8 miles. The trail goes only a few hundred feet farther, dead-ending at Boulder Creek, a huge gouge in the earth with no means of passage. This is your turnaround, but before you go, backtrack to the campsite and tiptoe out onto the old lakebed to get a feel for the new Elwha River from eye level.

EXPLORING FURTHER

Olympic National Park is in the process of building a trail onto the old lakebed. From the Glines Canyon Spillway Overlook and the Smokey Bottom trailhead, hikers can walk out onto the sandy bench and examine the changes up close. A mass of alder naturally revegetated the banks as the lake level was lowered, and you can see the work that the park has done to plant other vegetation closer to the river. It's fascinating and a bit miraculous how quickly life is coming back.

106 MARYMERE FALLS

BEFORE YOU GO
MAP Green Trails, Lake Crescent No. 101
CONTACT Olympic National Park
NOTES Dogs prohibited; restrooms, water, and picnic tables available
GPS N 48 03.480, W 123 47.343

ABOUT THE HIKE
SEASON Year-round
DIFFICULTY Easy to moderate
DISTANCE 1.8 miles roundtrip
HIGH POINT 940 feet
ELEVATION GAIN 340 feet

GETTING THERE

From Port Angeles, follow US Highway 101 west 20 miles to the turnoff for Lake Crescent Lodge and Marymere Falls. Turn right onto Lake Crescent Drive and turn right again at the four-way stop sign. Park in the large lot near the Storm King Ranger Station. Trailhead is accessible by bus.

ON THE TRAIL

Our family discovered Marymere Falls one summer when we were traveling to the coast. The drive was too long for our little ones to manage without stopping, so we picked this short hike near Lake Crescent to let them get their wiggles out. We couldn't have made a better choice. Its enormous firs, splendid nurse logs, and misty waterfall were a hit, and now we stop nearly every time we are in the vicinity.

The trail begins to the left of the Storm King Ranger Station on a broad lakeside path, but soon turns and goes through a corrugated steel tunnel under the highway. Emerge on the other side, amid bearded alders and maples that give way to Douglas firs and cedars. Some are enormous, blocking out the sun; others compete for light and life, with twisting root systems that latch onto downed logs and rocks.

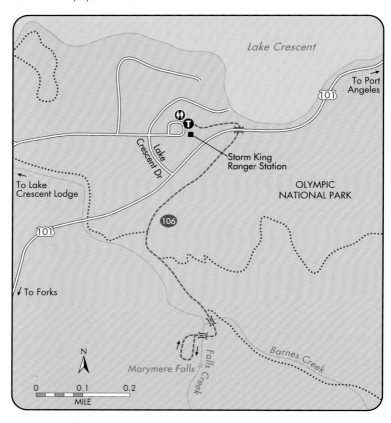

Stay on the main trail, ignoring side trails that go to Lake Crescent Lodge and Mount Storm King, and at 0.7 mile, reach the junction for Marymere Falls. Turn right. A large gravel bar along Barnes Creek may tempt kids into some rock-throwing or wading activity, and this is a good place to do it. When the kids have had their fun, cross the creek on the strong iron bridge and pass over another side stream on a narrow log bridge. Small children may need a hand on the latter.

A short loop trail provides a few different vantages. Take it in a clockwise direction so you approach the falls from below. The trail here climbs in earnest, with some handrails of dubious value along the sides, but it doesn't take long until you round a rock and, voilà! Marymere Falls plunges 90 feet from a small notch in the forested cliffs above. It starts as a spout, then fans out into a broader veil over the mossy rock face into a little pool below. Spend some time examining the micro environment created by this pretty waterfall, from the

Marymere Falls

ever-changing color of the moss to the maidenhair ferns and the foolhardy tree wedged into the cliff. Continue up to a second viewpoint (940 feet) to complete the short loop before heading back to Lake Crescent.

107 SPRUCE RAILROAD

BEFORE YOU GO
  MAP Green Trails, Lake Crescent No. 101
  CONTACT Olympic National Park
  NOTES Bicycles allowed; dogs must be leashed; privy available; bring flashlights
  GPS N 48 05.600, W 123 48.142

ABOUT THE HIKE
  SEASON Year-round
  DIFFICULTY Easy to moderate
  DISTANCE 2.5 to 8 miles roundtrip
  HIGH POINT 775 feet
  ELEVATION GAIN 150 feet

GETTING THERE

To reach the main trailhead from Port Angeles, drive US Highway 101 west for 17 miles to East Beach Road near the Olympic National Park entrance. Turn right on East Beach Road (signed Log Cabin Resort, East Beach) and drive 3.2 miles. At the intersection with Joyce-Piedmont Road, bear left onto Boundary Creek Road and follow it 0.8 mile to Spruce Railroad's Lyre River trailhead. (To reach the western trailhead, continue past East Beach Road an additional 11 miles to the far end of Lake Crescent. Turn right on Camp David Jr. Road and continue 3.3 miles to the end of the road.)

ON THE TRAIL

Change has come to the Spruce Railroad. The trail was originally a dirt path that largely followed the route of an abandoned rail corridor along the northern shore of glistening Lake Crescent. Now it is being incorporated into the 134-mile Olympic Discovery Trail, with some significant modifications. By the end of 2019 the trail will be universally accessible and multipurpose, providing welcome access for wheelchairs, strollers, and bikes, not to mention hikers. In addition, two long-closed train tunnels will be reopened on what will eventually be a 9.5-mile segment.

When complete, the Olympic Discovery Trail will stretch from Port Townsend to La Push—a byway for nonmotorized users through wild country and cute towns. The transformation is already taking shape, and bit by bit the vision is becoming a reality. The Spruce Railroad Trail has been rerouted and regroomed to 12 feet wide on the original trail corridor, and the first of two tunnels has been rehabilitated. Until the work is complete, expect rolling closures on the trail, especially on the western end of the trail.

Spruce Railroad can be hiked out and back or end-to-end with two vehicles. From the main parking area, climb above the lake on the smooth, newly engineered trail. If you have hiked here before, you may miss the intimacy and wildness of the former trail—the understory tickling your ankles, the big trees

Bridge over the Devils Punchbowl

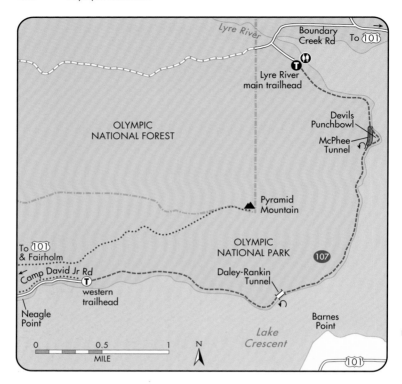

directly overhead, and the lake shimmering nearby. What hasn't changed is the Devils Punchbowl, now reachable from a side trail about 1.2 miles down the trail. A picturesque arching bridge spans a little pool set in a crescent bowl and framed by peeling, orange-barked madronas. Notice the color of the water and how it changes by depth. This is one of the best places to enjoy the lake.

Families with small children may find the Punchbowl a good place to turn around, but not before they explore the newly restored McPhee Tunnel. The trail now goes through the 450-foot tunnel, which bores through Pyramid Mountain. Bring a flashlight, because it can get dark inside, and it is important for bicyclists to be able to see you.

At the time of publication, the trail beyond this point is somewhat unclear. Olympic National Park will be closing the trail in sections as it connects this section to the paved trail at the western trailhead. A shorter tunnel will be restored directly across from Barnes Point, around the 2.9-mile mark. After the tunnel, the trail heads directly west for another 1.1 miles to the western trailhead at the end of Camp David Jr. Road, approximately 4 miles from the Lyre River trailhead where you began.

108 SOL DUC FALLS

BEFORE YOU GO
   MAP Green Trails, Seven Lakes Basin–Mt Olympus Climbing No. 133S
   CONTACT Olympic National Park
   NOTES National Park entrance fee; dogs prohibited; privy and
     picnic tables available
   GPS N 47 57.309, W 123 50.106

ABOUT THE HIKE
   SEASON March to November
   DIFFICULTY Easy to moderate
   DISTANCE 1.6 miles roundtrip
   HIGH POINT 2000 feet
   ELEVATION GAIN 100 feet

GETTING THERE

From Port Angeles, drive on US Highway 101 west 28 miles to Sol Duc Hot Springs Road. Turn left and drive 14 miles to a huge parking area at road's end.

ON THE TRAIL

If there is one single hike that best exemplifies the temperate rain forest of the Olympics, it is Sol Duc Falls. Magnificent old-growth trees, misty and moss-covered, tower overhead. Banana slugs creep across the trail, and red huckleberries glow in the understory. Then everything parts ways for a spectacular waterfall that plunges sideways into a basin before it rushes downstream.

The trailhead parking lot is enormous, but it fills in summer with hordes of day hikers and backpackers. This is the trunk trail for many hikes. Everyone passes by Sol Duc Falls on their way to Deer Lake or the High Divide. Along this short hike you'll hear a half-dozen different languages being spoken, be

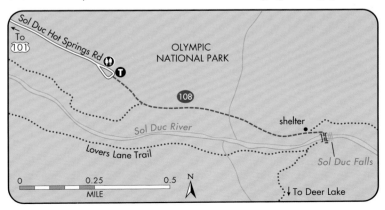

Counting the rings on a fallen Douglas fir tree (photo by Jon Stier)

passed by backpackers ripe from a week of hiking, and witness tiny tots hand-in-hand with their grandparents. It's a wondrous mix of generations and cultures intermingling in a single beautiful place.

At the far end of the lot, enter a green world of firs and hemlocks draped in moss. The trail is well-maintained, with gentle ups and downs. Even toddlers can walk its soft duff. When you reach the Sol Duc Falls Shelter, peer over the railing to the Sol Duc River in the canyon below where maidenhair ferns, vine maples, and moss hang precariously on cliff walls. Now listen closely for the drumming of the waterfall upstream. You're almost there.

A high wooden bridge spans the river, providing an impressive view of Sol Duc Falls (0.8 mile, 2000 feet). Always dramatic, the waterfall is even more so in springtime when the river is swollen with snowmelt and rainwater. It spills over a ledge in three cascades—sometimes four—and drops 30 feet into a narrow gorge. The frothy water then flows directly under the bridge into a magical canyon of moss, ferns, and devil's club.

For a different perspective, continue across the bridge and upstream. Olympic National Park has installed several viewing areas with protective fences. Even when the water is low, please keep all kids on the safe side of the railings. There is a big area to hang out in. Listen to the thundering sound of the waterfall and enjoy a snack before returning.

COASTAL BEACHES

OCEAN SAFETY TIPS

- Don't turn your back on the surf.
- Make sure your belongings are above the high tide line.
- Bring a tide table if you plan to hike around points accessible only in low tide.
- Stay away from floating drift logs.
- Beached drift logs can be slippery when wet.
- Set clear expectations when allowing kids to wade in the water.

109 OZETTE TRIANGLE: CAPE ALAVA–SAND POINT

BEFORE YOU GO
MAP Green Trails, La Push No. 163S
CONTACT Olympic National Park
NOTES National Park entrance fee; dogs prohibited; water and restrooms available; boardwalks slippery when wet; coastal section may be impassable at high tide
GPS N 48 09.272, W 124 40.135

ABOUT THE HIKE
SEASON Year-round
DIFFICULTY Moderate to difficult
DISTANCE 6 or 6.4 miles roundtrip; or to 9.2 miles loop
HIGH POINT 250 feet
ELEVATION GAIN Up to 250 feet

GETTING THERE

From Port Angeles, take US Highway 101 west for 5.5 miles to the intersection with State Route 112. Go right on SR 112, driving 38 miles to an intersection. Turn right, staying on SR 112, through the town of Sekiu, and drive 10.5 miles until you reach Hoko–Ozette Road. Turn left and drive 21 miles to the Ozette Ranger Station and parking area.

ON THE TRAIL

Boardwalks through coastal forest, miles of Pacific beach, a legion of majestic sea stacks, and a treasure hunt for mysterious petroglyphs await hikers who take on the Olympic Coast's iconic Ozette Triangle. It's one of Olympic National Park's most popular hikes, and it doesn't take long to see why. From Lake Ozette, trails depart in two directions: one to Sand Point, and the other to Cape Alava. Each can be hiked approximately 3 miles out to the beach via a string of boardwalks for an approximately 6-mile roundtrip, or they can be combined into a triangular loop for a strenuous 9.2-mile hike.

Lake Ozette to Sand Point (3 miles one-way)

Sand Point is a sandy, crescent-shaped beach protected by a shoal that keeps wave action offshore at low and medium tides. It's the easier of the two destinations, with little elevation gain as the trail snakes through coastal forest to

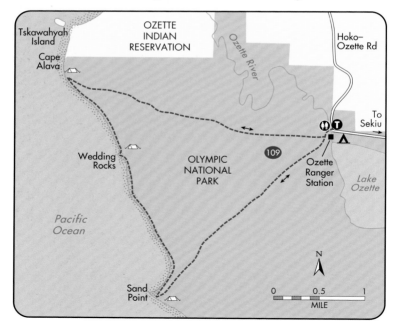

Sand Point and Cape Alava are excellent first backpacking trips for kids.

the ocean. From the trail junction beyond the ranger station, choose the path to the left. Walking the boardwalk is fun at first, and it certainly keeps your feet dry, but it also poses hazards. When wet, boardwalks can be slippery, and feet and hiking sticks can get stuck between boards and in rotten sections. It takes some vigilance to prevent a fall.

After hiking 2.5 miles, pay attention to your senses. First, smell the salt air, then hear the waves, and finally see the Pacific Ocean. Sand Point is a delight. A promontory can be carefully climbed to show how the land juts out into the sea and to view sea stacks that stick up like a bunch of thumbs from the water. Camping is allowed south of Sand Point and makes an excellent first backpacking destination for kids, but because campfires aren't allowed, many opt for Cape Alava.

Lake Ozette to Cape Alava (3.2 miles one-way)

Cape Alava is the westernmost place in the contiguous United States and the more popular of the two destinations. The tree-topped sea stacks offshore, grassy campsites, and abundant wildlife attract hikers. This section of beach is also open for campfires. The hike to Cape Alava, however, is more difficult than to Sand Point. The trail, with boardwalk, gains and loses more than 250 feet on its trek to the ocean, with numerous stairs. The ferns along this stretch are enormous, and the trail passes through an airy forest of cedar and spruce. At 2.2 miles, hike through Ahlstrom's Prairie, an old homestead now grown over. The final 0.5 mile is downhill to Cape Alava. To the north is distinctive Tskawahyah Island and to the west is Ozette Island. In between is a protected area that is excellent for finding crabs, anemones, and other sea creatures at low tide. Campsites are to the north, and beyond is the Ozette Indian Reservation.

Sand Point to Cape Alava (3 miles one-way)

Between Sand Point and Cape Alava are 3 miles of beach. Near the middle is Wedding Rocks, where Makah petroglyphs can be found etched into boulders strewn around a headland. For walkers, the beach throws up a few obstacles. Your feet sink into the deep drifts of surf-smoothed beach pebbles, which makes for a tiring slog. Occasionally you'll encounter a tree lodged perpendicular to the beach. And two headlands may require an upland detour at high tide. The Wedding Rocks are the prize of this section; you can spend hours searching the rocks for centuries-old petroglyphs of faces, ships, and whales. The Wedding Rocks are 1.9 miles north of Sand Point and 1.1 miles south of Cape Alava. A few campsites are located just to the north of the rocks, but there is no freshwater source.

110 HOLE-IN-THE-WALL

BEFORE YOU GO
   MAP Green Trails, Ozette No. 130S
   CONTACT Olympic National Park
   NOTES Dogs on leash allowed to Ellen Creek; privy available; bring a tide table
   GPS N 47 55.277, W 124 38.274

ABOUT THE HIKE
   SEASON Year-round
   DIFFICULTY Easy to moderate
   DISTANCE 3.4 miles roundtrip
   HIGH POINT 10 feet
   ELEVATION GAIN None

GETTING THERE

From Port Angeles, take US Highway 101 west for 54 miles to the Mora-La Push Road (State Route 110). (From Forks, drive 2 miles north to SR 110.) Turn right (west) on SR 110 and drive 7.9 miles to a crossroads. Bear right on Mora Road (SR 110 Spur) and travel 5.1 miles to the trailhead at Rialto Beach at road's end.

ON THE TRAIL

Let the kids scream with abandon as they sprint down this long, beautiful beach. A chorus line of loud breaking waves drowns out the kid noise as they dance at the edge of the foamy water. This is a truly wild beach. Even on calm days, the waves are big, and the drum of the ocean beats in your chest.

Rialto Beach is one of the most accessible on the Olympic Coast, and families can hike 1.7 miles to a sea-carved archway called Hole-in-the-Wall. During low tide you can climb through the arch and wander among tide pools filled with waving green anemone, colorful sea stars, cute little hermit crabs, and enormous barnacles.

To the south, James Island guards the mouth of the Quillayute River; it is part of the Quileute Indian Reservation. Known also as *A-Ka-Lat*, meaning

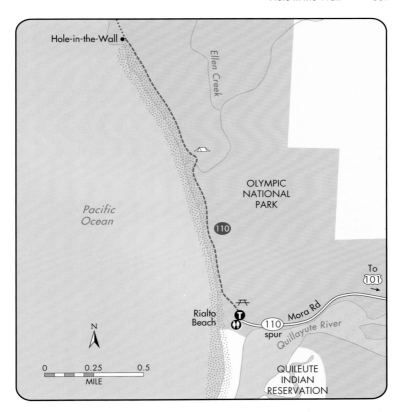

"Top of the Rock," it has served as a lookout point to spot whales and as an ancient burial ground for important tribal elders. It's one of the few area islands that is not part of the vast Quillayute Needles National Wildlife Refuge. The flat-topped island in the distance is fancifully called Cake Rock.

From the trailhead, the beach is only a hop, skip, and a jump through tumbled driftwood. At low tide the walking is easy on the wet sand, but at high tide walkers are routed onto a pebble beach and soft dry sand that makes travel more difficult. If you're able to time your visit, plan to reach Hole-in-the-Wall about a half hour prior to low tide. This provides the greatest opportunity for easy beach walking and successful tidepooling.

As you walk toward a dramatic beached sea stack, imagine storms that ravage the coast each year. The ocean has deposited huge root balls like popcorn among rows and rows of gargantuan trees. Skeletal snags stand stark on the edge of a contorted maritime forest. A fierce winter storm that coincides with high tide can rearrange all of it within a matter of hours.

At 0.8 mile, reach Ellen Creek. You may have to get your feet wet to cross it. Camping is allowed north of here, and the sites are not as crowded as those at Second or Third beaches. Proceed onward, reaching a big beached sea stack and then the Hole-in-the-Wall archway at 1.7 miles.

Go through Hole-in-the-Wall only if no water flows over its entry. Minus tides provide the best window of opportunity. Even if the water is too high for safe exploration, this is a lovely spot for a picnic. The beach here is sandy and protected from the largest waves—great for some well-deserved sand play. An overland trail—steep, with unforgiving drop-offs along a narrow catwalk at the top of a headland—offers unbeatable views above the salty mist in either direction. It's not appropriate for young kids (or older ones you don't fully trust), but adults may want to take turns climbing up for the photo opportunities.

Hole-in-the-Wall at low tide

On the return, make sure you keep an eye on the rising tide. Never turn your back on the ocean. Sneaker waves can wash over the unaware and knock them to the ground with great force.

EXPLORING FURTHER

Backpackers can trek north for miles, but it is not easy hiking. Impassable headlands require difficult overland routes, choked with mud, roots, and rickety ladders. Beaches can be full of driftwood and rocks. Timing the tides is essential. Those who brave the difficult conditions, however, are rewarded with empty beaches and the potential to see the remains of the wreckage of two old ships grounded offshore.

111 SECOND BEACH

BEFORE YOU GO
   MAP Green Trails, La Push No. 163S
   CONTACT Olympic National Park
   NOTES Dogs prohibited; privy available
   GPS N 47 53.892, W 124 37.425

ABOUT THE HIKE
   SEASON Year-round
   DIFFICULTY Easy
   DISTANCE 1.5 miles roundtrip
   HIGH POINT 160 feet
   ELEVATION GAIN 160 feet

GETTING THERE

From Port Angeles, take US Highway 101 west 54 miles to the Mora-La Push Road/State Route 110. (From Forks, drive 2 miles north to SR 110.) Turn right (west) on SR 110 and drive 7.9 miles to a crossroads. Remain left on SR 110 toward La Push. In 5.2 miles, look for a parking area on the left. A large overflow lot is accessible from the main parking lot. The trailhead is accessible by public transportation.

ON THE TRAIL

My kids have declared that Second Beach boasts the best sand on the coast. It's soft and moldable, with no rocks to get in the way of digging and building projects. The beach is a mile-long ribbon of this wonderful sand, with big breaking waves and piles of driftwood. You can go for an afternoon, a full day, or, best of all, a night. Backpackers are rewarded with brilliant sunsets, starry skies, and tidal changes.

At the trailhead, notice the enormous overflow parking lot. If it is full—most commonly on summer holiday weekends—expect company, especially if you're planning to backpack. Each car represents people on Second Beach, especially beginning backpackers. If you're day hiking, it is easy enough to spread out, but if you're camping, you will find only a limited number of guaranteed tide-free camping locations.

Enter the forest and feel the dampness immediately. The air is thick from fog, rain, and the concentration of spongy green plants. The tree shapes are fanciful, with multiple trunks, odd bulges, and twisty aboveground root systems. It's the kind of forest that inspires scary campfire tales—and story lines in the popular young adult *Twilight* series set in nearby Forks.

The well-maintained trail travels uphill a short distance before descending on a series of long steps to the ocean at 0.75 mile. The level beach expands and contracts markedly with the tides and is ideal for flying kites, throwing Frisbees, and constructing sandcastles. While Third Beach's sea stacks are off in the distance, Second Beach's are intimately arrayed close by. A natural arch peeps through the headland at the northwest end of the beach, and the Quillayute Needles pop up from the sea. The tree-topped sea stack, Crying Lady Rock, is the most prominent feature. Through binoculars you may be able to identify nesting and sheltering shorebirds on its cliffs. A few large rocky outcrops rise directly from the beach. These natural features break the waves, making the surf safer for wading, and they also provide habitat for sea stars, anemones, and other sea creatures that can be seen at low tide.

Take time to explore as much of Second Beach as possible. Wandering south, you'll shed the crowds and fall into the rhythm of the surf. Look to the

Fun in the sand at Second Beach (photo by Erika Schreder)

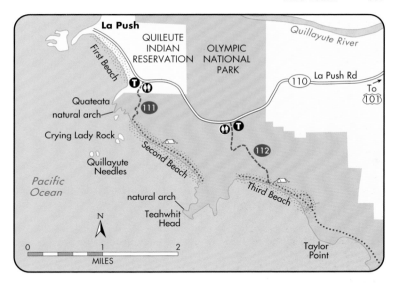

forest for eagles perched in the trees, to the surf for gulls scouting for their next meal, and to the far headland for another natural arch, bookending the one to the northwest. When you are ready, retrace your steps.

112 THIRD BEACH

BEFORE YOU GO
MAP Green Trails, La Push No. 163S
CONTACT Olympic National Park
NOTES Dogs prohibited; privy available; bring a tide table
GPS N 47 53.412, W 124 36.005

ABOUT THE HIKE
SEASON Year-round
DIFFICULTY Easy to moderate
DISTANCE 2.6 miles roundtrip
HIGH POINT 300 feet
ELEVATION GAIN 300 feet

GETTING THERE
From Port Angeles, take US Highway 101 west 54 miles to the Mora-La Push Road/State Route 110. (From Forks, drive 2 miles north to SR 110.) Turn right (west) on SR 110 and drive 7.9 miles to a crossroads. Remain left on SR 110 toward La Push. In 3.8 miles, look for a large parking area on the left. The trailhead to Third Beach is at the east end of the lot. This trail is accessible by public transportation.

ON THE TRAIL

Every visit to Third Beach is an adventure, with moody coastal weather arbitrarily summoning fog, wind, rain, and sun. A hike through the stunted maritime forest on a misty day is palpably different from a stroll here on a sunny afternoon. But one thing never changes: the appeal of this mile-long beach and the pantheon of dramatic sea stacks out at sea.

From the trailhead, wind through a humid coastal forest for a full mile before descending to the beach. The trees—mostly Sitka spruce, alder, and hemlock—grow larger the farther you get from the road. Look on the trunks for colorful shelf fungus and to the understory for the fruits of the forest: thimbleberries, red huckleberries, and salal.

At 1 mile, start your descent to the beach, the surf audible now with its soothing cadence. Small children will need help over some of the tall, rooty steps on the trail, as well as over a mass of driftwood between the trail and the beach. Once you've reached the beach at 1.3 miles, take off your shoes and socks and let the sand get between your toes. The kids will dash toward the surf with buckets and shovels, allowing you to take in the scene: Teahwhit Head, the impassable headland to the west, juts out into the ocean on one side and Taylor Point on the other. A dozen or more captivating sea stacks rise up from the water like scales on a dragon's back. When the kids return to your orbit, tell them it is called the Giants Graveyard.

If you have time, explore the half mile of beach south to a waterfall that plummets into the ocean off Taylor Point. A landslide across the beach, easily skirted during low tide, can present an obstacle during high water. A muddy trail over the slide has been carved by hikers, but the rest of the way is smooth sailing. A difficult overland trail—with rope ladders and ankle-twisting mud and roots—climbs over Taylor Point to access remote and spectacular ocean beaches beyond. Save that for an epic backpacking adventure when the kids are older.

Don't forget a bucket for sand play. (photo by Jon Stier)

WEST PENINSULA RAIN FORESTS

113 HOH RAIN FOREST NATURE TRAILS

BEFORE YOU GO
  MAP Green Trails, Seven Lakes Basin–Mt Olympus Climbing, No. 133S
  CONTACT Olympic National Park
  NOTES National Park entry fee required; dogs prohibited; restrooms available
  GPS N 47 51.635, W 123 56.082

ABOUT THE HIKE
  SEASON Year-round
  DIFFICULTY Easy
  DISTANCE 1 to 2.3 miles loops
  HIGH POINT 700 feet
  ELEVATION GAIN Up to 100 feet

GETTING THERE
From Forks, follow US Highway 101 south 12 miles to the Upper Hoh Road. Head east (left) and take the Upper Hoh Road 18 miles to the road's end at the Hoh Rain Forest Visitor Center.

ON THE TRAIL
In the Hoh Rain Forest, rainfall is measured by the foot, not the inch. Each year a prodigious 12 to 14 feet of rain feeds the forest's rivers and creeks, grows Sitka spruce and western hemlock to record-sized proportions, and thickens moss on every surface. It's one of the finest examples of a temperate rain forest remaining on the Pacific Coast. As such, it is home to critters big and small. The Hoh boasts the largest year-round population of Washington's state mammal, the Roosevelt elk, and is a great place to spot the yellow banana slug sliming its way across the trail.

Two short nature trails offer distinctly different rain forest experiences. The 1-mile Hall of Mosses Trail climbs uphill to a grove of big-leaf maple trees cloaked with long, mossy beards. The 1.3-mile Spruce Nature Trail, by contrast, travels across a forested old riverbed mowed low by grazing elk, reaching the shores of the Hoh River. This river is fed by rainfall and glaciers 7000 feet up on the slopes of Mount Olympus. The silt from those glaciers gives the river its milky look.

To make the most of a day in the Hoh, start at the Hoh Rain Forest Visitor Center. Get the kids started in the Junior Ranger program or consider picking up one of the Discovery Packs filled with field guides and binoculars. With these in hand, kids will slow down and be more observant of the little things that are so extraordinary within this environment. Because the nature hikes are short, you can hike both trails, or soldier forth on the Hoh River Trail (see Exploring Further).

From the universally accessible mini-loop, head off to the left for the Hall of Mosses Trail. Wind through a boggy wetland and cross over a green-bottomed creek. Search for fish among the wavy mermaid hair before proceeding to the loop junction. Go left, climbing uphill and into a primeval forest of giant, moss-draped trees and crazy root systems. Both the huge big-leaf maple and the shorter vine maple host a variety of epiphytes, air plants that grow off of other plants high above the ground. Wander and admire, then start descending to the loop junction and the Spruce Nature Trail.

There are several intersections to maneuver through to get to the Spruce Nature Trail. Follow the signs, and when you reach the loop trail, travel to the left. The difference between the two trails is obvious immediately. The forest

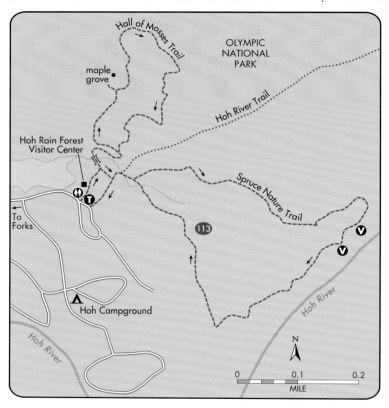

Working on a Junior Ranger badge along the banks of the Hoh River

floor here looks like a manicured park by comparison, cropped clean by elk. The trail traverses an old section of riverbed, now grown with alders and cottonwoods and spotted with sword ferns.

At 0.6 mile, the trail reaches the Hoh River, running at a good clip on its way to the Pacific Ocean. There are several places to stop for a picnic and even throw a few stones into its chalky current. The trail parallels the river for a quarter mile before returning to the forest. There are several examples of trees growing out of nurse logs; the most impressive boasts a row of eight mature trees emerging out of one rotting log, with the roots all intertwined aboveground. When you reach the end of the loop, return left for the visitor center.

GREAT GETAWAY: RAIN FOREST AND BEACHES

Build a sandcastle and hug a great big tree. The beauty of the west side of the Olympics is this diversity: wild coastal beaches with gigantic sea stacks and ocean surf, and a lush temperate rain forest that boasts some of the largest conifers in the country. Yes, it can rain here. Up to 14 feet of rain falls annually in the Hoh Rain Forest. But that's part of the allure. Why visit a rain forest when it's sunny?

Basic, but centrally located, accommodations can be found in Forks, and beachside cabins are located in La Push and Kalaloch. There are several campgrounds to choose from—Mora, Kalaloch, and Hoh are all favorites that provide plentiful nearby diversions. The coast is also the perfect place to try out backpacking. Each of the short coastal hikes can be done as a backpack, allowing for sunrises, sunsets, sandcastles, tidepooling, and relaxing on the beach.

EXPLORING FURTHER

A longer alternative to the busy nature trails near the visitor center is the Hoh River Trail, which leads 17.3 miles to the flanks of Mount Olympus. You need not walk its entire length to appreciate the Hoh Rain Forest. Nearly every turn reveals a new wonder: shamrock-leaved Oregon oxalis on the forest floor, downed logs nursing dozens of plants and trees, moss as thick as Santa's beard, and magnificent, enormous conifers. The trail nears the river at 1 mile for a short outing and reaches the Mount Tom Creek campsites at 2.3 miles. Backpackers can live for a short time in this Hoh fairyland by hiking to Mount Tom or to Five Mile Island, at 5.3 miles.

114 QUINAULT RAIN FOREST TRAILS

BEFORE YOU GO

MAP Green Trails, Lake Quinault No. 197; map available at ranger station and lodge
CONTACT Olympic National Forest
NOTES Northwest Forest Pass required; restrooms and water available
GPS N 47 27.586, W 123 51.717

ABOUT THE HIKE (RAIN FOREST NATURE TRAIL)

SEASON Year-round
DIFFICULTY Easy
DISTANCE 0.6 mile loop
HIGH POINT 300 feet
ELEVATION GAIN 100 feet

ABOUT THE HIKE (QUINAULT LOOP TRAIL)

SEASON Year-round
DIFFICULTY Easy to moderate
DISTANCE 1.7 miles loop
HIGH POINT 380 feet
ELEVATION GAIN 175 feet

GETTING THERE

From Hoquiam, drive north on US Highway 101 for 37 miles. Turn right on South Shore Road. To reach the Rain Forest Nature Trail parking area, drive 1.5 miles and turn right into the large lot. To reach the Quinault Loop trailhead, continue on the South Shore Road less than a mile farther to a small lot on the right just before the Lake Quinault Lodge. The trailhead is accessible by public transportation.

ON THE TRAIL

The opportunity to hug the world's largest Sitka spruce tree draws people to the Quinault Rain Forest each year. But what keeps them coming back is a fine trail system where they can choose their own adventure among delightful waterfalls, misty giants, and an intensely verdant understory. An extra treat is the gracious 1926 Lake Quinault Lodge, where hikers can warm up in front of the lobby's fireplace or cool off with a dip in the lake.

About 10 miles of well-maintained trails loop about on the mountainside south of Lake Quinault, linking three lakeside campgrounds and the lodge. Pick up a map at the ranger station or lodge to plot your route. To begin, I recommend two short loops: the Rain Forest Nature Trail (0.6 mile) and the Quinault Loop Trail (1.7 miles). These can also can be combined to create a longer 4.2-mile loop.

Rain Forest Nature Trail

This interpretive trail is an ideal orientation to the Quinault Rain Forest, providing context to the lush ecosystem of a temperate rain forest. Follow the trail clockwise. The first section, suitable for strollers, soon arrives at an immense Douglas fir with a deck built around it. A sign points out that most of the area's big Douglas firs are 250 to 550 years old, but some are much older.

The trail soon approaches Willaby Creek, then ascends and pulls away. Among the monster trees, you will see a few stumps from long-ago logging

Don't forget to look skyward for perspective.

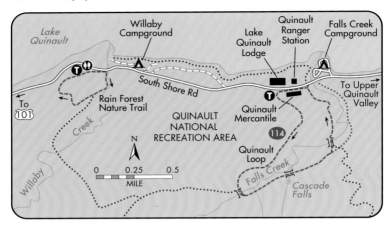

efforts. One in particular catches the eye: it sports a hemlock that has wrapped its roots around the top of the stump, as well as a notch where the loggers put a springboard where they could stand and cut higher on the trunk.

At a well-signed intersection at 0.3 mile, go right to complete the loop. There are some big, beautiful trees here, but it is hard to assess how tall they are until they fall. Check out the enormous root ball and seemingly endless length of a Douglas fir that fell perpendicular to the trail. Its trunk is thick all the way to the very top. Before you know it, the trail loops back to the trailhead at 0.6 mile, and it's time to seek another adventure.

Quinault Loop Trail

The showcase of the Quinault Loop is not the trees, or even the pleasant waterfall, but the incredibly lush understory—every square centimeter jam-packed with dozens of varieties of ferns, berries, moss, wildflowers, and more. Catch the well-groomed trail directly across from the Lake Quinault Lodge and immediately enter its green world. The first half mile of trail is uphill, topping out near an enormous red cedar that kids can climb inside.

The sound of the creek grows louder as you descend to a junction at 0.6 mile (365 feet). Go left for Cascade Falls. Cross Falls Creek and climb once again until you reach the waterfall, gently tumbling 20 feet beneath the bridge. A sturdy fence keeps hikers from tumbling down the steep hillside and provides a good vantage, but there is no place to sit and reflect.

Continue on, veering left at the junction with the Gatton Creek Trail to return via Falls Creek. Walk beneath the shaggy arms of big-leaf maples, crossing Falls Creek again, until you reach the road. Pick up a paved trail to the left of a small parking area and pass the ranger station, a store, and the lodge to reach the trailhead.

Opposite: Within reason, allow your kids to accessorize their hiking clothes.

COLUMBIA RIVER

LONG BEACH AND THE SOUTHWEST COAST

115 WILLAPA ART TRAIL

BEFORE YOU GO
MAP USGS Long Island
CONTACT Willapa National Wildlife Refuge
NOTES Dogs prohibited; privy available
GPS N 46 24.865, W 123 56.055

ABOUT THE HIKE
SEASON Year-round
DIFFICULTY Easy
DISTANCE 0.5 mile roundtrip
HIGH POINT 20 feet
ELEVATION GAIN None

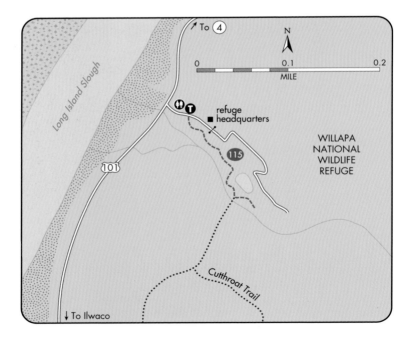

A frosty morning on the Willapa Art Trail (photo by Jon Stier)

GETTING THERE

From Kelso/Longview, take State Route 4 west 60 miles to US Highway 101. Turn left on US 101 South. In 4.7 miles, near milepost 24, arrive at the Willapa National Wildlife Refuge headquarters. Turn left into the parking lot.

ON THE TRAIL

Sculpture garden meets hiking trail at the headquarters property for Willapa National Wildlife Refuge. The Willapa Art Trail is a hidden treasure that you shouldn't miss on your journey to the coast. Dozens of sculptures—the work of art students at the University of Washington—line a 0.25-mile ADA-accessible boardwalk along tidal flats and a restored salmon-bearing stream.

Begin at the green Phytoplankton Entry Gate and begin a scavenger hunt for members of the animal kingdom rendered in wood, bronze, steel, and other materials. The artwork is all around—on a picnic table, taking flight from the tidal flats, swimming in the trees, perched on the handrail, climbing up rocks. Even the boardwalk itself is a work of art, gently sweeping and curving like a

WILLAPA SCAVENGER HUNT

Hummingbird	Caddisfly	Slug
Bear	Mussel	Snail
Dragonfly	Frog	Salamander
Salmon (how many?)	Feather	

sinuous stream. At the culmination of the boardwalk is the "Amphibitheater," where twenty-five bronze amphibians slither and hide. See if you can find all thirteen species that are present in the refuge.

EXPLORING FURTHER

Near the Amphibitheater, the Cutthroat Trail leads steeply uphill to the headwaters of the salmon stream. It is an additional two-thirds-of-a-mile loop trail among lush ferns and hemlocks. This trail, also dotted with interpretive signs and art, is worth exploring for older kids who have extra energy to burn before returning to the car for the long ride to or from the coast.

116 LEADBETTER POINT BAY LOOP

BEFORE YOU GO
MAP Available online
CONTACT Washington State Parks or Willapa National Wildlife Refuge
NOTES Discover Pass required; dogs prohibited; privy available
GPS N 46 36.412, W 124 02.622

ABOUT THE HIKE
SEASON Year-round
DIFFICULTY Easy to moderate
DISTANCE 1.2 miles loop
HIGH POINT 50 feet
ELEVATION GAIN 35 feet

GETTING THERE

From Kelso/Longview, take State Route 4 west 60 miles to US Highway 101. Turn left on US 101 South for 15 miles. In the town of Seaview, just before entering Long Beach, turn right on Sandridge Road (notice signs for Leadbetter Point). In just over 11 miles, connect with SR 103 and follow it north another 7.5 miles to the road's end in Leadbetter Point State Park.

ON THE TRAIL

The longest continuous sand beach in the United States is right here in Washington, running 28 miles up the Long Beach Peninsula. At the tip of the peninsula is Leadbetter Point, a wildlife-rich ecosystem of ocean beaches, salt marsh, and forested coastal dunes.

The area boasts more than 6 miles of quiet trails. The ones leading to the beach are impassable in all but the summer months, when hungry mosquitoes rule without mercy. It's best to visit in the mosquito-free season from September through May, when you're likely to have the place to yourself and can reach the water on the Willapa Bay side. Families will most enjoy the Bay Loop Trail, which combines the highlights of the maritime dune forest with a good opportunity to spot wildlife in the salt marshes of Willapa Bay. Five stations with interpretive displays provide context for this complex and dynamic environment and the creatures that live and visit here.

Leadbetter Point's Bay Loop Trail can be hiked in every season. (photo by Jon Stier)

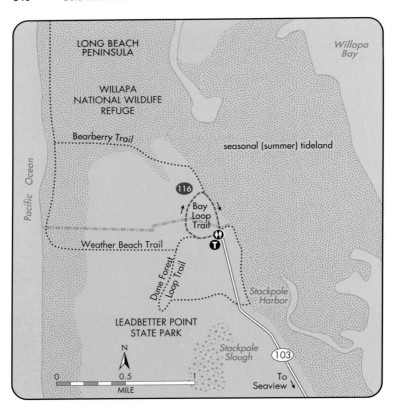

Begin the hike at the trailhead to the left of the privy. Hike a short distance along the Dune Forest Loop Trail. At the first intersection, veer right on the Bay Loop and enter the adjacent Willapa National Wildlife Refuge. Take time to examine this dune forest environment as you walk. The trunks and broken branches of shore pine appear spray-painted with light green lichen, and the understory is often thick with salal. It's quiet but for the thumping, unseen ocean and occasional birdsong.

At 0.6 mile, reach an intersection with the Bearberry Trail. This 1.3-mile spur, a portion of which is usually flooded from October to June, leads to the Pacific Ocean. Instead, stay right for the highlight of the hike along Willapa Bay's salt marsh. Look for motionless great blue herons, massing sandpipers, and playful marine-foraging river otters as you loop back along the bay. At the end of this section, climb to an observation platform for a good view of the bay before you return to your car.

117 CAPE DISAPPOINTMENT STATE PARK

BEFORE YOU GO
MAP Available online
CONTACT Washington State Parks
NOTES Discover Pass required; dogs must be leashed; restrooms and water available
GPS N 46 17.886, W 124 04.344

ABOUT THE HIKE
SEASON Year-round
DIFFICULTY Easy to moderate
DISTANCE 1.1 miles roundtrip
HIGH POINT 300 feet
ELEVATION GAIN 50 feet

GETTING THERE

From Kelso/Longview, take State Route 4 west 60 miles to US Highway 101. Turn left on US 101 South. In 13 miles, arrive at an intersection with US 101-Alt. Go left on US 101-Alt for just 0.6 mile and make a right onto US 101 North and drive 2.2 miles into Ilwaco. At 2nd Avenue SW (SR 100), turn left. This road becomes Robert Gray Drive and leads into Cape Disappointment State Park. Drive 2.7 miles, following signs for the Lewis and Clark Interpretive Center, and park in the center's lot.

ON THE TRAIL

Few parks pack in as much outdoor variety as Cape Disappointment State Park. There's enough to keep a family busy here for several days—hiking and biking trails, long beaches, a military fort, and an interpretive center, as well as an active maritime environment, two historic lighthouses, and one of the state's premier campgrounds. Most of the park's 8 miles of trails are family-friendly, and campers may want to try out each of them. One of the most crowd-pleasing is the short trek out to Cape Disappointment Lighthouse. Here you get a museum, historic battery, and hike all in one package.

LEWIS AND CLARK INTERPRETIVE CENTER

Exploring the top-notch Lewis and Clark Interpretive Center is an excellent addition to a visit to Cape Disappointment State Park. William Clark spent several days in November 1805 roaming all over Cape Disappointment. The center describes the explorers' route, especially the Washington portion, and has hands-on exhibits for all ages. Another exhibit details maritime history, with a big picture window overlooking the whitecapped waves at the mouth of the Columbia River, known to sailors as the "Graveyard of the Pacific."

From the parking area at the Lewis and Clark Interpretive Center, enter the adjacent labyrinthine military battery. As part of Fort Canby, the Battery Harvey Allen was built before World War I to defend the Columbia River. Interpretive kiosks describe the military history of the park, which dates to before the Civil War. Be sure to take some time to explore now or when you return. Kids will love exploring the maze of rooms, and it is fascinating to learn a bit about the history of the area. On the far side of the battery, pick up a dirt trail and turn left to descend the headland and an overlook of Deadman's Cove. It may be tempting to access the beach, but please heed the signs and stay off the steep terrain. The dirt trail ends at a Coast Guard gate.

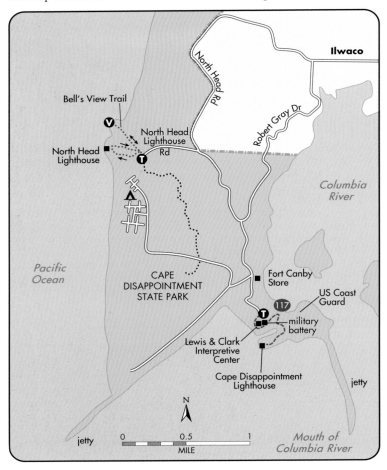

Exploring the trails near the North Head Lighthouse (photo by Jon Stier)

Curve around the cove to the right and walk up a road to the Cape Disappointment Lighthouse. Built in 1856, this is the oldest operating lighthouse on the Pacific Coast. Check out the elaborate system of manmade jetties that makes passage into the Columbia River safer. Look for ships navigating the currents and imagine the more than two thousand vessels wrecked by this treacherous passage over the past three hundred years. To the south is the Oregon Coast Range, with Saddle Mountain most prominent on the horizon. Retrace your steps when you are done.

EXPLORING FURTHER

Is the family up for more adventures? If so, hop back in the car and drive to the North Head Lighthouse. A quick 0.25-mile jaunt takes visitors to the North Head Lighthouse, which offers tours during summer months (kids age seven and up only). This is the "newer" of the park's two lighthouses, built in 1898 to alert vessels coming from the north to the hazardous waters at the mouth of the Columbia River. Peer out at the Pacific Ocean, watch waves slam against the rocky headlands, and contemplate the immense natural forces that sculpt the trees here.

Returning to the parking area, consider also taking the paved Bell's View Trail 0.3 mile to a large viewing platform where you can scan north along the Long Beach Peninsula and even to the Olympics. Interpretive signs about weather and a multitiered military bunker provide historical perspective.

VANCOUVER AREA

118 RIDGEFIELD NATIONAL WILDLIFE REFUGE–OAKS TO WETLANDS TRAIL

BEFORE YOU GO

MAP Available from refuge website
CONTACT Ridgefield National Wildlife Refuge
NOTES Refuge fee required; dogs prohibited; privy available
GPS N 45 49.876, W 122 44.917

ABOUT THE HIKE

SEASON Year-round
DIFFICULTY Easy
DISTANCE 2 miles loop
HIGH POINT 75 feet
ELEVATION GAIN 25 feet

GETTING THERE

From Vancouver, take Interstate 5 north to exit 14 (State Route 501/Pioneer Street). Follow SR 501 west 3 miles to the town of Ridgefield. Turn right on N Main Avenue and drive 1.1 miles to the Ridgefield National Wildlife Refuge office. Turn left into the parking area and park near the privies.

ON THE TRAIL

The Oaks to Wetlands Trail is known as much for its gorgeous old Oregon white oaks as for its preponderance of wildlife. These trees—some four hundred years old or more—are truly something to behold. In the winter, their bare branches create architectural silhouettes against a bright sky. In summer, they leaf out and offer habitat to birds and dense shade from the sun. Pass beneath their limbs on a looping trail that runs through wetland and forest

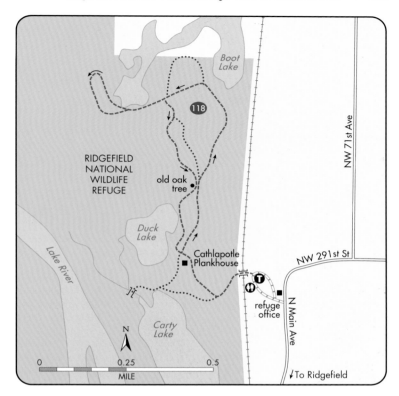

environments, with views across the Carty Unit of the Ridgefield National Wildlife Refuge.

Begin by crossing the railroad tracks on a high, arching pedestrian bridge. This is an extremely busy rail corridor, and it is almost certain that a train (or four) will blast through during your visit. If you're lucky or patient, you'll be standing on this bridge when one zooms beneath your feet. The paved trail leads first to the distinctive Cathlapotle Plankhouse, a full-scale replica based on archaeological evidence from a site on the refuge property. The plankhouse is open to the public on weekend afternoons from mid-April to October and provides a glimpse into the cultural heritage of native peoples in this area.

Continuing on your hike, take the forested pullouts on the right-hand side of the paved pathway. The trailside is sprinkled with helpful signs that identify common native plants in the refuge—Indian plum, Oregon grape, stinging nettle, western red cedar, and more. Joining up with the main trail again, reach a peaceful vista of the refuge and an enormous oak with remarkably long branches.

Bring binoculars to spot birds in the wetlands at Ridgefield National Wildlife Refuge.

Shortly thereafter at 0.5 mile, go right at a junction and follow a counter-clockwise loop. There are many trail junctions. It's a good rule of thumb (with one exception) to always choose the right-hand option, which will take you through the forest, past Boot Lake, and up near the refuge boundary. An additional trail north of the boundary, open seasonally, is less well-maintained. Skip it and curve around to the left, reaching a junction at 1 mile that takes hikers on a separate short loop to a lovely basalt outcrop. This is a wonderful place to break out some snacks, peer through the binoculars, and take in the expanse of the wetlands. In late April and May this knoll is flush with purple camas flowers, a staple in the historic diet of Native Americans. They harvested the bulbs and ate them like you would a potato.

Continue on your rightward journey, looping back toward the main paved path. Look for waterfowl swimming in Duck Lake or great blue herons posing frozen on its shores. Pass the plankhouse and return over the railroad tracks for a last opportunity to witness a train scream by.

EXPLORING FURTHER

Don't miss taking the 4.2-mile Auto Tour Route in the River "S" Unit of the Ridgefield National Wildlife Refuge on the other side of Ridgefield. Your car is your personal observation blind, allowing wildlife viewing and photography from the road that wouldn't otherwise be possible on foot. During a spring visit we saw egrets, river otters, herons, geese, sandpipers, and many ducks—all in the first five minutes of the drive. From May 1 to September 30, the Kiwa Trail is open for hikers. A 1.5-mile loop crosses sloughs and seasonal lakes, full of turtles, birds, and otters at the edge of an Oregon ash woodland. Climb inside a shedlike hunters' blind with binoculars and see what emerges from the cattails.

119 LACAMAS CREEK

BEFORE YOU GO
MAP Available from agency website
CONTACT Clark County Public Works
NOTES Dogs must be leashed; restroom and water at the playground
GPS N 45 36.217, W 122 24.413

ABOUT THE HIKE
SEASON Year-round
DIFFICULTY Easy to moderate
DISTANCE 2.5 miles roundtrip
HIGH POINT 200 feet
ELEVATION GAIN 100 feet

GETTING THERE

From Vancouver, take State Route 14 east to exit 12 toward Camas. Follow NW 6th Avenue to Division Street, about 1 mile. Turn left on Division Street and then right on NE 17th Avenue. At NE Everett Street (also SR 500), turn left and follow it nearly 0.9 mile to a medium-sized parking area on the right. The parking area comes up abruptly, so watch for NE Lake Road, and then take the first right into the lot. If this lot is full, there is another one on NE 35th Avenue.

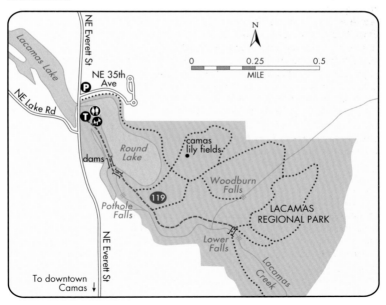

Lacamas Creek

ON THE TRAIL

A lake, three waterfalls, dense forest, and a bluff full of wildflowers in the middle of the city? Yes indeed! Lacamas Regional Park is one of the wildest city parks around and a great place to explore on foot. There are officially 6 miles of trails in the park, but the actual number is much higher, as hikers and bikers have struck their own paths to various destinations. The recommended route is an out-and-back across a dam and past two waterfalls to a picnic area, but it can be extended into a loop.

Begin your hike at the playground, where your kids can expend excess energy and use the restroom before striking off on the trail. Follow the shoreline of Round Lake counterclockwise on a wide trail to a set of two dams. The original dams, which created the lake, were built in 1883 to support logging operations. It's fun to cross the narrow catwalks on the dams. There is a big wheel you can pretend to turn and gears to maneuver around. Hikers are protected by a chain-link fence, so it's quite safe to watch the water pour out under your feet into Lacamas Creek.

Once across, turn right and follow the creek downstream away from the lake. The trail system is quite labyrinthine, and you will come to many junctions. Always choose the one that keeps the creek to your right. Lacamas Creek is a constant source of interest. During the rainy season, the creek rollicks with whitewater. During summer the water level lowers dramatically and large, smooth potholes emerge. You may see people playing in the creek, but be aware that each year there are several accidents from falls in this area.

The roar of water will build as you near modest Pothole Falls at 0.5 mile. Continuing on, arrive at a rocky bald. This isn't the park's main camas lily field, but it is a satisfying sampling of the lovely purple flower (in spring) for which the park and city were named. Please tread carefully to protect the delicate plants even when they are not in bloom.

Keep choosing the right option at each fork, now following signs for Lower Falls. The trail winds through impressive large stands of Douglas fir as it travels downhill. At 1.25 miles, reach Lower Falls. A long bridge spans the creek, allowing for a good view of this broad waterfall. Picnic tables on the far side of the creek beckon for a snack or lunch before your return upstream.

EXPLORING FURTHER

A loop of about 3.5 miles is a possible alternative. To hike the loop, start on the near side of the creek, and be sure and choose the trails that appear to be the most well-trodden as you make your way in a counterclockwise direction back to Round Lake. Two side trips are worth noting: a short 0.3 mile to a third waterfall, Woodburn Falls, and a 0.7-mile loop of the camas lily fields when they are blooming in April and May. If you choose the latter, stay on the trail to avoid poison oak. Note: There are many trails that are neither mapped nor signed throughout the park. It is easy to go astray and land in steep, muddy terrain.

COLUMBIA RIVER GORGE

120 STEIGERWALD LAKE NATIONAL WILDLIFE REFUGE

BEFORE YOU GO
MAP USGS Washougal; trail map available online
CONTACT Steigerwald Lake National Wildlife Refuge
NOTES Dogs prohibited; privy available; partial seasonal wildlife closure October to April
GPS N 45 34.221, W 122 18.889

ABOUT THE HIKE
SEASON Year-round
DIFFICULTY Easy
DISTANCE 1.6 miles roundtrip to 2.8 miles loop
HIGH POINT 25 feet
ELEVATION GAIN None

GETTING THERE

From Interstate 5 in Vancouver, follow State Route 14 east 18 miles. Just past the town of Washougal, signs will signal the entrance to Steigerwald Lake National Wildlife Refuge on the right. A short gravel driveway leads to a parking lot. Seasonal bus service may be available.

ON THE TRAIL

No matter when you visit Steigerwald Lake National Wildlife Refuge, you're guaranteed to see something that flies, slithers, creeps, or honks. More than two hundred bird species have been sighted here, from great blue herons and buffleheads to bald eagles and barn owls. There are also snakes (nonpoisonous), turtles, coyotes, bats, and deer. A sweet 2.8-mile loop makes for an ideal half-day outing from May through September, and a 1.6-mile out-and-back option is pleasing from October through April when a section of the Gibbons Creek Wildlife Art Trail closes for wildlife protection.

From the parking lot, follow the level, crushed gravel path alongside an earthen dike. A tangle of white gourds near the entrance is one of several nesting sites for purple martins when they migrate here for the summer from South America. Walking toward the grove of cottonwoods in the distance, look to the skies for raptors swooping in for a meal in the sea of wetland grasses.

In two-thirds of a mile, reach a bridge across Gibbons Creek and a wildlife gate. The segment of trail beyond the gate is closed from October through

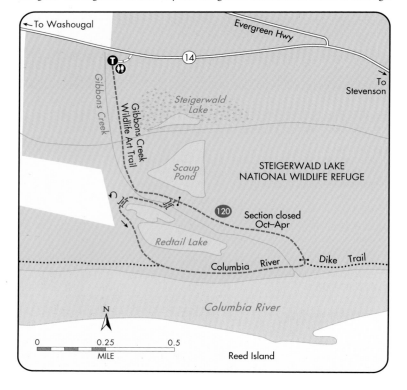

Goose perch

April for wintering birds. Never fear; plenty of wildlife can be spotted by crossing the bridge and continuing to Redtail Lake. Plan to linger on the 110-foot-long bridge spanning the lake's outlet. Look for families of ducks swimming in

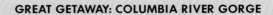

GREAT GETAWAY: COLUMBIA RIVER GORGE

The iconic image of the Columbia River Gorge is a mossy-rocked, towering waterfall in Oregon. That's all well and good, but the Washington side of the Columbia River has its own, lesser-known charms. I like it especially for the spring flower bloom that begins as early as February and peaks in April and May. The Washington side basks in the winter sun, with wide-open meadows, lofty river views, and a few of its own waterfalls. It used to be a secret, but now Portlanders regularly flock across the state line to play in an outdoor mecca less than an hour from home.

Between Portland, Vancouver, Hood River, The Dalles, and a string of little Washington towns, lodging is fairly easy to find. There are also a couple of good state park campgrounds: Beacon Rock to the west and Columbia Hills to the east. During your visit, bring bicycles to ride along the Klickitat Rail Trail near Lyle or explore your inner engineer with a visit to the Bonneville Dam. Young children will love just watching all of the modes of transportation along the Columbia River—trains, cars, boats, and barges.

the lake, pintails flying in for a landing, and painted turtles sunning themselves on logs. Members of the local birding community visit this place daily and are a great resource for identifying wildlife.

Some families will want to turn back here, for a 1.6-mile roundtrip. To complete the loop, or to catch a glimpse of the mighty Columbia, continue up to the Columbia River Dike Trail. This trail runs from the town of Washougal for 3.5 miles to just past the eastern refuge gate and provides an alternative entrance for families who want to combine a bike ride with a short hike (you must park your bikes to enter the refuge). Follow the dike trail left for 0.5 mile to the other end of the Gibbons Creek Trail. During summer months, this pathway offers a shaded return under the wispy cottonwoods and stately oaks. With all the birds competing for airspace, it can be downright noisy here.

Retracing your steps, look for a hollow tree in the middle of the trail. Inside is a sculpture of a giant beetle, one of a few art pieces along this trail. When you reach the parking lot, be sure to add your wildlife sightings to the whiteboard and start planning your next visit, when you may see new creatures both big and small.

WILDLIFE SIGHTING TIPS

- Bring binoculars.
- Be as quiet as possible.
- Listen for singing or rustling.
- Walk slowly.
- Look both high in the trees and low in the brush.
- Visit early in the morning or in the evening near dusk.
- Visit during migration season: March to May and September to December.

121 BEACON ROCK

BEFORE YOU GO

MAP Green Trails, Columbia River Gorge West No. 428S

CONTACT Washington State Parks

NOTES Discover Pass required; dogs must be leashed; restrooms and water at the second parking area; not appropriate for toddlers; winter storms can close the trail

GPS N 45 37.949, W 122 01.187

ABOUT THE HIKE

SEASON Year-round

DIFFICULTY Moderate to difficult

DISTANCE 1.5 miles roundtrip

HIGH POINT 848 feet

ELEVATION GAIN 600 feet

GETTING THERE

From Vancouver, travel east on State Route 14 approximately 35 miles to Beacon Rock State Park. Just past the state park headquarters building, look for the first of two parking areas on the right-hand side of the road. The trailhead is between the parking lots. Seasonal bus service may be available.

A series of catwalks climb up Beacon Rock.

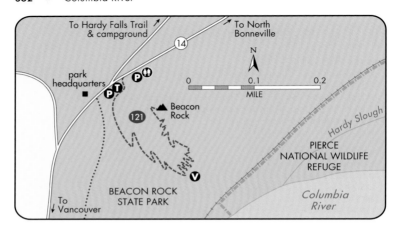

ON THE TRAIL

Geologic curiosity meets engineering showpiece at Beacon Rock. The most prominent natural landmark in the Columbia River Gorge Scenic Area can be scaled on a trail the likes of which you've never experienced. Fifty-three switchbacks zigzag up the side of a stone monolith high above the river on a series of catwalks and trail blasted into the rock. It's more exhilarating than frightening and easier than it sounds. Iron railings protect hikers the entire way, and while it may not be suitable for toddlers, its unique wow factor provides substantial motivation for older kids.

Thumblike Beacon Rock is believed to be either the core of an ancient volcano or the result of lava oozing through cracks in the earth's surface. In either case, the soft exterior of the formation was eroded by time and cataclysmic ice age floods that roared down the Columbia River. Named by Lewis and Clark in 1805, Beacon Rock was in private hands until it became a state park in 1935. Henry J. Biddle purchased the rock in 1915 with the sole purpose of building a trail to the top. As you walk the series of ramps, bridges, and steps, imagine what it took to build this trail more than one hundred years ago.

Begin your climb between the two parking areas, mere feet from Beacon Rock's vertical basalt walls. The views of the Columbia River begin almost immediately, revealing more with every hairpin turn. Spread below is a fascinating juxtaposition of the natural and built environments. There are two busy railroad corridors and two wildlife-rich islands, farms and mountains, barge traffic, and a wide river that once ran wild. With the trail snaking precariously along the mountainside, and sometimes on top of itself, it is breathtaking in more ways than one. You'll want to stop and check out the scene often.

The trail heads into forest as it curves around the southwest side of the mountain and makes its way to the top. The small rocky summit (0.75 mile, 848 feet) is surrounded by iron railings and can get crowded on busy summer days. You might find that you enjoy the views more from below.

122 HARDY AND RODNEY FALLS

BEFORE YOU GO
> **MAP** Green Trails, Columbia River Gorge West No. 428S
> **CONTACT** Washington State Parks
> **NOTES** Discover Pass required; dogs must be leashed; restrooms, water, picnic tables, and a playground available
> **GPS** N 45 37.732, W 122 01.295

ABOUT THE HIKE
> **SEASON** Year-round
> **DIFFICULTY** Moderate to difficult
> **DISTANCE** 2.2 miles roundtrip
> **HIGH POINT** 920 feet
> **ELEVATION GAIN** 500 feet

GETTING THERE

From Vancouver, travel east on State Route 14 approximately 35 miles to Beacon Rock State Park. Just past the state park headquarters building, turn left on the road to the campground. In 0.3 mile, turn right into the Hamilton Mountain Trailhead and Lower Picnic Area. If the parking lot is full, the trail can also be accessed from the campground. Seasonal bus service may be available.

On a summer's day, kids can cool off under the bridge over Hardy Creek.

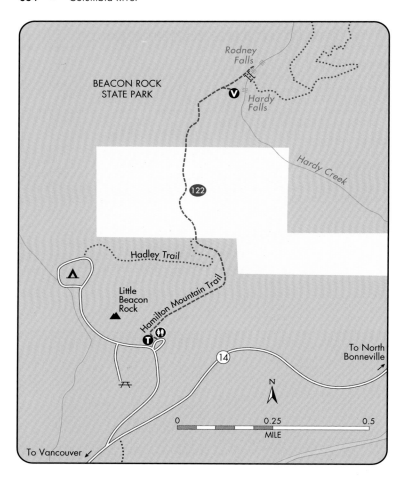

ON THE TRAIL

Who claims there are no waterfalls on the Washington side of the Columbia River Gorge? Beacon Rock State Park shows Oregon a thing or two, with a three-tiered set of two waterfalls that tumble down 170 feet. The Hamilton Mountain Trail can be hiked year-round, but the falls are most impressive—and loud—when full of snowmelt or rainwater in spring and fall.

Begin in cool, shaded forest, which makes this first uphill section more tolerable for little ones. At 0.4 mile, the trail breaks out of the trees and into a giant patch of salmonberry under powerlines and joins up with the Hadley Trail (the alternative access from the campground parking area). The looming peak visible from here is Hamilton Mountain, and many hikers will be hiking to its lofty summit.

Reenter forest and continue climbing, less steeply now. In the springtime, look for delicate pink and white wildflowers like bleeding heart, false Solomon's seal, and twinflower. In fall, enjoy the reds of the vine maple understory. Before you know it, your ears will pick up the sound of water. At 0.9 mile, reach the Hardy Falls Viewpoint. The upper deck provides a respectable view of this 90-foot cascade through the trees, but the steep descent to the lower viewpoint is simply not worth the effort.

A better choice is to go just a bit farther on the main trail to Rodney Falls (1.1 miles, 920 feet), where you get a much more intimate waterfall experience. Take a short side trail to the left up to a small platform that provides a peek into the aptly named Pool of Winds. Rodney Falls plunges through a 3-foot-wide ledge, pouring straight down 35 feet into a protected pool. The pool exits at your feet, then tumbles more gently another 45 feet, running under a handsome wooden bridge, until it reaches Hardy Falls below.

Every visit is different. When Hardy Creek is running at its highest, the Pool of Winds overflows, making it impossible to reach the platform. In late summer, the flow slows enough to reveal a tree trunk lodged vertically behind the waterfall. Most of the year, the strong spray blows a misty wind out of the alcove.

Before returning the way you came, do hike down to the bridge over the creek; Rodney Falls is photogenic from this vantage point. If the water is running low, kids can scamper down the rocks on either side of the bridge and perch themselves on boulders in the creek. It's a miniature tropical paradise, with kid-sized cascades, iridescent pools, and bright green moss and ferns.

123 FORT CASCADES HISTORIC SITE

BEFORE YOU GO
MAP Green Trails, Columbia River Gorge West No. 428S
CONTACT US Army Corps of Engineers–Portland District
NOTES Dogs must be leashed; privy and picnic tables available
GPS N 45 36.708, W122 03.129

ABOUT THE HIKE
SEASON Year-round
DIFFICULTY Easy
DISTANCE 1.5 miles loop
HIGH POINT 100 feet
ELEVATION GAIN 20 feet

GETTING THERE
From Vancouver, travel east on State Route 14 for 35 miles. Pass through North Bonneville and take a right at the Dam Access Road, distinguished by enormous red-and-white electric towers. Take an immediate right and follow signs to Fort Cascades Historic Site.

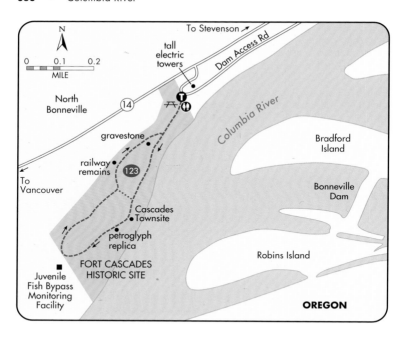

ON THE TRAIL

Take your children on a hike with a little history near a dam that has reshaped the Columbia River and region. The Fort Cascades Historic Site has been at the center of human activity for hundreds of years. Native Americans, fur traders, soldiers, travelers, railroad workers, fishermen, and dam builders all were drawn to this place by the power of the Columbia River and the prosperity that it brought. An interpretive kiosk details a great deal of the history, which is worth reviewing before you take this short hike.

Grab a Fort Cascades Trail guide, if available, and charge up your imagination as you head into the trees on the easy, level trail. In a short distance, reach a junction. Go left, walking downstream above the Columbia River. A mossy boulder field is a visible remnant of the Great Flood of 1894, when the river crested at its highest level ever. Take a moment to consider what it would have been like to face the massive river rising higher and higher, and what impacts a flood of such magnitude would have today.

At the next junction, stay straight and enter Cascades Townsite. From 1850 to 1894, more than one hundred residents called this place home. There was a hotel, a livery stable, and a blacksmith—all in service of building the Cascades Portage Railroad. It will take some imagination to envision a lively town among these tall trees today. No structures are visible—all were either wiped out by the flood or abandoned thereafter. One treat in this section is a mossy

Old railroad relics at Fort Cascades Historic Site

replica of a petroglyph. The original rock carving is now in front of the Skamania County Courthouse in Stevenson. No one knows what the designs mean, but it is a good reminder that Native Americans thrived in this area long before Euro-Americans arrived.

At 0.7 mile, curve back around and away from the river at the Juvenile Fish Bypass Monitoring Facility. The kids may be a bit frustrated that there have been no relics so far. Fortunately, that is about to change. You'll first come

BONNEVILE DAM

The Bonneville Dam area offers several opportunities for visitors. Traveling with a budding engineer? The Washington Shore Visitor Center at the Bonneville Dam offers views of the power generator and fish ladder. Weekend tours are available in summer. Kids more into nature can watch fishermen cast lines into the river or see salmon migrating in the fall. If you have a GPS unit or app on your phone, you may want to check out one of the facility's interpretive geocaches. You can spend the better part of a day poking around here.

across a small barrel and some rusty junk. Bear left at the junction and come across some railroad parts. Look closely at the wheels for dates, locations where they were forged, and the company that built them. These are old! Please leave all parts right where you find them for others to enjoy. The final stop on the tour is the gravestone of Thomas McNatt, a pioneer in the area who died in 1861. Then join up with the original trail and return to your car.

124 CATHERINE CREEK

BEFORE YOU GO
MAP Green Trails, Columbia River Gorge East No. 432S
CONTACT Columbia River Gorge National Scenic Area
NOTES Dogs must be leashed; seasonal portable toilet available; trail can be scaled for younger hikers; poison oak; ticks
GPS N 45 42.626, W 121 21.702

ABOUT THE HIKE
SEASON Year-round
DIFFICULTY Moderate
DISTANCE 2.7 miles in two loops
HIGH POINT 610 feet
ELEVATION GAIN 450 feet

GETTING THERE
From the west, drive State Route 14 east from the Hood Canal Bridge in White Salmon for 5.8 miles. Turn left on Old Highway 8 (County Road 1230) and drive around Rowland Lake, 1.5 miles to the large Catherine Creek parking area on the left. From the east, drive SR 14 west just 0.25 mile from Lyle, and after crossing the Klickitat River immediately turn right on Old Highway 8. Drive the Old Highway 4.7 miles to the trailhead on the right.

ON THE TRAIL
Sunny open meadows high above the Columbia River put on a long-lasting flower show each spring. As early as February, when purple grass widows begin

Wide-open exploring on the eastern side of the Columbia River Gorge

to bloom, the flora of Catherine Creek bursts forth. There are yellow bells and bachelor's buttons, desert parsley and death camas, bitterroot and balsamroot. There is also poison oak, and this is an ideal trail to learn about what it looks like and how to avoid it!

From the parking lot on the Old Cascades Highway, families can take a double loop that combines a paved 0.8-mile interpretive loop and a more primitive 1.9-mile loop that travels up an old farm road, passes a natural stone arch, and returns along a flower-filled bluff. Either of these two loops can be done independently for a shorter and easier outing.

To tackle the short, paved interpretive trail first, find the Universal Loop Trail opposite the parking area. Quickly reach a junction and go left on the interpretive loop. Catherine Creek is being managed to preserve its botanical diversity, and signs along the way identify and describe why this place in particular is so blossomy. Oddly, the interpretive signs never identify poison oak, but it most definitely grows alongside the trail!

At 0.2 mile is one of several benches and a view of a small waterfall on Catherine Creek. The trail descends more steeply until you can catch a glimpse of the highway and railroad tracks near the river. There's a trail on the right at 0.4 mile that provides a shortcut back to the trailhead. Following the longer loop to the left, however, adds only 0.2 mile for a 0.8-mile loop back to the trailhead.

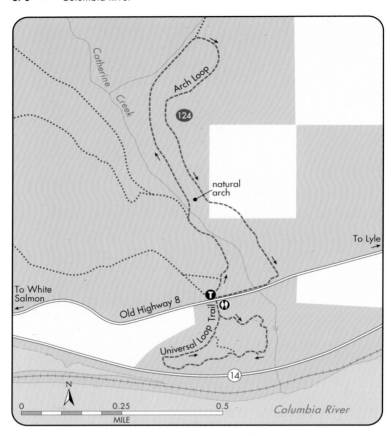

The 1.9-mile Arch Loop adds significantly to the hike, with an intriguing natural arch, more flowers, and windswept views of the Columbia River. On the north side of the road, pass through a fence, and choose the trail on the right that is ambiguously signed "020." This is an old gravel road that goes up an oak-filled draw choked with poison oak. If everyone remains on the wide trail, this nasty three-leafed plant will not be a problem. At 0.5 mile, reach fences and a partial view of a natural arch. Hikers used to be able to approach it, but the arch is now off-limits to protect its cultural significance.

Continue up the trail to an intersection under crackling powerlines at 0.8 mile. Leave the road on a narrow trail to the right and climb to the top of the ridge. This is my favorite section, dominated by views and flowers. If you have a field guide, see what you can identify. The seedpods linger long after the flowers are gone. Cresting the ridge also brings welcome breezes, views

POISON OAK

The eastern side of the Columbia River Gorge has excellent hiking, with big views and abundant wildflowers. It also has poison oak. Take the opportunity to learn how to identify this plant and prevent an itchy rash.

Poison oak loves the hot, oak-filled woodlands and meadows, and it can take on different looks: it can grow as vine, snaking up a tree; it can grow low to the ground, dangling leaves over the trail; and it can grow as a bush with woody stems. Poison oak's leaves can range from green to red, and it can sport white flowers in the springtime. My mantra when hiking in poison oak country is "leaves of three, let it be." We find examples to identify, and then avoid anything that resembles it. If the kids do brush up against poison oak, have them soak their exposed skin in cool water as soon as you can, using soap if possible. If poison oak gets on their clothes, bag up the clothes, then clean them by themselves in the washer with a degreasing detergent on a hot water cycle.

Poison oak (photo by Jon Stier)

of Mount Hood and Oregon's vineyards, as well as Catherine Creek's rolling, wooded hillsides.

Pass above the arch at 1.3 miles (500 feet), and then begin your descent on the east side of Catherine Creek. You'll emerge on the Old Highway at 1.8 miles. It's a short distance back to the parking area, and you'll need to walk the road to cross the creek and return to the trailhead. For safety, be sure to walk on the south side of the road, facing oncoming traffic.

125 HORSETHIEF BUTTE

BEFORE YOU GO
MAP Green Trails, Columbia River Gorge East No. 432S
CONTACT Washington State Parks
NOTES Discover Pass required; dogs must be leashed; privy available; rattlesnakes, poison oak, and ticks possible; drop-offs on butte
GPS N 45 39.035, W 121 05.914

ABOUT THE HIKE
SEASON Year-round
DIFFICULTY Easy
DISTANCE 1 mile roundtrip
HIGH POINT 290 feet
ELEVATION GAIN 20 feet

GETTING THERE
From Lyle, take State Route 14 east for 10 miles. Turn right into the Horsethief Butte trailhead near milepost 86.

Western fence lizard at Horsethief Butte (photo by Jon Stier)

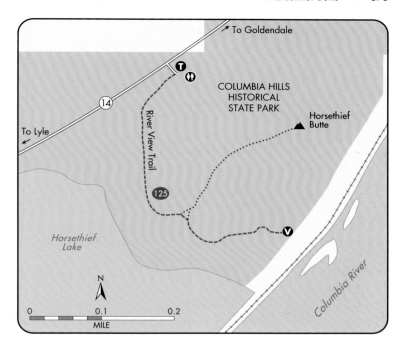

ON THE TRAIL

During the last ice age, floods of biblical proportions raced from Montana, carving a deep gouge through Washington and creating the Columbia River Gorge. On this sunny, dry section of the gorge, hexagonal tiers of dark basalt rise from the dammed river, providing sweeping views of two states and a dead-on look at pointy Mount Hood. Families can choose between a gentle mile-long stroll to a river viewpoint or a significantly more challenging hand-over-hand climb to the top of Horsethief Butte.

Despite hazards such as rattlesnakes, poison oak, and ticks (none of which are too prevalent), there are competing starring attractions that make this short hike kid-friendly: spring wildflowers, rock climbers in action, breathtaking views, and dozens of western fence lizards. Our hands-down favorite is the lizards. During warm months of the year, they are all over the rocks sunning themselves. The lizards are a bit skittish, but also curious, and they do not pose a threat. Scan the flat-topped rocks for the reptiles and sit quietly until they poke their little heads out.

Follow the main trail around the butte to the right on the River View Trail. Horsethief Lake lies below, separated from the Columbia River by busy railroad tracks. As you round the butte, look for swallows swooping in and out of the cliff walls. It's easy to identify them by their herky-jerky flying patterns.

At 0.3 mile, reach an intersection. Left takes hikers up Horsethief Butte. Right continues the easy path to a sweet river viewpoint at 0.5 mile. Make sure to stay well back from the edge and take in the eye candy, from Mount Hood, The Dalles, and the cars on I-84 across the water in Oregon, to the fascinating geology and busy rail corridor in Washington. For younger kids, this is as far as they should go. Return the way you came, and consider a visit to the other side of Horsethief Lake, where you can study Native American petroglyphs that were removed before the river was dammed.

EXPLORING FURTHER

Older kids may not be able to resist the temptation to climb Horsethief Butte. Use your best judgment. Reaching the top requires climbing over loose rocks and scaling walls 6 to 8 feet high. With many footholds, it may not be too hard for kids going up, but as with many precipitous climbs, it is significantly more difficult going down. And once they reach the top, there are numerous drop-offs. If your child lacks caution, this is not a good choice.

But for some kids, it provides just the right challenge and reward. Take the climbers' path up to a flat area and choose your own path to the top, staying to the right through the main draw. Set some ground rules once your reach the fragmented top, and stick close together. Then enjoy the expansive view.

ACKNOWLEDGMENTS

This book is a family affair. My husband, Jon Stier, and my children, Aidan and Aliza, accompanied me on seventy-five hikes over the course of twenty months of research. They acted as photographers and research assistants, and their images, voices, and opinions are woven throughout. I couldn't have done it without their patience, insight, and good humor.

My parents, Shearon and David Elderkin, took a special interest in this guide. They took me on my first real hike when I was three and introduced me to the mountains as a kid. My early introduction to hiking has shaped my passion for wild places and my work to protect them. They came along on several hikes for this book, enriching the experience with their grandchildren.

I was also fortunate to share the trail with many friends and family. Thank you to Jennifer Stier, Susan Gates, Gillian Maguire, Mike Delcamp, Melinda Luke, Randy White, Craig Romano, Marcy Grantor, Elizabeth Lunney, and Katie and Kelly Guenther—as well as all of their kids: Sunny, Naomi S., Simon, Naomi V., Conor, Eleanor, Giovanni, Malia, Marley, Nolan, Jameson, Matias, Chase, and Dakota—for making our hikes more fun, and also to Kindra Ramos and Kara Chin for their kid-free company on the trail. A special shout-out goes to Scott Rose's fourth and fifth graders at Pathfinder K–8 in West

Joan Burton, the author of the first Best Hikes with Kids: Western Washington, *joined me on the trail.*

Seattle. I spent twelve days hiking and camping with these kids, who displayed persistence, grit, and a good dose of glee in hiking some pretty tough trails!

I'd like to thank family and friends who contributed photographs to this guide: Jon Stier, Aidan Stier, David Elderkin, Eugene Lee, Ryan Ojerio, Kevin Hall and Erika Schreder. And also thank you to my editors at Mountaineers Books, Mary Metz and Kristi Hein, for their keen eyes for detail and enthusiastic support and to Green Trails Maps for keeping me oriented.

Last but not least, I'd like to thank Joan Burton, who penned the original Best Hikes with Kids guide for Washington in 1987. She had so much fun researching it that she wrote a second volume and then combined the two in 2006. It was the first hiking book I picked up when my son was born, and my copy is dog-eared from much use. Joan's hiking and climbing accomplishments are legendary, and I feel honored and humbled to walk in her shoes with this all-new volume of hikes for families. During my research, I was fortunate to share the trail with her twice, and I hope that my book shares a bit of her wise voice and extensive knowledge.

RESOURCES

CONTACT INFORMATION FOR LAND MANAGEMENT AGENCIES

Bureau of Land Management– Oregon/Washington
www.blm.gov/oregon-washington
(509) 536-1200

City of Anacortes–Parks and Recreation
www.cityofanacortes.org/parks_and
_recreation.php
(360) 293-1918

City of Bellevue–Parks and Community Services
www.ci.bellevue.wa.us/parks_intro.htm
(425) 452-6885

City of Federal Way–Parks and Recreation
www.cityoffederalway.com/node/1951
(253) 835-6911

City of Sammamish–Parks and Recreation
www.sammamish.us/parks-recreation
/parks-trails/
(425) 295-0500

City of Seattle–Parks and Recreation
www.seattle.gov/parks
(206) 684-4075

City of Tacoma–Metro Parks Tacoma
www.metroparkstacoma.org/parks
-alphabetical/
(253) 305-1000

Clark County Public Works
www.clark.wa.gov/parks
(360) 397-2285

Columbia River Gorge National Scenic Area
www.fs.usda.gov/main/crgnsa
(541) 308-1700

Cowiche Canyon Conservancy
www.cowichecanyon.org/
(509) 548-5065

Dungeness National Wildlife Refuge
www.fws.gov/refuge/dungeness/
(360) 457-8451

Ebey's Landing National Historical Reserve
www.nps.gov/ebla
(360) 678-6084

Gifford Pinchot National Forest
www.fs.usda.gov/activity
/giffordpinchot/recreation/hiking
(360) 891-5000

King County Parks
www.kingcounty.gov/services
/parks-recreation/parks
(206) 477-4527

Kitsap County Parks
www.kitsapgov.com/parks/
(360) 337-5350

Mount Baker–Snoqualmie National Forest
www.fs.usda.gov/activity/mbs
/recreation/hiking
(360) 627-6000

Mount Rainier National Park
www.nps.gov/mora/planyourvisit
/trails-of-mount-rainier.htm
(360) 569-6650

**Mount St. Helens National
Volcanic Monument**
www.fs.usda.gov/activity
/mountsthelens/recreation/hiking
(360) 449-7800

Nisqually National Wildlife Refuge
www.fws.gov/refuge/nisqually
(360) 534-9302

North Cascades National Park
www.nps.gov/noca/planyourvisit
/trailguide.htm
(360) 854-7200

**Okanogan–Wenatchee
National Forest**
www.fs.usda.gov/activity/okawen
/recreation/hiking
(509) 664-4900

Olympia Tumwater Foundation
www.olytumfoundation.org/
(360) 943-2550

Olympic National Forest
www.fs.usda.gov/activity/olympic
/recreation/hiking
(360) 956-2402

Olympic National Park
www.nps.gov/olym/planyourvisit
(360) 565-3130

Pierce County Parks and Recreation
www.piercecountywa.org/parks
(253) 798-4141

Ridgefield National Wildlife Refuge
www.fws.gov/refuge/ridgefield
(360) 887-4106

Seattle City Light
www.seattle.gov/light/damtours
/local.asp
(360) 854-2589

**Sehome Hill Arboretum
(Western Washington University)**
www.wwu.edu/share/map.html

Skagit County Parks and Recreation
www.skagitcounty.net/Departments
/ParksAndRecreation/parks
(360) 336-9414

**Snohomish County Parks
and Recreation**
www.snohomishcountywa.gov/1074
/Park-Directory
(425) 388-6600

**Steigerwald Lake National
Wildlife Refuge**
www.fws.gov/refuge/steigerwald_lake
(360) 835-8767

University of Washington
https://botanicgardens.uw.edu
/washington-park-arboretum
(206) 543-8800

**US Army Corps of Engineers–
Portland District**
www.nwp.usace.army.mil/Locations/
Columbia-River/Bonneville/
(541) 374-8820

**Washington Department of Fish
and Wildlife–Union River Unit**
http://wdfw.wa.gov/lands/wildlife
_areas/south_puget_sound
/Union%20River/
(360) 273-5126

**Washington Department of
Natural Resources**
www.dnr.wa.gov/managed-lands
(360) 902-1000

Washington State Parks
www.parks.wa.gov/
(360) 902-8844

**Whatcom County Parks
and Recreation**
www.co.whatcom.wa.us/1913
/Parks-Trails
(360) 384-3444

Willapa National Wildlife Refuge
www.fws.gov/refuge/willapa
(360) 484-3482

RESOURCES FOR
MAPS AND PERMITS

**America the Beautiful Pass and other
federal recreational lands passes**
www.nps.gov/planyourvisit/passes.htm

**Camping Reservations–
National parks and forests**
www.reserveamerica.com

Camping Reservations–State parks
http://parks.state.wa.us/223
/Reservations

Discover Pass
http://discoverpass.wa.gov/

**Friends of the Anacortes
Community Forest Lands**
www.friendsoftheacfl.org

Northwest Forest Pass
www.fs.usda.gov/detail/r6
/passes-permits/recreation
/?cid=fsbdev2_027010

ORGANIZATIONS

**Every Kid in a Park–Fourth graders
get free access to national parks**
www.everykidinapark.gov

Geocaching
www.geocaching.com
www.opencaching.us

Letterboxing
www.letterboxing.org
www.atlasquest.com

ORGANIZATIONS WITH
OUTDOOR PROGRAMS
FOR KIDS

Audubon Society of Portland
http://audubonportland.org/
(503) 292-6855

Hike It Baby
https://hikeitbaby.com/

Mazamas
www.mazamas.org
(503) 227-2345

The Mountaineers
www.mountaineers.org
(206) 521-6000

North Cascades Institute
www.ncascades.org/
(360) 854-2599

Seattle Audubon
www.seattleaudubon.org
(206) 523-4483

Washington Trails Association
www.wta.org
(206) 625-1367

Wild Whatcom
www.wildwhatcom.org/
(360) 389-3414

Wilderness Awareness School
www.wildernessawareness.org
(425) 788-1301

YMCA–BOLD and GOLD programs
www.ymcaleadership.com/

INDEX

ABOUT THE AUTHOR

Susan Elderkin has been hiking since she was three years old. As a child, she explored the trails of her native Iowa, the Great Lakes, and the Rocky Mountains on regular day hikes with her parents. This early exposure to the outdoors galvanized a lifelong love of hiking and commitment to the environment.

In 1995, while backpacking the 500-mile Colorado Trail, Susan realized two things: she wanted to give back to hiking trails and she wanted to write a guidebook. Susan moved to Seattle and joined the board of directors of Washington Trails Association (WTA) and later the staff, where she spent seven years as website editor and communications director. It took much longer—and some inspiration from her children—to write the guidebook.

Susan has worked for nonprofit environmental organizations, including National Wildlife Federation, Environmental Working Group, Earthjustice, and Futurewise, as well as WTA, for more than twenty-five years. She is currently a board member for Braided River and is active in her children's schools. Susan lives in Seattle, Washington, with her husband, Jon Stier, and two children, Aidan and Aliza.

recreation • lifestyle • conservation

MOUNTAINEERS BOOKS including its two imprints, Skipstone and Braided River, is a leading publisher of quality outdoor recreation, sustainability, and conservation titles. As a 501(c)(3) nonprofit, we are committed to supporting the environmental and educational goals of our organization by providing expert information on human-powered adventure, sustainable practices at home and on the trail, and preservation of wilderness.

Our publications are made possible through the generosity of donors, and through sales of more than 800 titles on outdoor recreation, sustainable lifestyle, and conservation. To donate, purchase books, or learn more, visit us online:

MOUNTAINEERS BOOKS
1001 SW Klickitat Way, Suite 201
Seattle, WA 98134
800-553-4453
mbooks@mountaineersbooks.org
www.mountaineersbooks.org

Leave No Trace strives to educate visitors about the nature of their recreational impacts and offers techniques to prevent and minimize such impacts. Leave No Trace is best understood as an educational and ethical program, not as a set of rules and regulations. For more information, visit www.lnt.org or call 800-332-4100.

OTHER MOUNTAINEERS BOOKS TITLES YOU MAY ENJOY!